John Mandeville

The voyage and travels of Sir John Maundeville

John Mandeville

The voyage and travels of Sir John Maundeville

ISBN/EAN: 9783337204785

Printed in Europe, USA, Canada, Australia, Japan

Cover: Foto ©Andreas Hilbeck / pixelio.de

More available books at **www.hansebooks.com**

The Voiage and Travaile

OF

Sir John Maundevile, Kt.

WHICH TREATETH OF THE

WAY TO HIERUSALEM; AND OF MARVAYLES OF INDE,
WITH OTHER ILANDS AND COUNTRYES.

Reprinted from the Edition of A.D. 1725.

WITH AN

INTRODUCTION, ADDITIONAL NOTES, AND GLOSSARY,

BY

J. O. HALLIWELL, Esq., F.S.A., F.R.A.S.

LONDON
REEVES AND TURNER
196, STRAND
1883

Advertisement to this Edition.

THE publisher thinks that it is due to Mr. HALLIWELL to state that he is in no way responsible for this re-impression of a work to which he contributed a few notes at the commencement of his literary career, more than twenty-five years since. This professes to be no more than a careful and accurate reprint of the edition of 1839.

Introduction.

THE text of the following volume is taken from MS. Cotton. Tit. C. xvi., as given in the edition of 1725 (Lond. 8vo), and was printed before the work was placed in my hands. This Introduction, then, the Additional Notes, and Glossary, are the only portions for which I am responsible. All, I believe, that is known of the author's life, is given in the preface of the former editor; and it will be only necessary here to notice the different MSS. and editions which I have been fortunate enough to meet with. Many other MSS. may also be found in the libraries of Oxford, Cambridge, and in almost every collection: so numerous, indeed, are they, owing to its great popularity, that it would be an endless labour to collate them all, though scarcely any two copies agree to any extent. I have consequently thought it a work of supererogation to point out the minor differences.

There are nineteen copies in the British Museum; and there may perhaps be more among the manuscripts not yet catalogued. In Heber's collection there was a very fine MS. of the French version; but I am not acquainted with its present possessor.

1. Bib. Reg. 17 C. xxxviii.

A small folio on vellum, written in double columns, of the latter end of the fourteenth century. It has a list of chapters at the commencement, and the following colophon:—"Here bygynneth the book of John Maundevile, Knyght of Ingelond, that was y bore in the toun of Seynt Albons, and travelidej aboute in the worlde in manye diverse contreis to se mervailes and customes of countreis, and diversiteis of folkys, and diverse shap of men, and of beistis, and all the mervaill that he say he wrot and tellith in this book, the which book conteyneth xxii chapiteris. And this knyght wente of Ingelond, and passid the see, the ӡer of our lord mcccxxxjj, and passid thorgh many londes contreis, and Iles, and compiled this book, and let write hit the ӡer of our lord mccclxvj, at xxxjjjj ӡer after that he wente out of his contre, ffor xxxjjjj ӡer he was in travelyng." It has several drawings, some agreeing with the woodcuts in this reprint: imperfect at the end.

2. Arundel. 140. f. 5 b.—41 b.

A folio of the fifteenth century, on paper: imperfect in various places. This MS. seems to be of little value.

3. Sloan. 1464. ff. 164.

An octavo on vellum, of the beginning of the fifteenth century, in French.

4. Sloan. 560. f. 2—55.

A folio on vellum, of the fifteenth century, in French.

5. Cotton. Tit. C. xvi. ff. 132.

A quarto on vellum, written about the year 1400, and from which the present text is taken. It ought to be observed, that the modern letter z had been substituted by the former editor for the middle-age character ӡ, as was commonly done till lately, and of course is retained in this reprint. Hearne uses the Saxon character ӡ; but that most generally employed now is the nondescript letter ӡ, which I have substituted in the Glossary for the sake of conformity with the present custom; and I do not think that the change will present any difficulty to the generality of readers.

6. Cotton. Append. iv. f. 59—102.

A folio on vellum, of the latter part of the fifteenth century, in Latin.

7. Bib. Reg. 17 B. xliii.

A quarto on vellum, of the fifteenth century, in English: imperfect at the end.

8. Harl. 3954.

A tall folio, of the end of the fourteenth century, on vellum. This is a very fine manuscript, and contains better and more numerous drawings than the one in the Royal Library, though they are none of them properly finished. The text is good.

9. Harl. 175.

A small quarto on vellum, of the fifteenth century, in Latin. At the end:—" Explicit Itinerarium domini Johannis de Maundeville militis de mirabilibus mundi."

10. Harl. 212. ff. 107.

A quarto on vellum, of the beginning of the fifteenth century, in French:—" Le geste de seigneur John Maundeville de mervailles de monde." This, in common with most of the French versions, has the date of 1332 instead of 1322, in the prologue. This manuscript has (f. 107) the copy of the letter from Maundeville to King Edward. From a manuscript note at the end, it appears that this copy must have been transcribed before the year 1425.

11. Harl. 82.

A folio on vellum, of the fifteenth century, in Latin. Imperfect both at the beginning and end. The forms of the Greek letters in this manuscript are worthy of observation.

12. Harl. 204. ff. 98.

A quarto on vellum, of the fifteenth century, in French; with the copy of the letter to King Edward at the end.

13. Harl. 1739.

Another French MS. on vellum and paper, in quarto, of the fifteenth century, and bound with the preceding. This MS. has the letter to King Edward.

14. Harl. 3589.

A folio on paper, of the fifteenth century, in Latin :—
"Incipit itinerarius magistri Johannis de Mandevelt ad partes Herosolumtanas et ad ulteriores partes transmarinas, qui obiit Leodii, anno domini mccclxxxjj.º" This MS. has a list of the chapters, and a larger prologue than I have observed in other Latin manuscripts.

15. Harl. 4383.

A folio on vellum, of the fifteenth century, in French : imperfect at the end. Some of the chapters have rubricated arguments.

16. Harl. 3940.

A quarto on vellum, of the fifteenth century, in French :—" Cy commenche le livre de Jeh. de Mandeville chevalier."

17. Bib. Reg. 20 A. i. ff. 119.

A quarto on vellum, of the fourteenth century, written in double columns, in French : a table of contents, and the letter to King Edward the Third, are at the end :—" Explicit le geste de sire John Maundevill Chivaler de Seint Albonz en Engletere." On the last leaf is an English poem on our Saviour, not mentioned in Casley's catalogue.

18. Bib. Reg. 20 B. x. ff. 83.

A folio on vellum, of the fourteenth century, in French, with the letter to King Edward. A list of the chapters is inserted at the commencement.

19. Bib. Reg. 13 E. ix. f. 40 a.—71 d.

A very large folio volume on vellum, finely written, about the year 1400, in double columns, in Latin. At the end :—" Explicit itinerarium domini Johannis de Maundevile militis de mirabiliis mundi, etc. Deo gracias."

At p. 5, Maundevile says, "And ȝee schulle undirstonde, that I have put this boke out of Latyn into Frensch, and translated it aȝen out of Frensch into Englyssche, that every man of my nacioun may undirstonde it." This passage, and what follows, I find only in the Cotton manuscript. In the Latin copies nothing is said on this point; but in MS. Sloan. 1464, and in many of the French versions, I find the following:—"Et sachetz que jeo usse mis ceste liverette en Latyn pur plus briefment deviser, mès pur ceo que plusours entendent mieultz Romanz que Latin, jeo l'ai mys en Romanz pur ceo que l'entende. Et que li seignours et li chivalers et les autres nobles hommes que ne scevent point Latin ou poi, et que ount eté outre mer, sachent et entendent si jeo dye voir ou noun, et jeo erre en disaunt, pus noun sovenanz ou autrement q'ils puissent atresser et amender. Car chose de longe temps passé par le vewe tournet en obli, et memorie de homme ne poet mie tout tenir et comprehendre." f. 4, r°.

The copy of the author's letter to King Edward the Third, already mentioned as being at the end of some of the French copies, is as follows:—

"*La copie de la lettre maundé ovesque cest escript, à très noble Prince Monsieur Edward de Wyndesore, roy de Engleterre et de Fraunce, par Monsieur John de Maundeville autour suisdit.*

"Principi excellentissimo, pre cunctis mortalibus precipue venerando, domino Edwardo, divina providentia, Francorum et Anglorum regi serenissimo, Hiberniæ domino, Aquitaniæ duci, mari ac ejus insulis occidentalibus dominanti, eufamie et ornatui, universorumque arma gerentium tutori, ac probitatis et strenuitatis exemplo; principi quoque invicto, mirabilis Alexandri sequaci, ac universo orbi tremendo; cum reverentia, non qua decet, cum ad talem et tantam reverentiam minus sufficientes extiterint, sed qua parvitas et possibilitas mittentis et offerentis se extendunt, contenta tradantur."

This letter is found only in the French copies, and in some of these it is omitted.

Much to illustrate these travels may be found in Marsden's edition of Marco Polo. Indeed the frequent agreements with Marco Polo would lead us to think that he had not been unacquainted with that author; and one person has suggested that Maundevile may never have gone to the East at all, but compiled his book out of previous journals. If the slightest negative evidence can be obtained, I grant that there may be sufficient room for carrying out the conjecture; but otherwise, I think that such a sweeping conclusion is wholly unjustifiable. It appears to me little less than certain, that if it had not been well known that Maundevile had travelled to the East before he published his book, it could never have been taken up with such general popular avidity; and so popular, that I will undertake to say that of no book, with the exception of the Scriptures, can more manuscripts be found of the end of the fourteenth and beginning of the fifteenth centuries.

The marvellous stories so readily credited by our author, and the great respect he pays to every relic, are not matters of surprise when we take into consideration the enthusiasm of a zealous Roman Catholic of the fourteenth century. He was treading on sacred ground, and credited, because he desired to credit, every idle story that came floating before his view. I transcribe from Chateaubriand's travels the translation of a tale respecting David's tomb, related by Benjamin of Tudela, because I think it affords a striking illustration of the sort of stories then circulated; and it is one which, from its very nature, is the kind of marvel that would have been most eagerly devoured, and credited without suspicion.

"Jerusalem is encompassed all round with lofty hills; but it is on Mount Sion that the Sepulchres of David's family must be situated, though the exact spot is not known. About fifteen years ago, one of the walls of the temple, which, as I have observed, stands on Mount Sion, fell down. Upon this the patriarch ordered a priest to repair it with such stones as were to be procured from the foundation of the walls of ancient Sion.

To this end, the latter hired about twenty workmen, between two of whom subsisted the closest friendship. One of these took the other home with him one morning to breakfast. Returning after their repast, the overseer inquired why they came so late: they replied that they would make up for it by working an hour over the regular time. Accordingly, while the rest of the men were at dinner, and these were continuing their work as they had promised, they raised a stone which closed the mouth of a cavern, and said to one another, 'Let us see if there be not some treasure concealed here.' Having entered, they went forward till they came to a palace supported by marble pillars, and covered with plates of gold and silver. Before it was a table, on which lay a crown and sceptre. This was the sepulchre of David king of Israel; that of Solomon, with similar ornaments was on the left, as were also the tombs of several other kings of Judah of the Family of David, who were interred in this place. They saw also chests which were locked up; so that what they contained is not known to this day. The two men were proceeding to enter the palace, when a violent whirlwind rushing in at the mouth of the cavern threw them upon the ground, where they remained as if dead till night. Another blast of wind roused them from this situation, and they heard a voice resembling that of a man, which said to them, 'Arise, and begone from this place.' Overcome with terror, they precipitately departed, and related all that had befallen them to the patriarch, who made them repeat the account in the presence of Abraham of Constantinople, the Pharisee, surnamed the Pious, who then resided at Jerusalem. He had sent for him to inquire what he thought of the matter; on which he replied, that this was the burial-place of the house of David, prepared for the kings of Judah. The following day the two men were found confined to their beds, and very ill in consequence of the fright. They refused to return to the spot for any reward whatever; declaring that it was vain for any mortal to attempt to penetrate into a place the entrance of which was defended by God himself; so that it was stopped up by the command of the patriarch, and it has thus been concealed from sight to this day."

This story seems to be a revival of that related by Josephus respecting the same tomb: Herod the Great having attempted to open David's coffin, flames issued from it, and prevented the accomplishment of his design. I remember when very young, that I was much excited by this same story of Benjamin of Tudela, and cried heartily because "papa" would not let me go immediately to the Holy Land, to let me try whether I could not be more successful than the two brother workmen.

The passage on Paradise is most singular; and, for the sake of the general reader, I will give it in modern language. It is at p. 303 of this reprint.

"Of Paradise I cannot speak properly, for I was never there. It is far beyond, and that I repented, and also I was not worthy. But as I have heard say of wise men beyond, I will tell you with good will. Earthly Paradise, as wise men say, is the highest point of the earth that is, in all the world; and it is so high, that it nearly touches the circle of the moon as the moon turns. For it is so high, that the flood of Noah could not reach it, but covered all the rest of the world above and below. And this Paradise is enclosed all round with a wall, and men know not whereof it is. For the walls are covered all over with moss, as it appears. And it appears that the wall is not of natural stone. And that wall stretches from the south to the north, and it has but one entrance, which is closed by burning fire, so that no mortal dare enter. And in the highest place of Paradise, in the middle, is a well, out of which issue four streams that run through different lands: of the which the first is called Phison or Ganges, which is all one, and it runs through India or Emlak, in which river are many precious stones, and much *lignum aloes*, and much gold-dust; and the next river is called the Nile, or Gyson, that goes through Ethiopia and Egypt; and the next is called Tigris, that runs by Assyria and Armenia the greater; and the next is called Euphrates, that runs through Media, Armenia, and Persia. And men there beyond say that all the sweet waters of the world, above and below, take their origin from the well of Paradise; and out of that well all waters come and go. The first river is called Phison; that is to say, in their language, assemblage; for many other rivers meet it, and join it there. And some men call it Ganges, for there was a king in India, who was called Gangeres, and it ran through his land. And that water is in some places clear, and in others thick; in some hot, and in others cool. The second river is called Nile or Gyson, for it is always rough; and Gyson, in the language of Ethiopia, is to say trouble; and in the language of Egypt also. The third river, which is called Tigris, is as much as to say swift running, for it runs faster than any other. And there is also a beast that is called a tiger, which is a swift runner. The fourth river is called Euphrates, that is to say, well-bearing; for many goods grow upon that river, as corn, fruit, and other goods in plenty."

This, I think, does not look much like plagiarism: the commencing words are too natural for us easily to admit the probability of such a conjecture; and, after a perusal of the whole volume, the judgment of any impartial reader would, I am sure, repudiate any such opinion.

Here I should have terminated, had I not been permitted, with the greatest kindness and liberality, to inspect and use the splendid collection of manuscripts and editions of this traveller preserved in the choice and magnificent library of the Right Hon. Thomas Grenville. I proceed, without further remark, to make a short enumeration of them, merely observing that, in a bibliographical point of view, nothing can exceed the beauty of their condition.

1. A small 4to, printed by Pynson, and one of the earliest productions of his press.

This is believed to be unique, and was purchased at

the sale of the library of Sir Francis Freeling, but is unfortunately rather imperfect. It possesses the following colophon at the end:—" Here endeth the boke of John Maundvyle knyght, of wayes to Jerusalem and of marveylys of ynde and of other countrees. Emprented by Rychard Pynson." Mr. Grenville remarks that "the text varies very much from Este's edition."

2. 4to. Lond. 1696. pp. 139.

This edition is rare, but there is nothing much worthy of observation about it except the woodcuts. It appears to be a reprint of the following:—

3. 4to. Lond. 1684.

4. 4to. Lond. 1618.

Not mentioned by Lowndes or by Watt.

5. 4to. T. Este. s. a.

See Ames, ii. 1022. It is of rare occurrence.

6. MS. fol. paper. xv. cent.

"Here begynnth the boke of Moundevyle knyȝt. that techyth the weyes to Jerusalem and of the mervelis of Ynde and of the londes of perstre John and of the grete Cham and of Constantynople and of many other contreys."

"Here endyth the boke of John Maundevyle knyȝte of dyvers wheys and many merveles," &c.

This MS. is in beautiful preservation, but omits the passage given at the end of the prologue in the Cotton MS.

7. MS. fol. vellum.

This is a beautiful and valuable manuscript, in the French language, of the beginning of the fifteenth century. It has the following colophon at the commencement:—" Ci commence le livre qui parle des diversités des pais qui sunt par universe monde, lequel livre fut copilé fait et ordonné par mesire Jehan Mandeville chevalier né d'Angleterre de la ville con dit Saint Albain."

It has the usual French passage relative to the languages in which the book was written, at the end of the prologue. The MS. came originally from the collection of some foreign prince.

8. Small 4to. Venet. 1521. *Ital.*

I should think that this Italian version is from the French, for the same variation occurs at the end of the prologue *ut supra*. See f. 2, v°.

9. 4to. Milano, 1517. *Ital.*

This edition is very rare, and is not to be found in the lists of Panzer, Pinelo, Meuselius, Haym, Richarderie, or Crofts.

10. 4to. Bologna, 1497. *Ital.*

11. 4to. Milano, 1497. *Ital.*

12. 4to. Venexia, 1496. *Ital.*

13. 4to. s. a. et. l. *Lat.*

This has the list of chapters at the commencement. The traveller is called in this edition Johannes de Monte Villa. It appears to have been printed about the close of the 15th century, and is not noticed by Panzer.

14. 4to. Antwerp, 1494. *Flem.*

15. 4to. Firenze, 1492. *Ital.*

The Italian editions vary very little. This book shews in its title-page its translation from the French, by calling the hero "Cavaliere *asperondoro*," meaning, I suppose, "*aux éperons d'or.*"

16. 4to. Bologn. 1492. *Ital.*

17. 4to. Venezia, 1491. *Ital.*

18. 4to. Bologna, 1488. *Ital.*

19. 4to. s. a. et l. *Lat.*

The first of the Latin editions, and printed probably about 1480.

20. 4to. Med. 1480. *Ital.*

This is the earliest date affixed to any of the printed editions. It may be mentioned here, that Laire supposes the first Latin edition (No. 19) to be printed between 1480 and 1490; and, in a MS. note, states that the author wrote his travels in French, Italian, and in Latin.

21. Folio. Strasburgh, 1484. *Germ.*

This very rare German version is attributed to Michelfeld, or, as he is sometimes called, Michelfelser. The illuminations are most curious, and very similar to those in the Harleian manuscript: the alphabets of the different nations are also very well worthy of observation.

22. Folio. 1480. *Français.*

This is splendidly printed in double columns; but without place, or name of printer. Nothing can exceed the beautiful condition of this exemplar.

Besides the editions here mentioned, several others were printed at different periods, all of which are very rare. For a further account of them, see Brunet, iii. p. 1355; Lowndes, p. 1204; or New Edit., p. 1463; Watt, ii. 639. Bergeron published an abridgment in 1735, in his "Voyages faits principalement en Asie dans les xii, xiii, xiv, et xv Siècles." 4to. A la Haye.

An article on our traveller will also be found in the Retrospective Review, vol. iii. p. 269-93.

The illustrations are fac-simile copies, by Mr. F. W. Fairholt, from the older editions, and from the MSS. in the Harleian collection; and have been engraved under his superintendance.

The Editor's Preface

TO THE EDITION OF 1727.

THE Reader has here an Edition of *The Voiage and Travaile of Sir John Maundevile, Kt.* published from a Manuscript in the Cottonian Library, (marked, Titus. C. XVI.) about 300 Years old; and collated with seven MSS. some near as old as the Author's time; and four old printed Editions. Two of the MSS. French, two English, and one Latin are in the King's Library; one Latin in the Cottonian; and one English in a private Hand. The printed Editions are two Latin; one Sans Date, the other in R. Hakluyts Collection, printed at London, 1598; one English, printed at London, 1568, and one Italian,—1537. The Variations of the Latin Copies are marked, L. 1, 2, 3, 4; of the English, E. 1, 2, 3, 4; of the French, F. 1, 2; and of the Italian, I. Here are also two Indices; one of the Contents, the other of obsolete Words.

This Edition agrees with the Latin and French MSS.; and appears to be the genuine Work of the Author; who says, that he translated it out of Latin into French, and out of French into English;[a] whereas all other printed Editions are so curtail'd and transpos'd, as to be made thereby other Books. The three English MSS. named above, as well as the English printed Edition, contain a third part less than this. For Instance; they wholly want, what is contain'd here, from Page 38 to 58.

The Author, according to the humour of the times of Ignorance he liv'd in, has put into his History abundance of Miracles and strange things; so that the Title of one of the Latin MSS. is *Itinerarium Johannis Maundevile, de Mirabilibus Mundi:* and his English Transcribers and Editors have taken care to preserve them all; but have dropt a great deal of what, now a days, will be counted the best part of the Book. He was ambitious of saying all he could, of the places he treats of; and therefore has taken Monsters out of Pliny, Miracles out of Legends, and strange Stories out of what will now be called Romances. Thus his Story of the Sparrow-hawk,[b] kept in a Castle

---

[a] Page 5.   [b] Pages 145, 146, 147.

in Armenia the less, he has from John of Arras's History of Melusine:[c] who after invocating the Divine Assistance, says, "The which Hystory I have bygonne, after the veray and true Cronykles, —and many other Bokes, that I have sought and overredde, for to accomplysshe hit." So that the falsities in this History are occasioned by other Authors, at that time accounted true; and the fault of the Historian, that he did not name his Authors. However, when he tells the most improbable Stories, he prefaces them with, "Thei seyn," or, "men seyn, but I have not sene it." And particularly, in Page 314 and 315, he owns, that his Book is made partly from Hear-say, and partly of his own Knowledge. Where he adds, that at his Request, the Pope caused it to be examined by his Council; who compar'd it with the Book, by which *Mappa Mundi* was made, and found it true: and thereupon it obtain'd the approbation of his Holiness. And if old Authors must be rejected for putting strange Stories and Improbabilities into their History, what will become of Venerable Bede, Gildas, Geoffry of Monmouth, and the rest of our English Historians?

Why then should not this Author have his due Place and Regard, amongst the Writers of the Age he liv'd in; and be believ'd, in what he says of his own Observation, as much as other His-

[c] Biblioth. Reg. 18. B. II.

torians of those times, and of such like Matters?
He had extraordinary Qualifications and Opportunities, and was the chief Traveller of his time;
having been 33 Degrees, 16 Minutes, Southern
Latitude, and 62 Degrees, 10 Minutes, Northern.[d]
He mentions one, that travail'd round the Globe;
which he had heard of when he was young:[e] this
probably inspir'd him with an early Passion for
Travell. He was of a Family, that came into
England with the Conqueror. He was a Man of
Learning and Substance, had studied Physic and
Natural Philosophy.[f] He was a conscientious
good Man; as appears from several Instances in
the Book:[g] particularly in p. 35; where he says,
that the Sultan of Egypt would have married him
to a great Prince's Daughter, if he would have
chang'd his Religion; and that he refus'd. He
had the Sultan's great Seal, which procur'd him
extraordinary Privileges, throughout his Dominions:[h] and was admitted to private Conversation
with him;[i] and "duelled with him, as Soudyour in
his Werres a gret while."[k] He also with his Fellow
Travellers were Soldiers under the Great Can of
Cathay fifteen Months.[l]

John Bale, in his Catalogue of British Writers,

---

[d] Page 181.   [e] Page 183.
[f] See Bale's Account of him below: and page 180 to 186.
[g] See the Prologue; and pages 19, 35, 84, 261, 283, 295, 296, 314, 315, and 316.   [h] Page 82.
[i] Page 137.   [k] Page 35.   [l] Page 220.

gives him a fine character: which follows, as translated by R. Hakluyt.

"John Mandevil Knight, borne in the Towne of S. Albans, was so well given to the study of Learning from his childhood, that he seemed to plant a good part of his felicitie in the same: for he supposed, that the honour of his Birth would nothing availe him, except he could render the same more honourable, by his knowledge in good letters. Having therefore well grounded himselfe in Religion, by reading the Scriptures, he applied his Studies to the Art of Physicke, a Profession worthy a noble Wit: but amongst other things, he was ravished with a mightie desire to see the greater parts of the World, as Asia and Africa. Having therefore provided all things necessary for his journey, he departed from his Countrey, in the Yeere of Christ 1322; and, as another Ulysses, returned home, after the space of 34 Yeeres, and was then knowen to a very fewe. In the time of his Travaile he was in Scythia, the greater and lesse Armenia, Egypt, both Libyas, Arabia, Syria, Media, Mesopotamia, Persia, Chaldæa, Greece, Illyrium, Tartarie, and divers other Kingdomes of the World: and having gotten by this meanes the knowledge of the Languages, least so many and great varieties, and things miraculous, whereof himself had bene an eie witnes, should perish in oblivion, he committed his whole Travell of 34 Yeeres to writing, in three divers tongues, English, French and Latine. Being arrived again in England, and having seene the wickednes of that Age, he gave out this Speech: 'In our time, (said he) it may be spoken more truly then of olde, that Vertue is gone, the Church is under foote, the Clergie is in errour, the Devill raigneth, and Simonie beareth the sway,' &c. He died at Leege, in the Yeere 1371, the 17 day of November, being there buried in the Abbie of the Order of the Gulielmites."

Abr. Ortelius, in his *Itinerarium Belgiæ* p. 16, has printed his Epitaph, which he found in the foresaid Abbie, thus: *Hic jacet Vir Nobilis, Dominus Johannes de Mandeville, aliter dictus, ad Barbam, Miles, Dominus de Campdi, natus de Anglia, Medicine Professor, devotissimus Orator, & bonorum largissimus pauperibus erogator: qui toto quasi Orbe lustrato, Leodii diem vite sue clausit extremum, anno Domini* 1371, *Mensis Novembris die* 17. And he says, that upon the same Stone with the Epitaph, is ingraven a Man in Armour, with a forked Beard, treading upon a Lion; and at the head of him, a hand of one blessing him, and these Words in French, *Vos ki paseis sor mi, pour l'amour Deix, proies por mi;* that is, *Ye that pass over me, for the love of God, pray for me.* There is also a void place, for a Scutcheon; wherein, he was told, was formerly a Brass Plate, with his Armes ingraven thereon; viz. a Lion Argent, with a Lunet Gules at his Breast, in a

Field Azure, and a Bordure ingraled Or.[m] The Churchmen there shewed him also, the Knives, the Furniture of his Horse, and the Spurs, which he used in his Travells.

It's not unlikely, but Sir John Mandevil might get the Nick-name of *ad Barbam*, from his using to wear a long Beard, when he was grown old. But at the end of the Latin printed Edition of his Travells, there is mentioned a venerable old Physician, called Johannes ad Barbam; whom he met with at Liege, and after some conversation, recollected that they had been acquainted at Cayro in Egipt; and that this Doctor, after having done him singular service, as a Physician, both persuaded and assisted him to write his Travells. However none of the above named MSS. have this Passage.

John Weever, in his ancient funeral Monuments, p. 568, says, he saw the foresaid Epitaph at Liege; and the Verses following, hanging by on a Table.

Aliud.

Hoc jacet in Tumulo, cui totus Patria vivo
    Orbis erat: totum quem peragrasse ferunt.
Anglus Equesque fuit: nunc Ille Britannus Ulysses
    Dicatur; Graio clarus Ulysse magis.
Moribus, ingenio, candore et sanguine clarus,
    Et vere cultor Relligionis erat.
Nomen si queras, est Mandevil: Indus Arabsque
    Sat notum dicet Finibus esse suis.

[m] This Coat was borne by Sir Roger Tyrell of Hartfordshire, in the time of Edward I. Cotton Lib. Tib. D. X. page 155.

And he ridicules the Inhabitants of St. Albans, for the following Epitaph, upon a Pillar of their Abbey; near to which, they suppose his Body to have been buried.

> All ye that passe, on this Pillar cast eye,
>   This Epitaph read, if you can:
> 'Twill tell you, a Tombe once stood in this roome,
>   Of a brave spirited man;
>
> John Mandevil by name, a Knight of great fame,
>   Born in this honoured Towne.
> Before him was none, that ever was knowne,
>   For travaile of so high renowne.
>
> As the Knights in the Temple crosse-legged in Marble,
>   In Armour with Sword and with Sheeld,
> So was this Knight grac't, which Time hath defac't,
>   That nothing but Ruines doth yeeld.
>
> His Travailes being donne, he shines like the Sun,
>   In heavenly Canaan,
> To which blessed Place, the Lord, of his grace,
>   Bring us all, man after man.

The Language of this History is such as our Ancestors spoke, three hundred Years ago: which is a Curiosity, will compensate the Reader for the Solecisms and uncouth Expressions, he will meet with. Before the Art of Printing was found out, there was no setled method of spelling: therefore the same Word here is often spelt different ways; and that even in the same Page; as, Heved, Heed, Hed, Hede; Awtier, Awtere, Awteer, Awtiere, &c.

Table of Contents.

	PAGE
The Prologue	1

Cap. I.
To teche zou the Weye out of Englond to Constantinoble 6

Cap. II.
Of the Crosse and the Croune of oure Lord Jesu Crist . 9

Cap. III.
Of the Cytee of Costantynoble, and of the Feithe of Grekis 15

Cap. IV.
Of the Weye fro Costantynoble to Jerusalem. Of Seynt John the Evaungelist; and of Ypocras Daughter, transformed from a Woman to a Dragoun . . 21

Cap. V.
Of manye Names of Soudans, and of the Tour of Babiloyn 34

Cap. VI.
Of the Desert betwene the Chirche of Seynte Kateryne and Jerusalem. Of the drie Tre; and how Roses cam first in the World 63

Cap. VII.
Of the Pilgrimages in Jerusalem, and of the Holy Places thereaboute 73

Cap. VIII.

Of the Temple of oure Lord. Of the Crueltee of Kyng Heroud. Of the Mount Syon. Of Probatica Piscina. And of Natatorium Siloe . . . 81

Cap. IX.

Of the Dede See; and of the Flom Jordan. Of the Hed of Seynt John the Baptist; and of the usages of the Samaritanes 99

Cap. X.

Of the Province of Galilee, and where Antecrist schalle be born. Of Nazarethe. Of the Age of oure Lady. Of the Day of Doom; and of the Customes of Jacobites, Surryenes; and of the Usages of Georgyenes . 110

Cap. XI.

Of the Cytee of Damasce. Of 3 Weyes to Jerusalem; on be Londe and be See; another more be Londe than be See; and the thridde Weye to Jerusalem, alle be Londe 122

Cap. XII.

Of the Customes of Sarasines, and of hire Lawe; and how the Soudan arresond me, Auctour of this Book. And of the begynnynge of Machomet . . 131

Cap. XIII.

Of the Londes of Albanye, and of Libye. Of the Wisshinges, for Wacchinge of the Sperhauk; and of Noes Schippe 142

Cap. XIV.

Of the Lond of Job; and of his Age. Of the Aray of men of Caldee. Of the Lond where Wommen duellen, with outen companye of men. Of the knouleche and vertues of the verray Dyamant . . . 151

Cap. XV.

Of the Customs of Yles abouten Ynde. Of the difference betwix Ydoles and Simulacres. Of 3 maner growing of Peper upon o Tree. Of the Welle, that chaungethe his odour, every hour of the day; and that is Mervaylle 161

Cap. XVI.

Of the Domes made be Seynt Thomas. Of Devocyoun and Sacrifice made to Ydoles there, in the Cytee of Calamye; and of the processioun in goynge aboute the Cytee 171

Cap. XVII.

Of the evylle customs used in the Yle of Lamary: and how the Erthe and the See ben of round Forme and schapp, be pref of the Sterre, that is clept Antartyk, that is fix in the Southe 178

Cap. XVIII.

Of the Palays of the Kyng of the Yle of Java. Of the Trees, that beren Mele, Hony, Wyn and Venym; and of othere Mervayilles and Customes, used in the Yles marchinge thereabouten 186

Cap. XIX.

How men knowen be the Ydole, zif the sike schalle dye or non. Of folk of dyverse schap and merveylously disfigured: And of the Monkes, that zeven hire releef to Babewynes, Apes and Marmesettes and to other Bestes 201

Cap. XX.

Of the grete Chane of Chatay. Of the Rialtee of his Palays, and how he sitt at Mete; and of the grete nombre of Officeres, that serven hym . . 215

Cap. XXI.

Wherefore he is clept the grete Chane. Of the Style of his Lettres, and of the Superscripcioun abowten his grete Sealle, and his pryvee Sealle . . . 222

Cap. XXII.

Of the governance of the grete Chanes Court, and whan he makethe solempne Festes. Of his Philosophres. And of his Array, whan he ridethe be the Contre . 232

Cap. XXIII.

Of the Lawe and the Customs of the Tartarienes, duellynge in Chatay; and how that men don, whan the Emperour schal dye, and how he schal be chosen . 247

Cap. XXIV.

Of the Roialme of Thurse and the Londes and Kyngdomes towardes the Septentrionale parties, in comynge down from the Lond of Cathay 255

Cap. XXV.

Of the Emperour of Persye, and of the Lond of Derknesse and of other Kyngdomes, that belongen to the grete Chane of Cathay, and other Londes of his, unto the See of Greece 257

Cap. XXVI.

Of the Contrees and Yles, that ben bezonde the Lond ot Cathay; and of the Frutes there; and of 22 Kynges enclosed within the Mountaynes . . . 263

Cap. XXVII.

Of the Ryalle estate of Prestre John; and of a riche man, that made a marveyllous Castelle, and cleped it Paradys; and of his Sotyltee 270

Cap. XXVIII.

Of the Develes Hede in the Valeye perilouse; and of the Customs of folk in dyverse Yles, that ben abouten, in the Lordschipe of Prestre John . . . 280

Cap. XXIX.

Of the Godenesse of the folk of the Yle of Bragma. Of Kyng Alisandre; and wherfore the Emperour of Ynde is clept Prestre John 291

Cap. XXX.

Of the Hilles of Gold, that Pissemyres kepen: and of the 4 Flodes, that comen from Paradys terrestre . 300

Cap. XXXI.

Of the Customs of Kynges, and othere that dwellen in the Yles costynge to Prestre Johnes Lond. And of the Worschipe, that the Sone dothe to the Fader, whan he is dede 306

Additional Notes 317

Glossary 320

The Prologue.

For als moche[a] as the Lond bezonde the See, that is to seye, the Holy Lond, that Men callen the Lond of Promyssioun, or of Beheste, passynge alle othere Londes, is the most worthi Lond, most excellent, and Lady and Sovereyn of alle othere Londes, and is blessed and halewed of the precyous Body and Blood of oure Lord Jesu Crist; in the whiche Lond it lykede him to take Flesche and Blood of the Virgyne Marie, to envyrone that holy Lond with his blessede Feet; and there he wolde of his blessednesse enoumbre him in the seyd blessed and gloriouse Virgine Marie, and become Man, and worche many Myracles, and preche and teche the Feythe and the Lawe of Cristene Men unto his Children; and there it lykede him to suffre many Reprevinges and Scornes for us; and he that was Kyng of Hevene, of Eyr, of Erthe, of See and of alle thinges that ben conteyned in hem, wolde alle only ben cleped Kyng of that Lond, whan he seyde, *Rex sum Judeorum*, that is to seyne, *I am Kyng of Jewes;* and that Lond he chees before alle other Londes, as the beste and most worthi Lond, and the most vertuouse

[a] *For als moche*] The Author makes his first Sentence of an unusual length; and the Causal, he begins with, hath its Inference no nearer than Page 3; *Wherefore every gode Cristene* &c. but the Latin Edition has them nearer together; wanting three Quarters of the Prologue.

Lond of alle the World: For it is the Herte and
the myddes of all the World; wytnessynge the
Philosophere, that seythe thus; *Virtus rerum in
medio consistit:* That is to seye, *The Vertue of
thinges is in the myddes;* and in that Lond he
wolde lede his Lyf, and suffre Passioun and Dethe
of Jewes, for us; for to bye and to delyvere us
from Peynes of Helle, and from Dethe withouten
ende; the whiche was ordeyned for us, for the
Synne of oure formere Fader Adam, and for oure
owne Synnes also: for as for himself, he hadde
non evylle deserved: For he thoughte nevere
evylle ne dyd evylle: And he that was Kyng of
Glorie and of Joye, myghten best in that Place
suffre Dethe; because he ches in that Lond, rathere
than in ony othere, there to suffre his Passioun
and his Dethe: For he that wil pupplische ony
thing to make it openly knowen, he wil make it
to ben cryed and pronounced in the myddel place
of a Town; so that the thing that is proclamed
and pronounced, may evenly strecche to alle Parties: Righte so, he that was formyour of alle the
World, wolde suffre for us at Jerusalem; that is
the myddes of the World; to that ende and entent,
that his Passioun and his Dethe, that was pupplischt there, myghte ben knowen evenly to alle
the Parties of the World. See now how dere he
boughte Man, that he made after his owne Ymage,
and how dere he azen boghte us, for the grete
Love that he hadde to us, and we nevere deserved
it to him. For more precyous Catelle ne gretter
Ransoum, ne myghte he put for us, than his blessede
Body, his precyous Blood, and his holy Lyf, that
he thralled for us; and alle he offred for us, that

nevere did Synne. A dere God, what Love hadde he to us his Subjettes, whan he that nevere trespaced, wolde for Trespassours suffre Dethe! Righte wel oughte us for to love and worschipe, to drede and serven suche a Lord; and to worschipe and preyse suche an holy Lond, that broughte forthe suche Fruyt, thorghe the whiche every Man is saved, but it be his owne defaute. Wel may that Lond be called delytable and a fructuous Lond, that was bebledd and moysted with the precyouse Blode of oure Lord Jesu Crist; the whiche is the same Lond, that oure Lord behighten us in Heritage. And in that Lond he wolde dye, as seised, for to leve it to us his Children. Wherfore every gode Cristene Man, that is of Powere, and hathe whereof, scholde peynen him with all his Strengthe[b] for to conquere oure righte Heritage, and chacen out alle the mysbeleevynge Men. For wee ben clept Cristene Men, aftre Crist our Fadre. And zif wee ben righte Children of Crist, we oughte for to chalenge the Heritage, that oure Fadre lafte us, and do it out of hethene Mennes hondes. But nowe Pryde, Covetyse and Envye han so enflawmed the Hertes of Lordes of the World, that thei are more besy for to disherite here Neyghbores, more than for to chalenge or to conquere here righte Heritage before seyd. And the comoun Peple, that wolde putte here Bodyes and here Catelle, for to conquere oure Heritage, thei may not don it withouten the Lordes. For a semblee of Peple withouten a Cheventeyn, or a chief Lord, is as a Flock of Scheep withouten a Schepperde;

[b] *Strengthe hem for to conquere.* E. 1, 2, 3; se deveroit pener et mettre en graunt. F. 1, 2.

the whiche departeth and desparpleth, and wyten never whidre to go. But wolde God, that the temporel Lordes and alle worldly Lordes weren at gode accord, and with the comen Peple woulden taken this holy Viage over the See. Thanne I trowe wel, that within a lityl tyme, oure righte Heritage before seyd scholde be reconsyled and put in the Hondes of the righte Heires of Jesu Crist.

And for als moche as it is longe tyme passed, that ther was no generalle Passage ne Vyage over the See; and many Men desiren for to here speke of the holy Lond, and han thereof gret Solace and Comfort; I John Maundevylle, Knyght, alle be it I be not worthi, that was born in Englond, in the Town of Seynt Albones, passed the See in the Zeer of our Lord Jesu Crist MCCCXXII, in the Day of Seynt Michelle; and hidre to have ben longe tyme over the See, and have seyn and gon thorghe manye dyverse Londes, and many Provynces and Kingdomes and Iles, and have passed thorghe Tartarye, Percye, Ermonye[c] the litylle and the grete; thorghe Lybye, Caldee and a gret partie of Ethiope; thorghe Amazoyne, Inde the lasse and the more, a gret partie; and thorghe out many othere Iles, that ben abouten Inde; where dwellen many dyverse Folkes, and of dyverse Maneres and Lawes, and of dyverse Schappes of Men. Of whiche Londes and Iles, I schalle speke more pleynly hereaftre. And I schalle devise zou sum partie of thinges that there ben, whan time schalle ben, aftre it may best come to my mynde; and specyally for hem, that wylle and are in purpos for to visite the Holy Citee of Jerusalem, and the holy

[c] Armenia.

Places that are thereaboute. And I schalle telle the Weye, that thei schulle holden thidre. For I have often tymes passed and ryden the way, with gode Companye of many Lordes: God be thonked.

And zee schulle undirstonde, that I have put this Boke out of Latyn into Frensche, and translated it azen out of Frensche into Englyssche, that every Man of my Nacioun may undirstonde it. But Lordes and Knyghtes and othere noble and worthi Men, that conne Latyn but litylle, and han ben bezonde the See, knowen and undirstonden, zif I erre in devisynge, for forzetynge, or elles; that thei mowe redresse it and amende it. For thinges passed out of longe tyme from a Mannes mynde or from his syght, turnen sone into forzetynge: Because that Mynde of Man ne may not ben comprehended ne witheholden, for the Freeltee of Mankynde.

Cap. I.

To teche zou the Weye out of Englond to Constantinoble.

IN the Name of God Glorious and Allemyghty. He that wil passe over the See, to go to the City of Jerusalem, he may go by many Weyes, bothe on See and Londe, aftre the Contree that hee cometh fro: manye of hem comen to on ende. But troweth[d] not that I wil telle zou alle the Townes and Cytees and Castelles, that Men schulle go by; for than scholde I make to longe a Tale: but alle only summe Contrees and most princypalle Stedes, that men schulle gone thorgh, to gon the righte Way. First, zif a Man come from the West syde of the World, as Engelond, Irelond, Wales, Skotlond or Norweye; he may, zif that he wole, go thorge Almayne,[e] and thorghe the Kyngdom of Hungarye, that marchethe[f] to the Lond of Polayne,[g] and to the Lond of Pannonye, and so to Slesie.[h] And the Kyng of Hungarye is a gret Lord and a myghty, and holdethe grete Lordschippes and meche Lond in his Hond. For he holdethe the Kyngdom of Hungarie, Solavonye[i] and of Comanye a gret part, and of Bulgarie, that men clepen the Lond of Bougiers, and of the Reme of

---

[d] *Troweth* for *trow*, is common in old English.
[e] Germany.   [f] Quod conterminum est, L. 1, 2.
[g] Poyalme, E. 1, 2, 3.
[h] Alleseye, E. 1, 2, 3; Swesie, L. 1, 2.
[i] Savoyze, E. 1; Savoye, E. 2, 3; Sclavoniam, L. 1.

Roussye a gret partie, whereof he hathe made a Duchee, that lasteth unto the Lond of Nyflan,[k] and marchethe to Pruysse. And men gon thorghe the Lond of this Lord, thorghe a Cytee that is clept Cypron,[l] and by the Castelle of Neaseburghe,[m] and be the evylle[n] Town, that sytt toward the ende of Hungarye. And there passe Men the Ryvere of Danubee. This Ryvere of Danubee is a fulle gret Ryvere; and it gothe into Almayne, undre the Hilles of Lombardye: and it receyvethe into him 40 othere Ryveres; and it rennethe thorghe Hungarie and thorghe Greece and thorghe Trachie, and it entreth into the See, toward the Est, so rudely[o] and so scharply, that the Watre of the See is fressche and holdethe his swetnesse 20 Myle within the See.

And aftre gon Men to Belgrave, and entren into the Lond of Bourgres;[p] and there passe Men a Brigge of Ston, that is upon the Ryver of Marrok.[q] And Men passen thorghe the Lond of Pyncemartz,[r] and comen to Greece to the Cytee of Nye,[s] and to the Cytee of Fynepape,[t] and aftre to the

[k] Neflond, E. 1; Nyflond, E. 2, 3; Nislan, L. 1, 2.
[l] Chippronne. E. 1, 2, L. 1; Schyppronne, E. 3, L. 2.
[m] Newbow, E. 1; Neuborewe, E. 2, 3.
[n] Same, E. 1; Ile, E. 2.
[o] *Swiftly*, E. 1; *stalworthly*, E. 2; *styflyche*, E. 3.
[p] Bruges, E. 1; Bugres, E. 2, 3; Bougres, F. 1, L. 2; Bungres, F. 2; Bulgrorum, L. 1. The Author means Bulgaria.
[q] Marrol, E. 3; Marroe: F. 1; Marroie, F. 2; De Marmore, L. 1, 2.
[r] Pynceras, E. 1, 3; Pyncoras, E. 2; Pynteras, L. 1.
[s] Sternes, E. 1, E. 3, L. 1; Scernys, E. 2; Sti, L. 2; Sternes ad fines Epapie, L. 1; Ny et puts a fine Pape, F. 1, 2.
[t] Affynpayn, E. 1, 2; Assynpayn, E. 3.

Cytee of Dandrenoble,[u] and aftre to Constantynoble, that was wont to be clept Bezanzon. And there dwellethe comounly the Emperour of Grece. And there is the most fayr Chirche and the most noble of alle the World: And it is of Seynt Sophie. And before that Chirche is the Ymage of Justynyan the Emperour, covered with Gold, and he sytt upon an Hors y crowned. And he was wont to holden

a round Appelle of Gold in his Hond: but it is fallen out thereof. And Men seyn there, that it is a tokene, that the Emperour hathe y lost a gret partie of his Londes, and of his Lordschipes: for he was wont to ben Emperour of Romayne and of Grece, of alle Asye the lesse, and of the Lond of Surrye, of the Lond of Judee, in the whiche is Jerusalem, and of the Lond of Egypt, of Percye, of Arabye. But he hathe lost alle, but Grece; and that Lond he holt alle only. And Men wolden

[u] Adrianople.

many tymes put the Appulle into the Ymages Hond azen, but it wil not holde it. This Appulle betokenethe the Lordschipe, that he hadde over alle the Worlde, that is round. And the tother Hond he lifteth up azenst the Est, in tokene to manace the Mysdoeres. This Ymage stont upon a Pylere of Marble at Costantynoble.

Cap. II.

Of the Crosse and the Croune of oure Lord Jesu Crist.

AT Costantynoble is the Cros of our Lord Jesu Crist, and his Cote withouten Semes, that is clept *Tunica inconsutilis,* and the Spounge, and the Reed,

of the whiche the Jewes zaven oure Lord Eyselle and Galle, in the Cros. And there is on of the Nayles, that Crist was naylled with on the Cros. And some Men tròwen, that half the Cros,[1] that Crist was don on, be in Cipres, in an Abbey of Monkes, that Men callen the Hille of the Holy Cros; but it is not so: For that Cros, that is in Cypre, is the Cros, in the whiche Dysmas the gode Theef was honged onne. But alle Men knowen not that; and that is evylle y don. For profyte of the Offrynge, thei seye, that it is the Cros of oure Lord Jesu Crist. And zee schulle undrestonde, that the Cros of oure Lord was made of 4 manere of Trees, as it is conteyned in this Vers,

In Cruce fit Palma, Cedrus, Cypressus, Oliva.

For that pece, that went upright fro the Erthe to the Heved, was of Cypresse; and the pece, that wente overthwart, to the whiche his Honds weren nayled, was of Palme; and the Stock, that stode within the Erthe, in the whiche was made the Morteys, was of Cedre; and the Table aboven his Heved, that was a Fote and an half long, on the whiche the Title was writen, in Ebreu, Grece and Latyn, that was of Olyve. And the Jewes maden the Cros of theise 4 manere of Trees: For thei trowed that oure Lord Jesu Crist scholde han honged on the Cros, als longe as the Cros myghten laste. And therfore made thei the Foot of the Cros of Cedre. For Cedre may not, in Erthe ne in Watre, rote. And therfore thei wolde, that it scholde have lasted longe. For thei trowed, that the Body of Crist scholde have stonken; therfore

[1] See pag. 28.

thei made that pece, that went from the Erthe upward, of Cypres: For it is welle smellynge; so that the smelle of his Body scholde not greve Men, that wenten forby. And the óverthwart pece was of Palme: For in the Olde Testament,[y] it was ordyned, that whan on overcomen, he scholde be crowned with Palme: And for thei trowed, that thei hadden the Victorye of Crist Jesus, therfore made thei the overthwart pece of Palme. And the Table of the Tytle, thei maden of Olyve; for Olyve betokenethe Pes. And the storye of Noe wytnessethe, whan that the Culver broughte the Braunche of Olyve, that betokened Pes made betwene God and Man. And so trowed the Jewes for to have Pes, whan Crist was ded: For thei seyd, that he made Discord and Strif amonges hem. And zee schulle undirstonde, that oure Lord was y naylled on the Cros lyggynge; and therfore he suffred the more peyne. And the Cristene Men, that dwellen bezond the See, in Grece, seyn that the Tree of the Cros, that we callen Cypresse, was of that Tree, that Adam ete the Appulle of: and that fynde thei writen. And thei seyn also, that here Scripture seythe, that Adam was seek, and seyed to his Sone Sethe, that he scholde go to the Aungelle, that kepte Paradys, that he wolde senden hym Oyle of Mercy, for to anoynte with his Membres, that he myghte have hele. And Sethe wente. But the Aungelle wolde not late him come in; but seyd to him, that he myghte not have of the Oyle of Mercy. But he toke him three Greynes of the same Tree, that his Fadre eet the Appulle offe; and bad him, als sone as his

[y] Rather, Olympick Games.

Fadre was ded, that he scholde putte theise three Greynes undre his Tonge, and grave him so: and he dide. And of theise three Greynes sprong a Tree, as the Aungelle seyde, that it scholde, and bere a Fruyt, thorghe the whiche Fruyt Adam scholde be saved. And whan Sethe cam azen, he fonde his Fadre nere ded. And whan he was ded, he did with the Greynes, as the Aungelle bad him; of the whiche sprongen three Trees, of the whiche the Cros was made, that bare gode Fruyt and blessed, oure Lord Jesu Crist; thorghe whom, Adam and alle that comen of him, scholde be saved and delyvered from drede of Dethe withouten ende, but it be here own defaute. This holy Cros had the Jewes hydde in the Erthe, undre a Roche of the Mownt of Calvarie; and it lay there 200 zeer and more, into the tyme that Seynt Elyne, that was Modre to Constantyn the Emperour of Rome. And sche was Doughtre of Kyng Cool[2] born in Colchestre, that was Kyng of Engelond, that was clept thanne, Brytayne the more; the whiche the Emperour Constance wedded to his Wyf, for here Bewtee, and gat upon hire Constantyn, that was aftre Emperour of Rome.

And zee schulle undirstonde, that the Cros of oure Lord was eyght Cubytes long, and the overthwart piece was of lengthe thre Cubytes and an half. And o partie of the Crowne of oure Lord, wherwith he was crowned, and on of the Nayles, and the Spere Heed, and many other Relikes ben in France, in the Kinges Chapelle. And the Crowne lythe in a Vesselle of Cristalle richely dyghte. For a Kyng of Fraunce boughte theise Relikes som-

[2] Coyle, E. 2; Coel, E. 4.

tyme of the Jewes; to whom the Emperour had leyde hem to wedde, for a gret summe of Sylvre. And zif alle it be so, that Men seyn, that this Croune is of Thornes, zee schulle undirstonde, that it was of Jonkes of the See, that is to sey, Rushes of the See, that prykken als scharpely as Thornes. For I have seen and beholden many tymes that of Parys and that of Costantynoble: For thei were bothe on, made of Russches of the See. But Men han departed hem in two Parties: of the whiche, o part is at Parys, and the other part is at Costantynoble. And I have on of tho precyouse Thornes, that semethe licke a white Thorn; and that was zoven to me for gret Specyaltee. For there are many of hem broken and fallen into the Vesselle, that the Croune lythe in: For thei breken for dryenesse, whan Men meven hem, to schewen hem to grete Lords, that comen thidre.

And zee schulle undirstonde, that oure Lord Jesu, in that Nyghte that he was taken, he was y lad in to a Gardyn; and there he was first examyned righte scharply; and there the Jewes scorned him, and maden him a Crowne of the Braunches of Albespyne, that is White Thorn, that grew in that same Gardyn, and setten it on his Heved, so faste and so sore, that the Blood ran down be many places of his Visage, and of his Necke, and of his Schuldres. And therfore hathe White Thorn many Vertues: For he that berethe a Braunche on him thereoffe, no Thondre ne no maner of Tempest may dere him; ne in the Hows, that it is inne, may non evylle Gost entre ne come unto the place that it is inne. And in that same Gardyn, Seynt Petre denyed oure Lord thryes.

Aftreward was oure Lord lad forthe before the Bisschoppes and the Maystres of the Lawe, in to another Gardyn of Anne; and there also he was examyned, repreved, and scorned, and crouned eft with a whyte Thorn, that Men clepethe Barbarynes, that grew in that Gardyn, and that hathe also manye Vertues. And aftreward he was lad in to a Gardyn of Cayphas, and there he was crouned with Eglentier.[a] And aftre he was lad in to the Chambre of Pylate, and there he was examynd and crouned. And the Jewes setten him in a Chayere and cladde him in a Mantelle; and there made thei the Croune of Jonkes of the See; and there thei kneled to him, and skornede him, seyenge, *Ave, Rex Judeorum,* that is to seye, *Heyl, Kyng of Jewes.* And of this Croune, half is at Parys, and the other half at Costantynoble. And this Croune had Crist on his Heved, whan he was don upon the Cros: and therfore oughte Men to worschipe it and holde it more worthi than ony of the othere.

And the Spere schaft hathe the Emperour of Almayne; but the Heved is at Parys. And natheles the Emperour of Costantynoble seythe that he hathe the Spere Heed: and I have often tyme seen it; but it is grettere than that at Parys.

[a] Englenter, E. 1, 2, F. 1, 2; Eglentine, E. 4.

Cap. III.

Of the Cytee of Costantynoble, and of the Feithe of Grekis.

AT Costantynoble lyethe Seynte Anne oure Ladyes Modre, whom Seynte Elyne dede brynge fro Jerusalem. And there lyethe also the Body of John Crisostome, that was Erchebisschopp of Costantynoble. And there lythe also Seynt Luke the Evaungelist: For his Bones werein broughte from Bethanye, where he was beryed. And many othere Relikes ben there. And there is the Vesselle of Ston, as it were of Marbelle, that Men clepen Enydros, that evermore droppeth Watre, and fillethe himself everiche zeer, til that it go over above, withouten that that Men take fro withinne.

Costantynoble is a fulle fayr Cytee, and a gode and a wel walled, and it is three cornered. And there is an Arm of the See Hellespont: and sum Men callen it the Mouthe of Costantynoble; and sum Men callen it the Brace of Seynt George: and that Arm closethe the two partes of the Cytee. And upward to the See, upon the Watre, was wont to be the grete Cytee of Troye, in a fulle fayr Playn: But that Cytee was destroyed by hem of Grece, and lytylle apperethe there of, be cause it so longe sithe it was destroyed.

Abouten Grece there ben many Iles, as Calistre,[a] Calcas,[b] Critige,[c] Tesbria,[d] Mynea,[e] Flaxon,[f] Melo, Carpate, and Lempne. And in this Ile is the Mount Athos, that passeth the Cloudes. And there ben many dyvers Langages and many Contreys, that ben obedyent to the Emperour; that is to seyn Turcople, Pyneynard, Cornange, and manye othere, as Trachye, and Macedoigne, of the whiche Alisandre was Kyng. In this Contree was Aristotle born, in a Cytee that Man clepen Stragers, a lytil fro the Cytee of Trachaye. And at Stragers lythe Aristotle; and there is an Awtier upon his Toumbe: And there maken Men grete Festes of hym every zeer, as thoughe he were a Seynt. And at his Awtier, thei holden here grete Conseilles and here Assembleez: And thei hopen, that thorghe inspiracioun of God and of him, thei schulle have the better Conseille. In this Contree ben righte hyghe Hilles, toward the ende of Macedonye. And there is a gret Hille, that Men clepen Olympus, that departeth Macedonye and Trachye: And it is so highe, that it passeth the Cloudes. And there is another Hille, that is clept Athos, that is so highe, that the Schadewe of hym

[a] Calastre, E. 1, 2, 3, 4. Calliste is one of the Cyclades.

[b] Colchos, L. 1, 3. It is wanting in E. 1, 2.

[c] Cetige, E. 1; Certyge, E. 2; Cectyge, E. 3; Crezitigia, L. 1, 2; Ortigo, L. 3; Settygo, E. 4; Ortigia, I.

[d] Tesbiria, E. 1, 2, 3; Thoysoria, E. 4; Tresbria, L. 1, 2; Tylbryâ, L. 3; Resoria, I.

[e] Arynona, E. 1; Mynona, E. 2, 3, 4; Athos, Minex, L. 1; Minex, L. 2; Minos, L. 3; Mirea, I. Mynia is a Town in the Isle Amorgus.

[f] Faxton, E. 1, 3, 4; Flexon, L. 3; Flazon, I. This Place and the three next are wanting in E. 2.

rechethe to Lempne,^g that is an Ile; and it is 76 Myle betwene. And aboven at the cop of the Hille is the Eir so cleer, that Men may fynde no Wynd there. And therfore may no Best lyve there; and so is the Eyr drye. And Men seye in theise Contrees, that Philosophres som tyme wenten upon theise Hilles, and helden to here Nose a Spounge moysted with Watre, for to have Eyr; for the Eyr above was so drye. And aboven, in the Dust and in the Powder of tho Hilles, thei wroot Lettres and Figures with hire Fingres: and at the zeres end thei comen azen, and founden the same Lettres and Figures, the whiche thei hadde writen the zeer before, withouten ony defaute. And therfore it semethe wel, that theise Hilles passen the Clowdes and joynen to the pure Eyr.

At Costantynoble is the Palays of the Emperour, righte fair and wel dyghte: and therein is a fair place for Justynges, or for other Pleyes and Desportes. And it is made with Stages and hath Degrees aboute, that every Man may wel se, and non greve other. And undre theise Stages ben Stables wel y vowted for the Emperours Hors; and alle the Pileres ben of Marbelle. And with in the Chirche of Seynt Sophie, an Emperour somtyme wolde have biryed the Body of his Fadre, whan he was ded; and as thei maden the Grave, thei founden a Body in the Erthe, and upon the Body lay a fyn Plate of Gold; and there on was writen, in Ebreu, Grece and Latyn, Lettres that seyden thus, *Jesu Cristus nascetur de Virgine Maria, et ego credo in eum:* That is to seyne, *Jesu*

^κ According to the old Greek Verse, Ἄθωος καλύπτει πλευρὰ λεμνίας βοός.

Crist schalle be born of the Virgyne Marie, and I trowe in hym. And the Date whan it was leyd in the Erthe, was 2000 zeer before oure Lord was born. And zet is the Plate of Gold in the Thresorye of the Chirche. And Men seyn, that it was Hermogene the Wise Man.

And zif alle it so be, that Men of Grece ben Cristene, zit they varien from oure Feithe. For thei seyn, that the Holy Gost may not come of the Sone; but alle only of the Fadir. And thei are not obedyent to the Chirche of Rome, ne to the Pope. And thei seyn, that here Patriark hathe as meche Power over the See, as the Pope hathe on this syde the See. And therfore Pope Johne the 22^d sende Lettres to hem, how Cristene Feithe scholde ben alle on; and that thei scholde ben obedyent to the Pope, that is Goddis Vacrie on Erthe; to whom God zaf his pleyn Power, for to bynde and to assoille: And therfore thei scholde ben obedyent to him. And thei senten azen dyverse Answeres; and amonges othere, thei seyden thus: *Potentiam tuam summam, circa tuos subjectos, firmiter credimus. Superbiam tuam summam tolerare non possumus. Avaritiam tuam summam satiare non intendimus. Dominus tecum: quia Dominus nobiscum est.* That is to seye: *We trowe wel, that thi Power is gret upon thi Subgettes. We mai not suffre thin high Pryde. We ben not in purpos to fulfille thi gret Covetyse. Lord be with The: For oure Lord is with us. Fare welle.* And other Answere myghte he not have of hem. And also thei make here Sacrement of the Awteer of Therf Bred: For oure Lord made it of suche Bred, whan he made his Mawndee. And on the

Scherethors Day make thei here Therf Bred, in tokene of the Mawndee, and dryen it at the Sonne, and kepen it alle the Zeer, and zeven it to seke Men, in stede of Goddis Body. And thei make but on Unxioun, whan thei Cristene Children. And thei anoynte not the seke Men. And thei saye, that there nys no Purgatorie, and the Soules schulle not have nouther Joye ne Peyne, tille the Day of Doom. And thei seye, that Fornicatioun is no Synne dedly, but a thing that is kyndely: and the Men and Women scholde not wedde but ones; and whoso weddethe oftere than ones, here Children ben Bastardis and geten in Synne. And here Prestis also ben wedded. And thei seye also, that Usure is no dedly Synne. And thei sellen Benefices of Holy Chirche: And so don Men in othere places: God amende it, whan his Wille is. And that is gret Sclaundre. For now is Symonye Kyng crouned in Holy Chirche: God amende it for his Mercy. And thei seyn, that in Lentone, Men schulle not faste, ne synge Masse; but on the Satreday and on the Sonday. And thei faste not on the Satreday, no tyme of the Zeer, but it be Cristemasse even on Estre even. And thei suffre not the Latynes to syngen at here Awteres: And zif thei done, be ony Aventure, anon thei wasschen the Awteer with holy Watre. And thei seyn, that there scholde be but o Masse seyd at on Awtier, upon o Day. And thei seye also, that oure Lord ne eet nevere Mete: But he made tokene of etyng. And also thei seye, that wee synne dedly, in schavynge oure Berdes. For the Berd is tokene of a Man, and Zifte of oure Lord. And thei seye, that wee synne dedly, in etynge of Bestes, that weren forboden in the Old Testement, and of the olde Lawe; as Swyn, Hares, and othere Bestes, that chewen not here Code. And thei seyn, that wee synnen, whan wee eten Flessche on the Dayes before Assche Wednesday, and of that that wee eten Flessche the Wednesday, and Egges and Chese upon the Frydayes. And thei accursen alle tho, that absteynen hem to eten Flessche the Satreday. Also the Emperour of Costantynoble makethe the Patriarke, the Erchebysschoppes and the Bisschoppes; and zevethe the Dignytees and the Benefices of Chirches, and deprivethe hem that ben worthy, whan he fyndethe ony Cause. And so is he Lord bothe temperelle and spirituelle, in his Contree. And zif zee wil wite of here A, B, C, what Lettres thei ben, here zee may seen hem, with the Names, that thei clepen hem there amonges hem.

a Alpha, β Betha, γ Gamma, δ Deltha, ϵ Epsilon, ζ Zeta, η Eta, θ Theta, ι Iota, κ Kappa, λ Lambda, μ My, ν Ny, ξ Xi, o Omicron, π Pi, ρ Rho, σ Sigma, τ Tau, υ Upsilon, ϕ Phi, χ Chi, ψ Psi, ω Omega.

And alle be it that theise thinges touchen not to o way, nevertheles thei touchen to that, that I have hight zou, to schewe zou a partie of Custumes and Maneres, and dyversitees of Contrees. And for this is the firste Contree, that is discordant in Feythe and in Beleeve, and variethe from oure Feythe, on this half the See, therefore I have sett it here, that zee may knowe the dyversitee that is betwene our Feythe and theires. For many Men han gret lykynge, to here speke of straunge thinges of dyverse Contreyes.

Cap. IV.

Of the Weye fro Costantynoble to Jerusalem. Of Seynt John the Evaungelist; and of Ypocras Daughter, transformed from a Woman to a Dragoun.

Now returne I azen, for to teche zou the Way from Costantynoble to Jerusalem. He that wol thorghe Turkye, he gothe toward the Cytee of Nyke, and passethe thorghe the zate of Chienetout,[h] and alle weyes Men seen before hem the Hille of Chienetout, that is righte highe: And it is a Myle and an half from Nyke. And whoso will go be Watre, be the Brace of Seynt George, and by the See, where Seynt Nycholas lyethe, and toward many other

Places: First Men gothe to an Ile, that is clept Sylo. In that Ile growethe Mastyck on smale

[h] Thoivitot, E. 1; Chivitot, E. 2, 3, 4; Chenetut, F. 1.

Trees: and out of hem comethe Gomme, as it were of Plombtrees or of Cherietrees. And aftre gon Men thorghe the Ile of Pathmos: And there wrot Seynt John the Evaungelist the Apocalips. And zee schulle undrestonde, that Seynt Johne was of Age 32 Zeer, whan oure Lord suffred his Passioun; and aftre his Passioun, he lyvede 67 Zeer, and in the 100th Zeer of his Age he dyede. From Pathmos Men gon unto Ephesim, a fair Citee and nyghe to the See. And there dyede Seynte Johne, and was buryed behynde the highe Awtiere, in a Toumbe. And there is a fair Chirche. For Cristene Men weren wont to holden that Place alweyes. And in the Tombe of Seynt John is noughte but Manna, that is clept Aungeles Mete. For his Body was translated into Paradys. And Turkes holden now alle that Place, and the Citee and the Chirche. And alle Asie the lesse is y cleped Turkye. And zee schulle undrestonde, that Seynt Johne leet make his Grave there in his Lyf, and leyd himself there inne alle quyk. And therefore somme Men seyn, that he dyed noughte, but that he restethe there til the Day of Doom.[1] And forsothe there is a great Marveyle: For Men may see there the Erthe of the Tombe apertly many tymes steren and meven, as there weren quykke thinges undre.

And from Ephesim Men gon throghe many

---

[1] Long before our Author's time, the Text, in John xxi. 22, 23, in the vulgar Latin, happen'd to be chang'd in favour of this Notion: For Jesus's Answer to Peter's Question about John; *Lord, and what shall this Man do?* is there, *Sic eum volo manere donec veniam;* the Conjunction *Si* being dropt, by means of *Sic* following.

Iles in the See, unto the Cytee of Paterane,[k] where Seynt Nicholas was born, and so to Martha,[l] where he was chosen to ben Bisschoppe; and there growethe right gode Wyn and strong; and that Men callen Wyn of Martha. And from thens gon Men to the Ile of Crete, that the Emperour zaf somtyme to Janeweys.[m] And thanne passen Men thorghe the Isles of Colos and of Lango;[n] of the whiche Iles Ypocras was Lord offe. And some Men seyn, that in the Ile of Lango is zit the Doughtre of Ypocras, in forme and lykeness of a gret Dragoun, that is a hundred Fadme of lengthe, as Men seyn: For I have not seen hire. And thei of the Isles callen hire, Lady of the Lond. And sche lyethe in an olde castelle, in a Cave, and schewethe twyes or thryes in the Zeer. And sche dothe none harm to no Man, but zif Men don hire harm. And sche was thus chaunged and transformed, from a fair Damysele, in to lyknesse of a Dragoun, be a Goddesse, that was clept Deane.[o] And Men seyn, that sche schalle so endure in that forme of a Dragoun, unto the tyme that a Knyghte come, that is so hardy, that dar come to hire and kiss hire on the Mouthe: And then schalle sche turne azen to hire owne Kynde, and ben a Woman azen: But aftre that sche schalle

[k] Pathan, E. 1; Patrau, F. 1; Patyran, E. 2; Pateran, L. 1, 2, 3, 4; Pataran, E. 3; Maiolica, I; Pateram Civitatem Pannonie, L. 4. It should be Patera, a City of Lycia.

[l] Marka, E. 2, 3, 4; Marrea, F. 2; Mirreorum, L. 1, 2; Myrrheam, L. 3, 4; Maretta, I. It should be Myra, and City of Lycia. [m] The Genoese.

[n] Lango is but another name of the Isle Cos or Cohos, where Hippocrates the famous Physician was born.

[o] Diana.

not liven longe. And it is not long siththen, that a Knyghte of the Rodes, that was hardy and doughty in Armes, seyde that he wolde kyssen hire. And whan he was upon his Coursere, and wente to the Castelle, and entred into the Cave, the Dragoun lifte up hire Hed azenst him. And whan the Knyghte saw hire in that Forme so hidous and so horrible, he fleyghe awey. And the Dragoun bare the Knyghte upon a Roche, mawgre his Hede; and from that Roche, sche caste him in to the See: and so was lost bothe Hors and Man. And also a zonge Man, that wiste not of the Dragoun, wente out of a Schipp, and wente thorghe the Ile, til that he come to the Castelle, and cam in to the Cave; and wente so longe, til that he fond a Chambre, and there he saughe a Damysele, that kembed hire Hede, and lokede in a Myrour; and sche hadde meche Tresoure abouten hire: and he trowed, that sche hadde ben a comoun Woman, that dwelled there to resceyve Men to Folye. And he abode, tille the Damysele saughe the Schadewe of him in the Myrour. And sche turned hire toward him, and asked hym, what he wolde. And he seyde, he wolde ben hire Limman or Paramour. And sche asked him, zif that he were a Knyghte. And he seyde, nay. And than sche seyde, that he myghte not ben hire Lemman: But sche bad him gon azen unto his Felowes, and make him Knyghte, and come azen upon the Morwe, and sche scholde come out of the Cave before him; and thanne come and kysse hire on the mowthe, and have no Drede; for I schalle do the no maner harm, alle be it that thou see me in Lyknesse of a Dragoun. For thoughe thou see me hidouse and

horrible to loken onne, I do the tô wytene, that it
is made be Enchauntement. For withouten doute,
I am non other than thou seest now, a Woman;
and therfore drede the noughte. And zif thou
kysse me, thou schalt have alle this Tresoure, and
be my Lord, and Lord also of alle that Ile. And
he departed fro hire and wente to his Felowes to
Schippe, and leet make him Knyghte, and cam
azen upon the Morwe, for to kysse this Damysele.
And whan he saughe hire comen out of the Cave,
in forme of a Dragoun, so hidouse and so horrible,
he hadde so grete drede, that he fleyghe azen to the

Schippe; and sche folewed him. And whan sche
saughe, that he turned not azen, sche began to
crye, as a thing that hadde meche Sorwe: and
thanne sche turned azen, in to hire Cave; and
anon the Knyghte dyede. And siththen hidre-

wards, myghte no Knyghte se hire, but that he dyede anon. But whan a Knyghte comethe, that is so hardy to kisse hire, he schalle not dye; but he schalle turne the Damysele in to hire righte Forme and kyndely Schapp, and he schal be Lord of alle the Contreyes and Iles aboveseyd.

And from thens Men comen to the Ile of Rodes, the whiche Ile Hospitaleres [p] holden and governen; and that token thei sumtyme from the Emperour: And it was wont to be clept Collos;[q] and so callen it the Turks zit. And Seynt Poul,[r] in his Epistles, writeth to hem of that Ile, *ad Colossenses*. This Ile is nyghe 800 Myle from Costantynoble.

And from this Ile of Rodes, Men gon to Cipre, where bethe many Vynes, that first bene rede, and aftre o Zeer, thei becomen white: and theise Wynes that ben most white, ben most clere and best of smelle. And Men passen be that Way, be a Place that was wont to ben a gret Cytee and a gret Lond: and the Cytee was clept Cathaillye:[s] the whiche Cytee and Lond was lost, thorghe Folye of a zonge Man. For he had a fayr Damysele, that he loved wel, to his Paramour; and sche

[p] An order of Knights, called also Knights of St. John of Jerusalem.

[q] From the Colossus there, an Image of Jupiter, 70 Cubits or 105 Foot high; being one of the Wonders of the World.

[r] The Author had the concurring Opinion of some modern Greeks, that this was the Place, to which St. Paul directs his Epistle to the Colossians. But that it was not the Place, but Colossæ, a City of Phrygia Major, appears from the Conclusion of the Epistle, where mention is made of Laodicea and Hierapolis, two neighbouring Cities of Phrygia Major.

[s] Catala, E. 1; Sathalay, E. 2, 3, 4; Sathalie, L. 3, 4; Chatalie, F. 2; Cataillie, F. 1; Cattalie, L. 2; ......lie, L. 1: Sotalia, I.

dyed sodeynly, and was don in a Tombe of Marble: and for the grete Lust, that he had to hire, he wente in the Nyghte unto hire Tome and opened it, and went in and lay be hire, and wente his wey. And whan it came to the ende of nine Monethes, there com a Voys to him, and seyde, Go to the Tombe of that Woman, and open it and beholde what thou hast begoten on hire; and zif thou lette to go, thou schalt have a gret harm. And he zede and opened the Tombe; and there fleyghe out an

Eddere[1] righte hidous to see; the whiche als swythe fleighe aboute the Cytee and the Contree; and sone aftre the Cytee sank down. And there ben manye perilouse passages.

Fro Rodes to Cypre ben 500 Myle and more. But Men may gon to Cypre, and come not at Rodes. Cypre is righte a gode Ile and a fayr and a gret, and it hathe 4 princypalle Cytees within him. And there is an Erchebysshoppe at Ni-

---

[1] All the Manuscripts but that the Book is printed from, have it, *an Head*.

chosie,ᵘ and 4 othere Bysschoppes in that Lond. And at Famagost is on of the princypalle Havenes of the See, that is in the World: and there arryven Cristene Men and Sarazynes and Men of alle Naciouns. In Cipre is the Hille of the Holy Cros; and there is an Abbeye of Monkis blake; and there is the Cros of Dismas the gode Theef, as I have seyd before.ˣ And summe Men trowen, that there is half the Crosse of oure Lord: but it is not so: and thei don evylle, that make men to beleeve so. In Cipre lythe Seynt Zenomyne :ʸ of whom Men of that Contree maken gret Solempnytee. And in the Castelle of Amours lythe the Body of Seynt Hyllarie; and Men kepen it righte worschipfully. And besyde Famagost was Seynt Barnabee the Apostle born. In Cipre Men hunten

ᵘ Famagusta, all the Latin Manuscripts have it, and that right.
ˣ Page 10.   ʸ Genonoun, E. 1.

with Papyonns,[z] that ben lyche Lepardes : and thei taken wylde Bestes righte welle, and thei ben somdelle more than Lyouns ; and thei taken more scharpely the Bestes and more delyverly than don Houndes. In Cipre is the manere of Lordis and alle othere Men, alle to eten on the Erthe. For thei make Dyches in the Erthe alle aboute in the Halle, depe to the Knee, and thei do pave hem : and whan thei wil ete, thei gon there in and sytten there. And the Skylle is, for thei may ben the more fressche : For that Lond is meche more hottere than it is here. And at grete Festes and for Straungeres, thei setten Formes and Tables, as Men don in this Contree : but thei had lever sytten in the Erthe.

From Cypre, Men gon to the Lond of Jerusalem be the See : and in a Day and in a Nyghte, he that hathe gode Wynd may come to the Havene of Thire, that now is clept Surrye. There was somtyme a gret Cytee and a gode, of Crystene Men : but Sarazins han destroyed it a gret partye; and thei kepe that Havene right welle, for drede of Cristene Men. Men myghte go more right to that Havene, and come not in Cypre : but thei gon gladly to Cypre, to reste hem on the Lond, or elles to bye thingis, that they have nede to here lyvynge. On the See syde, Men may fynde many Rubyes. And there is the Welle, of the whiche Holy Writt spekethe offe, and seythe, *Fons Ortorum, et Puteus Aquarum viventiun :*[a] That is to seye, *The Welle of Gardyns, and the Dyche of lyvynge Watres.* In this Cytee of Thire, seyde

---

[z] Pampyons, E. 4.   [a] Canticles iv. 15.

the Woman to oure Lord, *Beatus Venter qui te portavit, et Ubera que succisti :* That is to seye, *Blessed be the Body that the baar, and the Pappes that thou sowkedest.* And there oure Lord forzaf the Woman of Chananee hire Synnes. And before Tyre was wont to be the Ston, on the whiche oure Lord sat and prechede : and on that Ston was founded the Chirche of Seynt Savyour.

And 8 Myle from Tyre, toward the Est, upon the See, is the Cytee of Sarphen, in Sarept of Sydonyeus. And there was wont for to dwelle Helye the Prophete; and there reysed he Jonas the Wydwes Sone from Dethe to Lyf. And 5 Myle fro Sarphen is the Cytee of Sydon : of the whiche Citee, Dydo was Lady, that was Eneas Wyf aftre the Destruccioun of Troye ; and that founded the Cytee of Cartage in Affrick, and now is cleped Dydon Sayete.[b] And in the Cytee of Tyre regned Agenore the Fadre of Dydo. And 16 Myles from Sydon is Beruthe. And from Beruthe to Sardenare is 3 Journeys. And from Sardenar is 5 Myle to Damask.

And whoso wil go longe tyme on the See, and come nerrer to Jerusalem, he schal go fro Cipre, be See, to the Port Jaff. For that is the nexte Havene to Jerusalem. For fro that Havene is not but o Day Journeye and an half to Jerusalem. And the Town is called Jaff; for on of the Sones of Noe, that highte Japhet, founded it ; and now it is clept Joppe. And zee schulle undrestonde, that it is on of the oldest Townes of the World : For it was founded before Noes Flode. And zitt there schewethe in the Roche ther, as the Irene Cheynes

[b] Didonsarte, E. 4.

were festned, that Andromade, a gret Geaunt was bounden with, and put in Presoun before Noes Flode: of the whiche Geaunt, is a rib of his Syde, that is 40 Fote longe.^c

And whoso wil arryve at the firste Port of Thire or of Surre, that I have spoken of before, may go be Londe, zif he wil, to Jerusalem. And Men gothe fro Surre unto the Citee of Dacoun in a Day. And it was clept somtyme Tholomayde. And it was somtyme a Cytee of Cristenemen, fulle fair; but it is now destroyed: and it stont upon the See. And fro Venyse to Akoun, be See, is 2080 Myles of Lombardye. And fro Calabre or fro Cecyle to Akoun, be See, is 1300 Myles of Lombardye. And the Ile of Crete is right in the myd weye. And besyde the Cytee of Akoun, toward the See, 120 Furlonges on the right syde, toward the Southe, is the Hylle of Carmelyn, where Helyas the Prophete dwellede: and there was first the Ordre of Freres Carmes founded. This Hille is not right gret, ne fulle highe. And at the Fote of this Hille was somtyme a gode Cytee of Cristene Men, that Men cleped Cayphas: For Cayphas first founded it: but it is now alle wasted. And on the lift syde of the Hille Carmelyn is a Town, that Men clepen Saffre: and that is sett on another Hille. There Seynt James and Seynt Johne were born: and in the Worschipe of hem, there is a fair Chirche. And fro Tholomayde, that Men clepen now Akoun, unto a gret Hille, that is

^c And there be Bones of a Geant's Syde 40 Foot long, E. 1, 2, 3, 4; but the French and Latin Manuscripts agree with this Text. Such was the Ignorance of those Times, as to mistake Andromeda, for the Monster that was to have devoured her.

clept Scalle of Thires, is 100 Furlonges. And besyde the Cytee of Akoun renneth a lytille Ryvere,
that is clept Belon. And there nyghe is the Fosse
of Mennon, that is alle round; and it is 100 Cubytes of largenesse, and it is alle fulle of Gravelle,
schynynge brighte, of the whiche Men maken fair
Verres and clere. And Men comen fro fer, by
Watre in Schippes, and be Londe with Cartes, for
to fetten of that Gravelle. And thoughe there be
nevere so moche taken awey there of, on the
Day, at Morwe it is as fulle azen as evere it
was. And that is a gret Mervaille. And there is
evermore gret Wynd in that Fosse, that sterethe
everemore the Gravelle, and makethe it trouble.
And zif ony Man do thereinne ony maner Me-
talle, it turnethe anon to Glasse. And the Glasse,

that is made of that Gravelle, zif it be don azen
in to the Gravelle, it turnethe anon in to Gra-

velle as it was first. And therfore somme Men seyn, that it is a sweloghe of the gravely See.

Also fro Akoun aboveseyd gon Men forthe 4 Journees to the Citee of Palestyn, that was of the Philistyenes, that now is clept Gaza, that is a gay Cytee and a riche; and it is righte fayr, and fulle of Folke, and it is a lytille fro the See. And from this Cytee broughte Sampson the stronge the Zates upon an highe Lond, whan he was taken in that Cytee: and there he slowghe in a Paleys the King and hymself, and gret nombre of the beste of the Philistienes, the whiche had put out his Eyen, and schaven his Hed, and enprisound him, be Tresoun of Dalida his Paramour. And therefore he made falle upon hem a gret Halle, whan

thei were at Mete. And from thens gon Men to the Cytee of Cesaire, and so to the Castelle of Pylgrymes, and so to Ascolonge, and than to Jaffe, and so to Jerusalem.

Cap. V.

Of manye Names of Soudans, and of the Tour of Babiloyn.

AND whoso wille go be Londe thorghe the Lond of Babyloyne, where the Sowdan dwellethe comonly, he moste gete Grace of him and Leve, to go more sikerly thorghe tho Londes and Contrees. And for to go to the Mount of Synay, before that Men gon to Jerusalem, thei schalle go fro Gaza to the Castelle of Daire. And after that, Men comen out of Surrye, and entren in to Wyldernesse, and there the Weye is sondy. And that Wyldernesse and Desert lastethe 8 Journeyes. But alleweyes Men fynden gode Innes, and alle that hem nedethe of Vytaylle. And Men clepen that Wyldernesse Achelleke.[d] And whan a Man comethe out of that Desert, he entrethe in to Egypt, that Men clepen Egypt Canopac: and aftre other Langage, Men clepen it Morsyn.[e] And there first Men fynden a gode Toun, that is clept Belethe;[f] and it is at the ende of the Kyngdom of Halappee. And from thens Men gon to Babyloyne and to Cayre.

At Babyloyne there is a faire Chirche of oure Lady, where sche dwelled 7 Zeer, whan sche fleyghe out of the Lond of Judee, for drede of Kyng Heroude. And there lythe the Body of Seynt Barbre the Virgine and Martyr. And there duelled Josephe, whan he was sold of his Bre-

---

[d] Alhylet, F, 2; Abylet, F. 1; Alhelet, L. 1, 2; Abylech, L. 3.
[e] Mersin, L. 1, 2; Mersur, L. 3, 4.
[f] Balbeor, L. 1, 2; F. 1, 2.

theren. And there* made Nabugodonozor the Kyng putte three Children in to the Forneys of Fuyr; for thei weren in the righte Trouthe of Beleeve: The whiche Children Men cleped, Ananya, Azaria, Mizaelle; as the Psalm of *Benedicite* seythe. But Nabugodonozor cleped hem other wise, Sydrak, Misak, and Abdenago: that is to seye, God glorious, God victorious, and God over alle Thinges and Remes. And that was for the Myracle, that he saughe Goddes Sone go with the Children thorghe the Fuyr, as he seyde. There duellethe the Soudan in his Calahelyke, (for there is comounly his See) in a fayr Castelle strong and gret and wel sett upon a Roche. In that Castelle duellen alle wey, to kepe it and to serve the Sowdan, mo than 6000 Persones, that taken alle here Necessaries of the Sowdanes Court. I oughte right wel to knowen it; for I duelled with him as Soudyour in his Werres a gret while, azen the Bedoynes.[g] And he wolde have maryed me fulle highely, to a gret Princes Daughtre, zif I wolde han forsaken my Lawe and my Beleve. But I thanke God, I had no wille to don it, for no thing, that he behighten me. And zee schulle undrestonde, that the Soudan is Lord of 5 Kyngdomes, that he hathe conquered and apropred to him be Strengthe: And theise ben the Names, the Kyngdom of Canapak, that is Egypt; and the Kyngdom of Jerusalem, where that David and Salomon were Kynges; and the Kyngdom of Surrye, of the whiche the Cytee of Damasc was chief; and the Kyngdom of Alappe, in the Lond of Mathe,[h]

---

* In Babylon of Chaldæa, and not in that of Egypt.

[g] Bedones, L.   [h] Dameth, E. 2, 3, 4.

and the Kyngdom of Arabye, that was to on of the
3 Kynges, that made Offryng to oure Lord, whan
he was born. And many othere Londes he
holdethe in his Hond. And there with alle he
holdethe Calyffes, that is a fulle gret thing in here
Langage: And it is als meche to seye as Kyng.
And there were wont to ben 5 Soudans: but now
there is no mo but he of Egypt. And the firste
Soudan was Zarocon,[i] that was of Mede, (as was
Fadre to Sahaladyn) that toke the Califfe of Egypt
and sloughe him, and was made Soudan be
Strengthe. Aftre that was Soudan Sahaladyn, in
whoos tyme the Kyng of Englonde, Richarde the
firste, with manye othere, kepten the passage, that
Sahaladyn ne myghte not passen. Aftre Sahaladyn, regned his Sone Boradyn;[k] and aftre him his
Nephewe. Aftre that the Comaynz,[l] that weren in
Servage in Egypt, felten hem self, that thei weren
of gret Power, thei chesen hem a Soudain amonges
hem: the whiche made him[m] to ben cleped Mele-
thesalan.[n] And in his tyme entred in to the Contree, of the Kynges of France, Seynt Lowyz, and
foughte with him: and the Soudan toke him and
enprisound him. And this was slayn of his owne
Servauntes. And aftre thei chosen an other to be
Soudan, that thei cleped Tympieman. And he let
delyveren Seynt Lowys out of Presoun, for certeyn
Ransoum. And aftre on of theise Comaynz regned, that highte Cachas, and sloughe Tympieman,
for to be Soudan: and made him ben cleped Mele-

---

[i] Yaracon, L. 1, 2; Saracon, L. 3, 4.
[k] Baradyn, L. 1, 2.   [l] Comunitas, L. The Comons.
[m] Himself.   [n] Melochsala, L. 1.

chemes.º And aftre, another that hadde to Name Bendochdare,ᵖ that sloughe Melechemes, for to be Soudan; and cleped himself Melechdare.ᑫ In his tyme entred the gode Kyng Edward of Englond in Syrye, and dide gret harm to the Sarrazines. And aftre was this Soudan enpoysound at Damasce; and his Sone thoghte to regne aftre him be Heritage, and made him to ben clept Meleschsache.ʳ But another, that had to Name Elphy, chaced him out of the Contree, and made him Soudan. This Man toke the Cytee of Tripollee and destroyede manye of the Cristene Men, the Zeer of Grace 1289: but he was anon slayn. Aftre that was the Sone of Elphy chosen to ben Soudan, and cleped him Mellethasseraff :ˢ and he toke the Citee of Akoun, and chaced out the Cristene Men : And this was also enpoysond. And than was his Brother y made Soudan, and was cleped Melechnasser. And aftre, on that was clept Guytoga,ᵗ toke him and put him in Prisoun, in the Castelle of Mountryvalle;ᵘ and made him Soudan be strengthe, and cleped him Melechcadelle :ˣ And he was of Tartaryne. But the Comaynz chaced him out of the Contree, and diden hym meche Sorwe; and maden on of hem self Soudan, that hadde to Name Lachyn.ʸ And he made him to ben clept Melechmanser :ᶻ the whiche on a Day pleyed at the Chesse, and his Swerd lay besyde him; and so befelle, that on wratthed him, and with his owne

º Melethemeos, L. 1, 2.   ᵖ Bendothdar, L. 1, 2.
ᑫ Molothdaer, L. 1, 2.   ʳ Melechsait, L. 1, 2.
ˢ Melethasserak, L. 1.   ᵗ Gutoga, L. 1, 2.
ᵘ De Monte regali, L. 1, 2. ˣ Mellethedelle, L. 1.
ʸ Bachin, L. 1, 2.   ᶻ Mellethmanser, L. 1, 2.

propre Swerd he was slayn. And aftre that, thei weren at gret Discord, for to make a Soudan. And fynally thei accordeden to Melechnasser, that Guytoga had put in Prisoun at Mountrivalle. And this regnede longe and governed wisely; so that his eldest Sone was chosen aftre him, Melechemader; the whiche his Brother leet sle prevyly,[a] for to have the Lordschipe, and made him to ben clept Melechmadabron.[b] And he was Soudan, whan I departed fro the Contrees. And wyte zee wel, that the Soudan may lede out of Egipt mo than 20000 Men of Armes. And out of Surrye, and out of Turkye, and out of other Contrees, that he holt, he may arrere mo than 50000. And alle tho ben at his Wages: and thei ben alle weys at him, withouten the Folke of his Contree, that is withouten Nombre. And everyche of hem hath be Zere the mountance of 6 score Floreynes. But it behovethe, that every of hem holde 3 Hors and a Cameylle. And be the Cytees and be the Townes ben Amyralles, that han the Governance of the Peple. On hath to governe 4, and another hath to governe 5, another mo, and another wel mo. And als moche takethe the Amyralle be him allone, as alle the other Souldyours han undre hym. And therfore whan the Soudan wille avance ony worthi Knyghte, he makethe him a Amyralle. And whan it is ony Derthe, the Knyghtes ben right pore, and thanne thei sellen bothe here Hors and here Harneys. And the Soudan hathe 4 Wyfes, on Cristene and 3 Sarazines: of the whiche, on dwellethe at Jerusalem, and another at Damasce, and another at Ascalon. And whan hem lyst, thei re-

---

[a] Fecit occidi, L.   [b] Mellethmandabron, L. 1, 2.

mewen to other Cytees. And whan the Soudan wille, he may go visite hem. And he hathe as many Paramours, as hym lykethe. For he makethe to come before him, the fairest and the nobleste of Birthe and the gentylleste Damyseles of his Con-

tree, and he maketh hem to ben kept and served fulle honourabely, and whan he wole have on to lye withe him, he makethe hem alle to come before him; and he beholdethe in alle, whiche of hem is most to his plesance, and to hire anon he sendethe or castethe a Ryng fro his Fyngre: And thanne anon sche schalle ben bathed and richely atyred, and anoynted with delicat thinges of swete smelle, and than lad to the Soudanes Chambre. And thus he dothe, als often as him list, when he wil have ony of hem. And before the Soudan comethe no Strangier, but zif he be clothed in

Clothe of Gold or of Tartarye or of Camaka, in the Sarazines guyse, and as the Sarazines usen. And it behovethe, that anon at the firste sight, that Men see the Soudan, be it in Wyndowe, or in what place elles, that Men knele to him and kysse the Erthe: for that is the manere to do Reverence to the Soudanne, of hem that speken with him. And whan that Messangeres of straunge Contrees comen before him, the Meynee of the Soudan,[c] whan the Straungeres speken to hym, thei ben aboute the Souldan with Swerdes drawen and Gysarmez and Axes, here Armes lift up in highe with the Wepenes, for to smyte upon hem, zif thei seye ony Woord, that is displesance to the Soudan. And also, no Straungere comethe before him, but that he makethe him sum Promys and Graunt, of that the Straungere asketh resonabely, beso it be not azenst his Lawe. And so don othere Prynces bezonden. For thei seyn, that no Man schalle come before no Prynce, but that he be bettre, and schalle be more gladdere in departynge from his presence, thanne he was at the comynge before hym.

And undirstonde zee, that that Babyloyne that I have spoken offe, where that the Soudan duellethe, is not that gret Babyloyne, where the Dyversitee of Langages was first made for Vengeance, by the Myracle of God, when the grete Tour of Babel was begonnen to ben made; of the whiche the Walles weren 64 Furlonges of heighthe;[d] that is in the grete Desertes of Arabye, upon the Weye as Men gon toward the Kyngdom of Caldee. But it is fulle long sithe that ony Man durste neyhe to the Tour: for it is alle deserte and fulle of Dra-

[c] Gens ipsius, L. [d] So both Latin and French MSS.

gouns and grete Serpentes, and fulle of dyverse venymouse Bestes alle abouten. That Tour, with the Cytee, was of 25 Myle in cyrcuyt of the Walles; as thei of the Contree seyn, and as Men may demen by estymatioun, aftre that Men tellen of the Contree. And though it be clept the Tour of Babiloyne, zit natheles there were ordeyned with inne many Mansiouns and many gret duellynge Places, in lengthe and brede: And that Tour conteyned gret Contree in circuyt: For the Tour allone conteyned 10 Myle sqware. That Tour founded Kyng Nembrothe, that was Kyng of that Contree: and he was firste Kyng of the World. And he leet make an Ymage in the lyknesse of his Fadre, and constreyned alle his Subgettes for to worschipe it. And anon begonnen othere Lordes to do the same. And so begonnen the Ydoles and the Symulacres first. The Town and the Cytee weren fulle wel sett in a fair Contree and a Playn; that Men clepen the Contree of Samar:[e] of the whiche the Walles of the Cytee werein 200 Cubytes in heighte,[f] and 50 Cubytes in breadthe. And the Ryvere of Euphrate ran thorghe out the Cytee and aboute the Tour also. But Cirus the Kyng of Perse toke from hem the Ryvere, and destroyede all the Cytee and the Tour also. For he departed that Ryvere in 360 smale Ryveres; because that he had sworn, that he scholde putte the Ryvere in suche poynt, that a Woman myghte wel passe there, withouten castynge of of hire Clothes; for als moche as he hadde lost many worthi Men,

[e] Sennaar, L. 1, 2.
[f] Herodotus makes them 350 Foot high, 87 Foot thick, and 480 Furlongs or 60 Miles about.

that troweden to passen that Ryvere by swymmynge.

And from Babyloyne, where the Soudan dwellethe, to go right betwene the Oryent[g] and the Septemtryon, toward the grete Babyloyne, is 40 Journeyes to passen be Desart. But it is not the grete Babiloyne, in the Lond and in the Powere of the seyd Soudan; but it is in the Power and the Lordschipe of Persye. But he holdethe it of the grete Cham, that is the gretteste Emperour and the most Sovereyn Lord of alle the parties bezonde: and he is Lord of the Iles of Cathay and of many othere Iles, and of a gret partie of Inde. And his Lond marchethe unto Prestre Johnes Lond; and he holt so moche Lond, that he knowethe not the ende. And he is more myghty and grettre Lord withoute Comparisoun, than is the Soudan. Of his ryalle Estate and of his myghte, I schalle speke more plenerly, when I schalle speke of the Lond and of the Contree of Ynde.

Also the Cytee of Methone[h] where Machomet lythe, is of the grete Desertes of Arabye. And there lithe the Body of hym fulle honourabely in here Temple, that the Sarazines clepen Muskethe. And it is fro Babyloyne the lesse, where the Soudan duellethe, unto Methon aboveseyd, in to a 32 Journeyes. And wytethe wel, that the Rewme of Arabye is a fulle gret Contree: but there in is over moche Dysert. And no Man may dwelle there in that Desert, for Defaute of Watre. For that Lond is alle gravelly and fulle of Sond. And it is drye and nothing fructuous; because that it hathe no Moysture: and therfore is there so meche Desart.

[g] East and North. [h] Mecca. Medina

And zif it hadde Ryveres and Welles, and the Lond also were, as it is in other parties, it scholde ben als fulle of Peple and als fulle enhabyted with Folk, as in other Places. For there is fulle gret Multitude of Peple, where as the Lond is enhabyted. Arabye durethe fro the endes of the Reme of Caldee, unto the laste ende of Affryk, and marchethe to the Lond of Ydumee, toward the ende of Botron. And in Caldee, the chief Cytee is Baldak.[i] And of Affryk, the Chief Cytee is Cartage, that Dydo, that was Eneas Wyf, founded. The whiche Eneas was of the Cytee of Troye, and aftre was Kyng of Itaylle. Mesopotamye strecchethe also unto the Desertes of Arabye; and it is a gret Contree. In this Contree is the Cytee of Araym, where Abrahames Fadree duelled, and from whens Abraham departed, be Commandement of the Aungelle. And of that Cytee was Effraym,[k] that was a gret Clerk and a gret Doctour. And Theophylus was of that Cytee also, that oure Ladye savede from oure Enemye. And Mesopotame durethe fro the Ryvere of Eufrates, unto the Ryvere of Tygris. For it is betwene tho 2 Ryveres. And bezonde the Ryvere of Tygre, is Caldee, that is a fulle gret Kyngdom. In that Rewme, at Baldak aboveseyd, was wont to duelle the Calyffeez, that was wont to ben bothe as Emperour and Pope of the Arabyenez; so that he was Lord Spirituelle and Temporelle. And he was Successour to Machomete, and of his Generatioun. That Cytee of Baldak was wont to ben cleped Sutis:[l] and Nabugodonozor founded it. And there duelled the Holy Prophete Daniel; and there he saughe Visionnes

[i] Bagdad.   [k] Efraim Çyrus. ∫   [l] Susa.

of Hevene; and there he made the Expositioun of Dremes. And in old tyme, there were wont to be 3 Calyffez; and thei dwelleden in the Cytee of Baldak aboveseyd.

And at Cayre besides Babyloyne duelled the Calyffee of Egypt. And at Marrok, upon the West See, duelte the Calyffee of Barbaryenes and of Affrycanes. And now is there non of the Calyffeez, ne noughte han ben, sithe the tyme of Sowdan Sahaladyn. For from that tyme hidre, the Sowdan clepethe him self Calyffee. And so han the Calyffeez y lost here Name. Also wytethe wel, that Babyloyne the lesse, where the Soudan duellethe, and at the Cytee of Cayr, that is nyghe besyde it, ben grete huge Cytees manye and fayr; and that on sytt nyghe that other. Babyloyne sytt upon the Ryvere of Gyson, somtyme clept Nyle, that comethe out of Paradys terrestre. That Ryvere of Nyle, alle the zeer, whan the Sonne entrethe in to the Signe of Cancer, it begynnethe to wexe; and it wexethe alle weys, als longe as the Sonne is in Cancro, and in the Signe of Lyoune. And it wexethe in suche manere, that it is somtyme so gret, that it is 20 Cubytes or more of depnesse; and thanne it dothe gret Harm to the Godes, that ben upon the Lond. For thanne may no Man travaylle to ere the Londes, for the grete Moystnesse: And therfore is there dere Tyme in that Contree. And also whan it wexethe lytylle, it is dere Tyme in that Contree: For defaute of Moysture. And whan the Sonne is in the Signe of Virgo, thanne begynnethe the Ryvere for to wane and to decrece lytyl and lytylle; so that whan the Sonne is entred in to the Signe of Libra, thanne thei entren betwene theise Ryveres. This Ryvere comethe rennynge from Paradys terrestre, betwene the Desertes of Ynde; and aftre it smytt unto Londe, and rennethe longe tyme many grete Contrees undre Erthe: And aftre it gothe out undre an highe Hille, that Men clepen Alothe, that is betwene Ynde and Ethiope, the distance of five Moneths journeyes fro the entree of Ethiope. And aftre it envyronnethe alle Ethiope and Morekane,[m] and gothe alle along fro the Lond of Egipte; unto the Cytee of Alisandre, to the ende of Egipte; and there it fallethe into the See. Aboute this Ryvere, ben manye Briddes and Foules, as Sikonyes, that thei clepen Ibes.

Egypt is a long Contree; but it is streyt, that is to seye narow; for thei may not enlargen it toward the Desert, for defaute of Watre. And the Contree is sett along upon the Ryvere of Nyle; be als moche as that Ryvere may serve be Flodes or otherwise, that whanne it flowethe, it may spreden abrood thorghe the Contree: so is the Contree large of Lengthe. For there it reyneth not but lityIle in that Contree: and for that Cause, they have no Watre, but zif it be of that Flood of that Ryvere. And for als moche as it ne reynethe not in that Contree, but the Eyr is alwey pure and cleer, therfore in that Contree ben the gode Astronomyeres; for thei fynde there no Cloudes, to letten hem. Also the Cytee of Cayre is righte gret, and more huge than that of Babyloyne the lesse: And it sytt aboven toward the Desert of Syrye, a lytille above the Ryvere aboveseyd. In Egipt there ben 2 parties; the Heghte, that is to-

[m] Mauritania.

ward Ethiope; and the Lowenesse, that is towardes Arabye. In Egypt is the Lond of Ramasses and the Lond of Gessen. Egipt is a strong Contree: for it hathe manye schrewede Havenes, because of the grete Roches, that ben stronge and daungerouse to passe by. And at Egipt, toward the Est, is the rede See, that durethe unto the Cytee of Coston: and toward the West, is the Contree of Lybye, that is a fulle drye Lond, and lityll of Fruyt: for it is over moche plentee of Hete. And that Lond is clept Fusthe. And toward the partie Meridionalle is Ethiope. And toward the Northe is the Desart, that durethe unto Syrye: And so is the Contree strong on alle sydes. And it is wel a 15 Journeyes of Lengthe, and more than two so moche of Desert: and it is but two Journeyes in Largenesse. And between Egipt and Nubye, it hathe wel a 12 Journees of Desert. And Men of Nubye ben Cristene: but thei ben blake as the Mowres, for grete Hete of the Sonne.

In Egipt there ben 5 Provynces; that on highte Sahythe, that other highte Demeseer,[n] another Resithe, that is an Ile in Nyle, another Alisandre, and another the Lond of Damiete. That Cytee was wont to be righte strong: but it was twyes wonnen of the Cristene Men: And therfore after that the Sarazines beten down the Walles. And with the Walles and the Tour thereof, the Sarazenes maden another Cytee more fer from the See, and clepeden it the newe Damyete. So that now no Man duellethe at the rathere Toun of Damyete. And that Cytee of Damyete is on of the Havenes of Egypt: and at Alisandre is that

[n] Deveorser, L. 1, 2; Damaser, F. 2.

other, that is a fulle strong Cytee. But there is no Watre to drynke, but zif it come be Condyt from Nyle, that entrethe in to here Cisternes. And who so stopped that Watre from hem, thei myghte not endure there. In Egypt there ben but fewe Forcelettes or Castelles, be cause that the Contree is so strong of him self. At the Desertes of Egypte was a worthi Man, that was an holy Heremyte; and there mette with hym a Monstre, (that is to seyne, a Monstre is a thing difformed azen Kynde both of Man or of Best or of ony thing elles: and that is cleped a Monstre). And this Monstre, that mette with this holy Heremyte, was as it hadde ben a Man, that hadde 2 Hornes trenchant on his Forehede; and he hadde a Body lyk a Man, unto the Nabele; and benethe he hadde the Body lyche a Goot. And the Heremyte asked him, what he was. And the Monstre answerde him, and seyde, he was a dedly Creature, suche as God hadde formed, and duelled in tho Desertes in purchasynge his Sustynance; and besoughte the Heremyte, that he wolde preye God for him, the whiche that cam from Hevene for to saven alle Mankynde, and was born of a Mayden, and suffred Passioun and Dethe, (as we well knowen) be whom we lyven and ben. And zit is the Hede with the 2 Hornes of that Monstre at Alisandre for a Marveyle.°

In Egypt is the Cytee of Elyople, that is to seyne, the Cytee of the Sonne. In that Cytee there is a Temple made round, aftre the schappe of the Temple of Jerusalem. The Prestes of that

° *Nota, Of a Merveyle.* This Story is in the Life of Paul the Hermite, writ by St. Jerom; and there is a Copy thereof in the Cotton Library 1000 Years old.

Temple han alle here Wrytynges, undre the Date of the Foul that is clept Fenix: and there is non but on in alle the World. And he comethe to brenne him self upon the Awtere of the Temple, at the ende of 5 Hundred Zeer: for so longe he lyvethe. And at the 500 Zeres ende, the Prestes arrayen here Awtere honestly, and putten there upon Spices and Sulphur vif and other thinges, that wolen brenne lightly. And than the Brid Fenix comethe, and brennethe him self to Ashes. And the first Day next aftre, Men fynden in the Ashes a Worm; and the secunde Day next aftre, Men funden a Brid quyk and perfyt; and the thridde Day next aftre, he fleethe his wey.[p] And so there is no mo Briddes of that Kynde in alle the World, but it allone. And treuly that is a gret Myracle of God. And Men may well lykne that Bryd unto God; be cause that there nys no God but on; and also, that oure Lord aroos fro Dethe to Lyve, the thridde Day. This Bryd Men seen often tyme, fleen in tho Contrees: And he is not mecheles more than an Egle. And he hathe a Crest of Fedres upon his Hed more gret than the Poocok hathe; and his Nekke is zalowe, aftre colour of an Orielle, that is a Ston well schynynge; and his Bek is coloured blew, as Ynde; and his Wenges ben of Purpre Colour, and the Taylle is zelow and red, castynge his Taylle azen in travers. And he is a fulle fair Brid to loken upon, azenst the Sonne: for he schynethe fully gloriously and nobely.[q]

Also in Egypt ben Gardyns, than han Trees

[p] The Author has this Story from Pliny's Natural History, Lib. X. Cap. 2.

Plin. Nat. Hist. L. XI. Cap. 37.

and Herbes, the whiche beren Frutes 7 tymes in the Zeer. And in that Lond Men fynden many fayre Emeraudes and y nowe, And therefore thei ben there grettere cheep. Also whan it reynethe ones in the Somer, in the Lond of Egipt, thanne is alle the Contree fulle of grete Myrs. Also at Cayre, that I spak of before, sellen Men comounly bothe Men and Wommen of other Lawe, as we don here Bestes in the Markat. And there is a comoun Hows in that Cytee, that is alle fulle of smale Furneys; and thidre bryngen Wommen of the Toun here Eyren of Hennes, of Gees and of Dokes, for to ben put in to tho Furneyses. And thei that kepen that Hows coveren hem with Hete of Hors Dong, with outen Henne, Goos or Doke or ony other Foul; and at the ende of 3 Wekes or of a Monethe, thei comen azen and taken here Chickenes and norissche hem and bryngen hem forthe: so that alle the Contree is fulle of hem. And so Men don there bothe Wyntre and Somer.

Also in that Contree, and in othere also, Men fynden longe Apples to selle, in hire cesoun: and Men clepen hem Apples of Paradys; and thei ben righte swete and of gode Savour. And thoghe zee kutte hem in never so many Gobettes or parties, overthwart or end longes, evermore zee schulle fynden in the myddes the figure of the Holy Cros of oure Lord Jesu. But thei wil roten within 8 Days: And for that Cause Men may not carye of the Apples to no fer Contrees. And thei han grete Leves, of a Fote and an half of lengthe: and thei ben covenably large. And Men fynden there also the Appulle Tree of Adam, that han a byte at on

E

of the sydes. And there ben also Fyge Trees, that beren no Leves, but Fyges upon the smale Braunches: and Men clepen hem Figes of Pharoon. Also besyde Cayre, withouten that Cytee, is the Feld where Bawme growethe: And it comethe out on smale Trees, that ben non hyere than a Mannes breek Girdille; and thei semen as Wode that is of the wylde Vyne. And in that Feld ben 7 Welles, that oure Lord Jesu Crist made with on of his Feet, whan he wente to pleyen with other Children. That Feld is not so well closed, but that Men may entren at here owne list. But in that Cesonne, that the Bawme is growynge, Men put there to gode kepynge, that no Man dar ben hardy to entre. This Bawme growethe in no Place, but only there. And thoughe that Men bryngen of the Plauntes, for to planten in other Contrees, thei growen wel and fayre, but thei bryngen forthe no fructuous thing: and the Leves of Bawme ne fallen noughte. And Men kutten the Braunches with a scharp Flyntston or with a scharp Bon, whanne Men wil go to kutte hem: For who so kutte hem with Iren, it wolde destroye his Vertue and his Nature. And the Sarazines clepen the Wode Enonch balse; and the Fruyt, the whiche is as Quybybes,[r] thei clepen Abebissam; and the Lycour, that droppethe fro the Braunches, thei clepen Guybalse. And Men maken alle weys that Bawme to ben tyled of the Cristenemen, or elles it wolde not fructifye; as the Sarazines seyn hem self: for it hathe ben often tyme preved. Men seyn also, that the Bawme growethe in Ynde the more, in that Desert where the Trees of the

[r] Cubeba, L.

Sonne and of the Mone spak to Alisaundre. But I have not seen it. For I have not ben so fer aboven upward: because that there ben to many perilouse Passages. And wyte zee wel, that a Man oughte to take gode kepe for to bye Bawme, but zif he cone knowe it righte wel: for he may righte lyghtely be disceyved. For Men sellen a Gome, that Men clepen Turbentyne, in stede of Bawme; and thei putten there to a littille Bawme for to zeven gode Odour. And sume putten Wax in Oyle of the Wode of the fruyt of Bawme, and seyn that it is Bawme: and sume destyllen Clowes of Gylofre and of Spykenard of Spayne and of othere Spices, that ben well smellynge; and the Lykour that gothe out there of, thei clepe it Bawme: and thei wenen, that thei han Bawme; and thei have non. For the Sarazines countrefeten it be sotyltee of Craft, for to disceyven the Cristene Men, as I have seen fulle many a tyme. And aftre hem, the Marchauntis and the Apotecaries countrefeten it eftsones, and than it is lasse worthe, and a gret del worse. But zif it lyke zou, I schalle schewe, how zee schulle knowe and preve, to the ende that zee schulle not ben disceyved. First zee schulle wel knowe, that the naturelle Bawme is fulle cleer, and of Cytrine colour, and stronge smellynge: And zif it be thykke, or reed or blak, it is sophisticate, that is to seyne, contrefeted and made lyke it, for disceyt. And undrestondethe, that zif zee wil putte a litylle Bawme in the Pawme of zoure hond, azen the Sonne, zif it be fyn and gode, zee ne schulle not suffre zoure hand azenst the hete of the Sonne. Also takethe a lytille Bawme, with the poynt of a Knif, and touche it to the fuyr, and zif it brenne, it is a gode signe. Aftre take also a drope of Bawme, and put it in to a Dissche or in a Cuppe with Mylk of a Goot; and zif it be naturelle Bawme, anon it wole take and beclippe the Mylk. Or put a Drope of Bawme in clere Watre, in a Cuppe of Sylver or in a clere Bacyn, and stere it wel with the clere Watre; and zif that the Bawme be fyn and of his owne kynde, the Watre schalle nevere trouble: And zif the Bawme be sophisticate, that is to seyne countrefeted, the Watre schalle become anon trouble: And also zif the Bawme be fyn, it schalle falle to the botme of the Vesselle, as thoughe it were Quyksylver: For the fyn Bawme is more hevy twyes, than is the Bawme that is sophisticate and countrefeted. Now I have spoken of Bawme: and now also I schalle speke of an other thing, that is bezonde Babyloyne, above the Flode of Nyle, toward the Desert, betwene Affrik and Egypt: that is to seyn, of the Gerneres of Joseph, that he leet make, for to kepe the Greynes for the perile of the dere Zeres. And thei ben made of Ston, fulle wel made of Masonnes craft: of the whiche two ben merveylouse grete and hye; and the tothere ne ben not so grete. And every Gerner hathe a Zate, for to entre with inne, a lytille hyghe fro the Erthe. For the Lond is wasted and fallen, sithe the Gerneres were made. And with inne thei ben alle fulle of Serpentes. And aboven the Gerneres with outen ben many scriptures of dyverse Langages. And sum Men seyn, that thei ben Sepultures of grete Lordes, that weren somtyme; but that is not trewe: for alle the comoun rymour and speche is of alle the peple there, bothe fer and nere, that thei ben the Garneres of Joseph. And so fynden thei in here Scriptures and in here Cronycles. On that other partie, zif thei werein Sepultures, thei scholden not ben voyd with inne. For zee may well knowe, that Tombes and Sepultures ne ben not made of suche gretnesse, ne of such highnesse. Wherfore it is not to beleve, that thei ben Tombes or Sepultures. In Egypt also there ben dyverse Langages and dyverse Lettres, and of other manere condicioun, than there ben in other parties. As I schalle devyse zou, suche as thei ben, and the names how thei clepen hem; to suche entent, that zee mowe knowe the difference of hem and of othere. Athoimis, Bunchi, Chinok, Durain, Eni, Fin, Gomor, Heket, Janny, Karacta, Luzanim, Miche, Naryn, Oldache, Pilon, Quyn, Yron, Sichen, Thola, Urmron, Yph and Zarm, Thoit.

Now will I retourne azen, or I procede ony ferthere, for to declare zou the othere weyes, that drawen toward Babiloyne, where the Soudan him self duellethe, that is at the entree of Egypt; for als moche as mony folk gon thidre first, and aftre that to the Mount Synay, and aftre retournen to Jerusalem, as I have seyd zou here beforn. For thei fulfillen first the more long Pilgrymage, and aftre retournen azen be the nexte Weyes; because that the more nye Weye is the more worthi, and that is Jerusalem. For no other Pylgrymage is not lyk, in comparsoun to it. But for to fulle fylle here Pilgrymages more esily and more sykerly, men gon first the longer weye. But whoso wil go to Babyloyne be another weye, more schort from the Contrees of the West, that I have reherced before; or from other Contrees next fro hem; than Men gon by Fraunce, be Burgoyne and be Lombardye.

It nedethe not to telle zou the names of the Cytees, ne of the Townes that ben in that Weye: For the Weye is comoun, and it is knowen of many Naciouns. And there ben many Havenes, that Men taken the See. Sume Men taken the See at Gene, some at Venyce, and passen by the See Adryatyk, that is clept the Goulf of Venyse, that departethe Ytaylle and Greece on that syde. And some gon to Naples, some to Rome, and from Rome to Brandys,[1] and there thei taken the See: and in many othere places, where that Havenes ben. And Men gon be Tussye, be Champayne, be Calabre, be Appuille, and be the Hilles of Ytaylle, Chorisqe, be Sardyne, and be Cycile, that is a gret Ile and a gode. In that Ile of Cycile there ys a maner of a Gardyn, in the whiche ben many dyverse Frutes. And the Gardyn is alweys grene and florisshing, alle the cesouns of the Zeer, als wel in Wyntre es in Somer. That Yle holt in compas aboute 350 Frensche Myles. And betwene Cycele and Itaylle there is not but a lytille Arm of the See, that Men clepen the Farde of Mescyne. And Cycile is betwene the See Adryatyk and the See of Lombardye. And fro Cycyle in to Calabre is but 8 Myles of Lombardye. And in Cycile there is a manere of Serpentes, be the whiche Men assayen and preven, where here Children ben Bastardis or none, or of lawefulle Mariage. For zif thei ben born in righte Mariage, the Serpentes gon aboute hem, and don hem non harm: and zif thei ben born in Avowtrie, the Serpentes byten hem and envenyme hem. And thus manye wedded Men preve, zif the Children ben here owne. Also in that Ile

[1] Brindisi, Brundusiñ.

is the Mount Ethna, that Men clepen Mount Gybelle; and the Vulcanes that ben everemore brennynge. And there ben 7 places, that brennen and that casten out dyverse flawmes and dyverse colour. And be the chaungynge of tho Flawmes, Men of that Contree knowen, whanne it schalle be Derthe or gode tyme, or cold or hoot, or moyst or drye, or in alle othere maneres, how the tyme schalle be governed. And from Itaille unto the Vulcanes nys but 25 Myle. And Men seyn, that the Vulcanes ben Weyes of Helle.

Also whoso gothe be Pyse, zif that Men list to go that Weye, there is an Arm of the See, where that Men gon to othere Havenes in tho Marches. And than Men passen be the Ile of Greaf, that is at Gene: And aftre arryvethe Men in Grece at the Havene of the Cytee of Myrok, or at the Havene of Valone, or at the Cytee of Duras; and there is a Duk at Duras, or at othere Havenes in tho Marces: And so Men gon to Costantynoble. And aftre gon Men be Watre to the Ile of Crete and to the Ile of Rodes, ond so to Cypre, and so to Athens, and fro thens to Costantynoble.

To holde the more righte Weye be See, it is wel a 1880 Myle of Lombardye. And aftre fro Cipre Men gon be See, and leven Jerusalem and alle the Contree on the left hond, unto Egypt, and arryven at the Cytee of Damyete, that was wont to be fulle strong, and it sytt at the entree of Egypt. And fro Damyete gon Men to the Cytee of Alizandre, that sytt also upon the See. In that Cytee was seynte Kateryne beheded. And there was seynt Mark the Evangelist martyred and buryed.

But the Emperour Leoun made his Bones to ben broughte to Venyse. And zit there is at Alizandre a faire Chirche, alle white withouten peynture: and so ben alle the othere Chirches; that weren of the Cristene Men, alle white with inne. For the Panemes and the Sarrazynes maden hem white, for to fordon the Ymages of Seyntes, that weren peynted on the Walles. That Cytee of Alizandre is wel 30 Furlonges in lengthe: but it is but 10 on largenesse. And it is a full noble Cytee and a fayr. At that Cytee entrethe the Ryvere of Nyle in to the See; as I to zou have seyd before. In that Ryvere Men fynden many precyouse Stones, and meche also of Lignum Aloes: and it is a manere of Wode, that comethe out of Paradys terrestre, the whiche is good for manye dyverse Medicynes: and it is righte dereworthe. And fro Alizandre Men gon to Babyloyne, where the Soudan dwellethe; that sytt also upon the Ryvere of Nyle. And this Weye is most schort, for to go streyghte unto Babiloyne.

Now schall I seye зou also the Weye, that gothe fro Babiloyne to the Mount of Synay, where Seynte Kateryne lythe. He moste passe be the Desertes of Arabye; be the whiche Desertes Moyses ladde the Peple of Israel: and thanne passe Men be the Welle, that Moyses made with his hond in the Desertes, whan the People grucched, for thei fownden no thing to drynke. And than passe Men be the Welle of Marache, of the whiche the Watre was first byttre: but the Children of Israel putten there inne a Tree; and anon the Watre was swete and gode for to drynke. And thanne gon Men be Desart unto the Vale of Elyn; in the whiche Vale be 12 Welles: and there ben 72 Trees of Palme, that beren the Dates, the whiche Moyses fond with the Children of Israel. And fro that Valeye is but a gode Journeye to the Mount of Synay.

And whoso wil go be another Weye fro Babiloyne, than Men gothe be the Rede See, that is an Arm of the See Occean. And there passed Moyses, with the Children of Israel, overthwart the See, alle drye, whan Pharao the Kyng of Egypt chaced hem. And that See is wel a 6 Myle of largenesse in bredthe. And in that See was Pharao drowned and alle his Hoost, that he ladde. That See is not more reed than another See; but in some place thereof is the Gravelle reede: and therfore Men clepen it the Rede See. That See rennethe to the endes of Arabye and of Palestyne. That See lastethe more than 4 Journeyes. And then gon Men be Desert unto the Vale of Elyn: and fro thens to the Mount of Synay. And зee may wel undirstonde, that be this Desert, no Man may go on

Hors back, be cause that there nys nouther Mete for Hors ne Watre to drynke. And for that cause Men passen that Desert with Camelle. For the Camaylle fynt alle wey Mete in Trees and on Busshes, that he fedethe him with. And he may well faste fro Drynk 2 dayes or 3 : and that may non Hors don.

And wyte wel, that from Babiloyne to the Mount Synay is wel a 12 gode Journeyes : and som Men maken hem more : and some Men hasten hem and peynen hem ; and therefore thei maken hem lesse. And alle weys fynden Men Latyneres to go with hem in the Contrees, and ferthere bezonde, in to tyme that Men conne the Langage. And it behovethe Men to bere Vitaille with hem, that schalle duren hem in tho Desertes, and other necessaries for to lyve by.

And the Mount of Synay is clept the Desert of Syne, that is for to seyne, the Bussche brennynge : because there Moyses sawghe oure Lord God many tymes, in forme of Fuyr brennynge upon that Hille; and also in a Bussche brennynge ; and spak to him. And that was at the Foot of the Hille. There is an Abbeye of Monks, wel bylded and wel closed with Zates of Iren, for drede of the wylde Bestes. And the Monkes ben Arrabyenes, or Men of Greece : and there is a gret Covent ; and alle thei ben as Heremytes ; and thei drynken no Wyn, but zif it be on principalle Festes : and thei ben fulle devoute Men, and lyven porely and sympely, with Joutes and with Dates : and thei don gret Abstynence and Penaunce. There is the Chirche of Seynte Kateryne, in the whiche ben manye Lampes brennynge. For thei han of Oyle

of Olyves y now, bothe for to brenne in here
Lampes, and to ete also: And that plentee have
thei be the Myracle of God. For the Ravenes and

the Crowes and the Choughes, and other Foules of
the Contree assemblen hem there every Zeer ones,
and fleen thider as in pilgrymage: and everyche
of hem bringethe a Braunche of the Bayes or of
Olyve, in here Bekes, in stede of Offryng, and leven
hem there; of the whiche the Monkes maken gret
plentee of Oyle.; and this is a gret Marvaylle.
And sithe that Foules, that han no kyndely Wytt
ne Resoun, gon thidre to seche that gloriouse Virgyne; wel more oughten Men than to seche hire
and to worschipen hire. Also behynde the Awtier
of that Chirche is the place where Moyses saughe
oure Lord God in a brennynge Bussche. And
whanne the Monkes entren in to that place, thei
don of bothe Hosen and Schoon or Botes alweys;
be cause that oure Lord seyde to Moyses, *Do of
thin Hosen and thi Schon: for the place that thou
stondest on is Lond holy and blessed.* And the

Monkes clepen that place Bezeleel, that is to seyne, the Schadew of God. And besyde the highe Awtiere, 3 degrees of heighte, is the Fertre[t] of Alabastre, where the Bones of Seynte Kateryne lyzn. And the Prelate of the Monkes schewethe the Relykes to the pilgrymes. And with an Instrument of Sylver, he frotethe the Bones; and thanne ther gothe out a lytylle Oyle, as thoughe it were a maner swetynge, that is nouther lyche to Oyle ne to Bawme; but it is fulle swete of smelle: And of that thei zeven a litylle to the Pilgrymes; for there gothe out but litylle quantitee of the Likour. And aftre that thei schewen the Heed of Seynte Kateryne, and the Clothe that sche was wrapped inne, that is zit alle blody. And in that same Clothe so y wrapped, the Aungeles beren hire Body to the Mount Synay, and there thei buryed hire with it. And thanne thei schewen the Bussche, that brenned and wasted nought, in the whiche oure Lord spak to Moyses, and othere Relikes y nowe. Also whan the Prelate of the Abbeye is ded, I have undirstonden, be informacioun, that his Lampe quenchethe. And whan thei chesen another Prelate, zif he be a gode Man and worthi to be Prelate, his Lampe schal lighte, with the Grace of God, withouten touchinge of ony Man. For everyche of hem hathe a Lampe be him self. And be here Lampes thei knowen wel whan ony of hem schalle dye. For whan ony schalle dye, the Lyghte begynnethe to chaunge and to wexe dym. And zif he be chosen to ben Prelate, and is not worthi, is Lampe quenchethe anon. And other Men han told me, that he that syngethe the Masse for the

[t] Feretrum.

Prelate that is ded, he schalle fynde upon the Awtier the Name writen of him that schalle be Prelate 'chosen. And so upon a day I asked of the Monkes, bothe on and other, how this befelle. But thei wolde not telle me no thing, in to the tyme that I seyde, that thei scholde not hyde the Grace, that God did hem; but that thei scholde publissche it, to make the Peple to have the more Devocioun; and that thei diden synne, to hide Goddis Myracle, as me seemed. For the Myracles, that God hathe don, and zit dothe every Day, ben the Wytnesse of his Myghte and of his Merveylles; as David seythe in the Psaultere; *Mirabilia Testimonia tua, Domine:* that is to seyn, *Lord, thi Merveyles ben thi Wytnesse.* And thanne thei tolde me, bothe on and other, how it befelle fulle many a tyme: but more I myghte not have of hem. In that Abbeye ne entrethe not no Flye ne Todes ne Ewtes, ne suche foule venymouse Bestes, ne Lyzs ne Flees, be the Myracle of God and of oure Lady. For there were wont to ben many suche manere of Filthes, that the Monkes werein in wille to leve the Place and the Abbeye, and weren gon fro thens, upon the Mountayne aboven, for to eschewe that Place. And oure Lady cam to hem, and bad hem tournen azen: And fro this forewardes nevere entred suche Filthe in that Place amonges hem, ne nevere schalle entre here aftre. Also before the Zate is the Welle, where Moyses smot the Ston, of the whiche the Watre cam out plenteously.

Fro that Abbeye Men gon up the Mountayne of Moyses, be many degrees: and there Men fynden first a Chirche of oure Lady, where that sche mette the Monkes, whan thei fledden awey for the

Vermyn aboveseyd. And more highe upon that Mountayne is the Chapelle of Helye the Prophete. And that Place thei clepen Oreb, where of Holy Writt spekethe. *Et ambulavit in fortitudine Cibi illius. usq; ad Montem Oreb:* that is to seyne, *And he wente in Strengthe of that Mete, unto the Hille of God, Oreb.* And there nyghe is the Vyne that Seynt Johne the Evaungelist planted, that Men clepen Reisins, *Staphis.* And a lytille aboven is the Chapelle of Moyses, and the Roche where Moyses fleghe to, for drede, whan he saughe oure Lord face to face. And in that Roche is prented the forme of his Body; for he smot so strongly and so harde him self in that Roche, that alle his body was dolven with inne, thorghe the Myracle of God. And there besyde is the Place where oure Lord toke to Moyses the 10 Comandementes of the Lawe. And there is the Cave undre the Roche, where Moyses duelte, whan he fasted 40 Dayes and 40 Nyghtes. And from that Mountayne Men passen a gret Valeye, for to gon to another Mountayne, where Seynt Kateryne was buryed of the Aungeles of oure Lord. And in that Valey is a Chirche of 40 Martyres: and there singen the Monkes of the Abbeye often tyme. And that Valey is right cold. And aftre Men gon up the Mountayne of Seynt Kateryne, that is more highe then the Mount of Moyses. And there, where seynt Kateryne was buryed, is nouther Chirche ne Chapelle, ne other duellynge place: But there is an heep of Stones aboute the place, where the body of hire was put of the Aungeles. There was wont to ben a Chapelle: but it was casten downe, and zit lyggen the Stones there. And alle be it that the Collect of Seynte

Kateryne seye, that it is the Place where oure
Lord betaughten the Ten Comandementes to Moy-
ses, and there where the blessed Virgyne seynte
Kateryne was buryed; that is to undrestonde, in o
Contree, or in o Place berynge o Name. For bothe
that on and that othre is clept the Mount of Synay.
But there is a grete weye from that on to that othre,
and a gret deep Valeye betwene hem.

Cap. VI.

Of the Desert betwene the Chirche of Seynte Kate-
ryne and Jerusalem. Of the drie Tre; and how
Roses cam first in the World.

Now aftre that Men had visited tho holy Places,
thanne will thei turnen toward Jerusalem. And
than wil thei take leve of the Monkes, and recom-
menden hem to here Preyeres. And than thei
zeven the Pilgrimes of here Vitaylle, for to passe
with the Desertes, toward Surrye. And tho
Desertes duren wel a 13 Journeyes. In that
Desert duellyn manye of Arrabyenes, that Men
clepen Bedoynes and Ascopardes. And thei ben
folke fulle of alle evylle Condiciouns. And thei
have none Houses, but Tentes, that thei maken of
Skynnes of Bestes, as of Camaylles and of othere
Bestes, that thei eten; and there benethe thei
couchen hem and duellen, in Place, where thei
may fynden Watre, as on the Rede See or elles
where. For in that Desert is fulle gret defaute of

Watre: and often time it fallethe, that where Men fynden Watre at o tyme in a Place, it faylethe another tyme. And for that skylle, thei make none Habitaciouns there. Theise folk, that I speke of, thei tylen not the Lond, ne thei laboure noughte; for thei eten no Bred, but zif it be ony that dwellen nyghe a gode Toun, that gon thidre and eten Bred som tyme. And thei rosten here Flesche and here Fische upon the hote Stones azenst the

Sonne. And thei ben stronge Men and wel fyghtynge. And there is so meche multytude of that folk, that thei ben withouten nombre. And thei ne recchen of no thing, ne don not, but chacen aftre Bestes, to eten hem. And thei recchen no thing of here Lif: and therfore thei dowten not the Sowdan, ne non othre Prince; but thei dar wel werre with hem, zif thei don ony thing that is grevance to hem. And thei han often tyme Werre with the Soudan; and namely, that tyme that I was with him. And thei beren but o Scheld and o

Spere, with outen other Armes. And thei wrappen
here Hedes and here Necke with a gret quantytee

of white lynnen Clothe. And thei ben righte
felonouse and foule, and of cursed kynde.

And whan Men passen this Desert, in comynge
toward Jerusalem, thei comen to Bersabee, that
was wont to ben a fulle fair Town and a delytable of Cristene Men: And zit there ben summe
of here Chirches. In that Toun dwelled Abraham
the Patriark, a long tyme. In that Toun of Bersabee, founded Bersabee the Wif of Sire Urye, the
Knyghte; on the whiche, Kyng David gatt Salomon the wyse, that was Kyng aftre David,
upon[u] the 12 Kynredes of Jerusalem, and regned
40 Zeer. And fro thens gon Men to the Cytee
of Ebron, that is the montance of 2[x] gode Myle.
And it was clept somtyme the Vale of Mambree,
and sumtyme it was clept the Vale of Teres, because that Adam wepte there, an 100 Zeer, for

[u] Super.   [x] The rest of the English MSS. have it 12.

the dethe of Abelle his Sone, that Cayn slowghe. Ebron was wont to ben the princypalle Cytee of Philistyenes: and there duelleden somtyme the Geauntz. And that Cytee was also Sacerdotalle, that is to seyne, seyntuarie, of the Tribe of Juda: And it was so fre, that Men resceyved there alle manere of Fugityfes of other places, for here evyl Dedis. In Ebron, Josue, Calephe, and here Companye comen first to aspyen, how thei myghte wynnen the Lond of Beheste. In Ebron regned first Kyng David 7 Zeer and an half: And in Jerusalem he regnede 33 zeer and an half. And in Ebron ben alle the Sepultures of the Patriarkes, Adam, Abraham, Ysaac, and of Jacob; and of here Wyfes, Eve, Sarre, and Rebekke, and of Lya: the whiche Sepultures the Sarazines kepen fulle curyously, and han the place in gret reverence, for the holy Fadres, the Patriarkes, that lyzn there. And thei suffre no Cristene man entre in to that Place, but zif it be of specyalle grace of the Soudan. For thei holden Cristene men and Jewes as Dogges. And thei seyn, that thei scholde not entre in to so holy Place. And men clepen that Place, where they lyzn, Double Spelunke, or double Cave or double Dyche; for als meche as that on lyethe above that other. And the Sarazines clepen that Place in here Langage, Karicarba;[y] that is to seyne, the Place of Patriarkes. And the Jewes clepen that Place, Arbothe. And in that same Place was Abrahames Hous: and there he satt and saughe 3 Persones, and worschipte but on; as Holy Writt seythe, *Tres vidit et unū adoravit:* that is to seyne, *He saughe 3, and worschiped on:* and of tho same

[y] Cariatarba, L. &c.

resceyved Abraham the Aungeles in to his Hous. And righte faste by that Place is a Cave in the Roche, where Adam and Eve duelleden, whan

thei weren putt out of Paradyse; and there goten thei here Children. And in that same Place was Adam formed and made; aftre that that sum men seyn. For Men werein wont for to clepe that Place, the Feld of Damasce; because that it was in the Lordschipe of Damask. And fro thens was he translated in to Paradys of Delytes, as thei seyn: and aftre that he was dryven out of Paradys, he was there left. And the same Day that he was putt in Paradys, the same Day he was put outt: for anon he synned. There begynnethe the Vale of Ebron, that durethe nyghe to Jerusalem. There the Aungelle commaunded Adam, that he scholde duelle with his Wyf Eve: of the whiche he gatt Sethe; of whiche Tribe, that is to seye, Kynrede, Jesu Crist was born. In that Valeye is a Feld, where Men drawen out of the Erthe a thing, that men clepen Cambylle: and thei ete it in stede of Spice, and thei bere it to selle. And Men may

not make the hole ne the Cave, where it is taken
out of the Erthe, so depe ne so wyde, but that it
is, at the Zeres ende, fulle azen up to the sydes,
thorgh the Grace of God.

And 2 Myle from Ebron is the Grave of Lothe,
that was Abrahames Brother. And a lytille fro
Ebron is the Mount of Mambre, of the whiche the
Valeye takethe his name. And there is a Tree of
Oke, that the Sarazines clepen Dirpe,² that is of
Abrahames tyme, the whiche Men clepen the drye
Tree. And thei seye, that it hathe ben there sithe

the beginnynge of the World; and was sumtyme
grene, and bare Leves, unto the tyme that oure
Lord dyede on the Cros; and thanne it dryede;
and so dyden alle the Trees, that weren thanne in
the World. And summe seyn, be here Prophecyes, that a Lord, a Prynce of the West syde of
the World shalle wynnen the Lond of Promyssioun, that is the Holy Lond, withe helpe of Cristene Men; and he schalle do synge a Masse undir

² Drip, L.

that drye Tree, and than the Tree schalle wexen grene and bere bothe Fruyt and Leves. And thorghe that Myracle manye Sazarines and Jewes schulle ben turned to Cristene Feythe. And therfore thei don gret Worschipe thereto, and kepen it full besyly. And alle be it so, that it be drye, natheles zit he berethe gret vertue: for certeynly he that hathe a litille there of upon him, it helethe him of the fallynge Evylle: and his Hors schalle not ben a foundred: and manye othere Vertues it hathe: where fore Men holden it fulle precyous.

From Ebron, Men gon to Bethelem, in half a day: for it is but 5 Myle; and it is fulle fayre Weye, be Pleynes and Wodes fulle deletable. Betheleem is a lityll Cytee, long and narwe and well walled, and in eche syde enclosed with gode Dyches; and it was wont to ben cleped Effrata; as Holy Wrytt seythe, *Ecce audivimus eum in Effrata;*[a] that is to seye, *Lo, wee herde him in Effrata.* And toward the Est ende of the Cytee, is a fulle fair Chirche and a gracyouse; and it hathe many Toures, Pynacles and Corneres, fulle stronge and curiously made: and with in that Chirche ben 44 Pyleres of Marble, grete and faire. And betwene the Cytee and the Chirche is the Felde Floridus; that is to seyne, the Feld florisched: For als moche as a fayre Mayden was blamed with wrong, and sclaundred, that sche hadde don Fornycacioun; for whiche cause sche was demed to the Dethe, and to be brent in that place, to the whiche sche was ladd. And as the Fyre began to brenne aboute hire, sche made hire Preyeres to oure Lord, that als wissely as sche was not gylty of

[a] Psalm cxxxii. 6.

that Synne, that he wold helpe hire, and make it to be knowen to alle men, of his mercyfulle grace. And whan sche hadde thus seyd, sche entred in to the Fuyer: and anon was the Fuyr quenched and oute: and the Brondes that weren brennynge, becomen rede Roseres; and the Brondes that weren not kyndled, becomen white Roseres, fulle of Roses. And theise weren the first Roseres and Roses, both white and rede, that evere ony Man saughe. And thus was this Mayden saved be the Grace of God. And therfore is that Feld clept the Feld of God florysscht: for it was fulle of Roses. Also besyde the Queer of the Chirche, at the right syde, as men comen dounward 16 Greces, is the place where oure Lord was born, that is fulle welle dyghte of Marble, and fulle richely peynted with Gold, Sylver, Azure and other Coloures. And 3 Paas besyde, is the Crybbe of the Ox and the Asse. And besyde that, is the place where the Sterre felle, that ladde the 3 Kynges, Jaspar, Melchior and Balthazar: but Men of Grece clepen hem thus, Galgalathe, Malgalathe and Saraphie: and the Jewes clepen in this manere, in Ebrew, Appelius, Amerrius and Damasus. Theise 3 Kynges offreden to oure Lord, Gold, Ensence and Myrre: and thei metten to gedre, thorghe Myracle of God: for thei metten to gedre in a Cytee in Ynde, that Men clepen Cassak, that is 53 Journeyes fro Betheleem; and thei weren at Betheleem the 13 Day. And that was the 4 Day aftre that thei hadden seyn the Sterre, whan thei metten in that Cytee: and thus thei weren in 9 Dayes, fro that Cytee at Betheleem; and that was gret Myracle. Also undre the Cloystre of the Chirche, be 18 Degrees, at the righte syde, is the Charnelle of the Innocentes, where here Bones lyzn. And before the place where oure Lord was born, is the Tombe of Seynt Jerome, that was a Preest and a Cardynalle, that translatede the Bible and the Psaultere from Ebrew in to Latyn : and witheoute the Mynstre ; is the Chayere that he satt in, whan he translated it. And faste besyde that Chirche, a 60 Fedme, is a Chirche of Seynt Nicholas, where oure Lady rested hire, aftre sche was lyghted of oure Lord. And for as meche as sche had to meche Mylk in hire Pappes, that greved hire, sche mylked hem on the rede Stones of Marble ; so that the traces may zit be sene in the Stones alle whyte. And zee schulle undrestonde, that alle that duellen in Betheleem ben Cristene Men. And there ben fayre Vynes about the Cytee, and gret plentee of Wyn, that the Cristene Men han don let make.[b] But the Sarazines ne tylen not no Vynes, ne thei drynken no Wyn. For here Bokes of here Lawe, that Makomete betoke hem, whiche thei clepen here Alkaron, and sume clepen it Mesaphe ; and in another Langage it is cleped Harme ; and the same Boke forbedethe hem to drinke Wyn. For in that Boke, Machomete cursed alle tho that drynken Wyn, and alle hem that sellen it. For sum men seye, that he sloughe ones an Heremyte in his Dronkenesse, that he loved ful wel : and therefore he cursed Wyn, and hem that drynken it. But his Curs be turned in to his owne Hed ; as Holy Wrytt seythe ; *Et in verticem ipsius iniquitas ejus descendet ;* that is for to seye, *His Wykkednesse schalle turne and falle in*

[b] Operatione Cristianorū, L.

his owne Heed. And also the Sarazines bryngen forthe[c] no Pigges, nor thei eten no Swynes Flessche : for thei seye, it is brother to Man, and it was forboden be the olde Lawe : and thei holden hem alle accursed that eten thereof. Also in the Lond of Palestyne and in the Lond of Egypt, thei eten but lytille or non of Flessche of Veel or of Beef; but he be so old, that he may no more travayle for elde ; for it is forbode : and for because thei have but fewe of hem, therfore thei norisschen hem, for to ere here Londes. In this Cytee of Betheleem was David the Kyng born : and he hadde 60 Wyfes; and the firste Wyf hihte Michol : and also he hadde 300 Lēmannes.

An fro Betheleem unto Jerusalem nys but 2 Myle. And in the Weye to Jerusalem, half a Myle fro Betheleem is a Chirche, where the Aungel seyde to the Scheppardes, of the Birthe of Crist. And in that Weye is the Tombe of Rachelle, that was Josephes Modre, the Patriarke; and sche dyede anon, aftre that sche was delyvered of hire Sone Beniamyn ; and there sche was buryed of Jacob hire Husbonde : and he leet setten 12 grete Stones on here, in tokene that sche had born 12[d] Children. In the same Weye, half Myle fro Jerusalem, appered the Sterre to the 3 Kynges. In that Weye also ben manye Chirches of Cristene Men, be the whiche Men gon towardes the Cytee of Jerusalem.

[c] Nutriunt, L.
[d] Rachel had but two Children, Joseph and Benjamin : but by them she had 12 Grand-children. Gen. xlvi. 20, 21, 22.

Cap. VII.

Of the Pilgrimages in Jerusalem and of the Holy Places thereaboute.

AFTER for to speke of Jerusalem, the Holy Cytee, zee schulle undirstonde, that it stont fulle faire betwene Hilles: and there ben no Ryveres ne Welles; but Watre comethe be Condyte frō Ebron. And zee schulle undirstonde, that Jerusalem of olde tyme, unto the tyme of Melchisedeche, was cleped Jebus; and aftre it was clept Salem, unto the tyme of Kyng David, that putte theise 2 Names to gidere, and cleped it Jebusalem; and aftre that Kyng Salomon cleped it Jerosolomye: and aftre that, Men cleped it Jerusalem; and so it is cleped zit. And aboute Jerusalem is the Kyngdom of Surrye: and there besyde is the Lond of Palestyne: and besyde it is Ascolone: and besyde that is the Lond of Maritaine. But Jerusalem is in the Lond of Judee; and it is clept Jude, for that Judas Machabeus was Kyng of that Contree; and it marchethe[e] Estward to the Kyngdom of Arabye; on the Southe syde, to the Lond of Egipt; and on the West syde, to the grete See; on the North syde, toward the Kyngdom of Surrye, and to the See of Cypre. In Jerusalem was wont to be a Patriark, and Erchebysshoppes and Bisshoppes abouten in the Contree. Abouten Jeru-

[e] Confinis est.

salem ben theise Cytees: Ebron, at 7 Myle; Jerico, at 6 Myle; Bersabee, at 8 Myle; Ascalon, at 17 Myle: Jaff, at 16 Myle; Ramatha, at 3 Myle; and Betheleem, at 2 Myle. And a 2 Myle from Betheleem, toward the Sowthe, is the Chirche of Seynt Karitot,[f] that was Abbot there; for whom thei maden meche Doel amonges the Monkes, whan he scholde dye; and zit thei ben in moornynge, in the wise that thei maden here Lamentacioun for him the firste tyme: and it is fulle gret pytee to beholde.

This Contree and Lond of Jerusalem hathe ben in many dyverse Naciounes Hondes: and often therfore hathe the Contree suffred meche Tribulacioun, for the Synne of the Poeple, that duellen there. For that Contree hathe ben in the Hondes of alle Nacyouns: that is to seyne, of Jewes, of Chananees, Assiryenes, Perses, Medoynes, Macedoynes, of Grekes, Romaynes, of Cristene Men, of Sarazines, Barbaryenes, Turkes, Tartaryenes, and of manye othere dyverse Nacyouns. For God wole not, that it be longe in the Hondes of Traytoures ne of Synneres, be thei Cristene or othere. And now have the Hethene Men holden that Lond in here Hondes 40 Zeere and more: but thei schull not holde it longe, zif God wole.

And zee schulle undirstond, that whan Men comen to Jerusalem, here first Pilgrymage is to the Chirche of the Holy Sepulcre, where oure Lord was buryed, that is with oute the Cytee, on the Northe syde: but it is now enclosed in, with the Toun Walle. And there is a fulle fayr

---

[f] Karocati, L. 1, 2; Mercaritot, E. 1, 2, 3; Markertot, E. 4.

Chirche, alle rownd, and open above, and covered with Leed.^g And on the West syde is a fair Tour and an highe, for Belles, strongly made. And in the myddes of the Chirche is a Tabernacle, as it were a lytylle Hows, made with a low lytylle Dore: and that Tabernacle is made in manere of half a Compas, righte curiousely and richely made, of Gold and Azure and othere riche Coloures, fulle nobelyche made. And in the righte syde of that Tabernacle is the Sepulcre of oure Lord. And the Tabernacle is 8 fote longe, and 5 fote wyde, and 11 fote in heighte. And it is not longe sithen the Sepulcre was alle open, that Men myghte kisse it and touche it. But for Pilgrymes that comen thidre, peyned hem to breke the Ston in peces or

^g Que in circuitu operitur Plumbo, L.

in poudre, therfore the Soudan hathe do make a Walle aboute the Sepulcre, that no man may towche it. But in the left syde of the Walle of the Tabernacle is well the heighte of a man, a gret Ston to the quantytee of a mannes Hed, that was of the Holy Sepulcre: and that Ston kissen the Pilgrymes, that comen thidre. In that Tabernacle ben no Wyndowes: but it is alle made lighte with Lampes, that hangen before the Sepulcre. And there is a Lampe, that hongethe before the Sepulcre, that brennethe lighte: and on the Gode Fryday it gothe out be him self; and lyghtith azen be him self at that Oure, that oure Lorde roos fro Dethe to lyve. Also within the Chirche, at the righte syde, besyde the Queer of the Chirche, is the Mount of Calvarye, where oure Lord was don on the Cros: and it is a Roche of white Colour, and a lytille medled with red: And the Cros was set in a Morteys, in the same Roche: and on that Roche dropped the Woundes of our Lord, whan he was payned on the Crosse; and that is cleped Golgatha. And Men gon up to that Golgatha be Degrees: and in the place of that Morteys was Adames Hed founden, aftre Noes flode; in tokene that the Synnes of Adam scholde ben boughte[h] in that same place. And upon that Roche made Abraham Sacrifice to oure Lord. And there is an Awtere: and before that Awtere lyzn Godefray de Boleyne and Bawdewyn, and othere Cristene Kynges of Jerusalem. And there nyghe, where oure Lord was crucyfied, is this written in Grew: 'Ο Θεὸς Βασιλεὺς ἡμῶν πρὸ αἰώνων εἰργάσατο σωτηρίαν ἐν μέσῳ τῆς γῆς· that is to seyne, in Latyn,

[h] Redimenda essent, L.

Deus Rex noster ante Secula operatus est Salutem, in medio Terræ; that is to seye, *God oure Kyng, before the Worldes, hathe wroughte Hele in myddis of the Erthe.* And also on that Roche, where the Cros was sett, is writen with in the Roche theise Wordes; "Ο εἶϛεις, ἐστὶ βάσις τῆς πίστεως ὅλης τοῦ κόσμου τούτον· that is to seyne in Latyn, *Quod vides, est fundamentū totius Fidei hujus Mundi;* that is to seye, *That thou seest, is ground of alle the Feythe of this World.* And zee schulle undirstonde, that whan oure Lord was don upon the Cros, he was 33 zere and 3 Monethes of elde. And the Prophecye of David[i] seythe thus: *Quadraginta annis proximus fui*[k] *generationi huic;* that is to seye, *Fourty zeer was I neighebore to this Kynrede.* And thus scholde it seme, that the Prophecyes ne were not trewe: but thei ben bothe trewe: for in old tyme men maden a Zeer of 10 Monethes; of the whiche, Marche was the firste, and Decembre was the laste. But Gayus, that was Emperour of Rome, putten theise 2 Monethes there to, Janyver and Feverer; and ordeyned the Zeer of 12 Monethes; that is to seye, 365 Dayes, with oute Lepe Zeer, aftre the propre cours of the Sonne. And therfore, aftre cowntynge of 10 Monethes of the Zeer, he dyede in the 40 Zeer; as the Prophete seyde: and aftre the Zeer of 12 Monethes, he was of age 33 Zeer and 3 Monethes. Also with in the Mount of Calvarie, on the right side, is an Awtere, where the Piler lyzthe, that oure Lord Jesu was bounden to, whan he was scourged. And there besyde ben 4 Pileres

---

[i] Psalm xcv. 10.
[k] The vulgar Latin has it, *offensus fui.*

of Ston, that alle weys droppen Watre: and sum men seyn, that thei wepen for our Lordes Dethe.

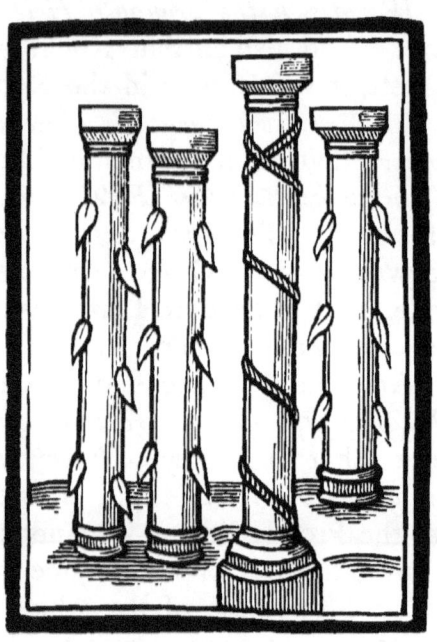

And nyghe that Awtier is a place undre Erthe, 42 Degrees of depnesse, where the Holy Croys was founden, be the Wytt of Seynte Elyne, undir a Roche, where the Jewes had hidde it. And that was the verray Croys assayed: for thei founden 3 Crosses; on of oure Lord, and 2 of the 2 Theves: and Seynte Elyne preved hem on a ded Body, that aros from Dethe to lyve, whan that it was leyed on it that oure Lord dyed on. And there by in the Walle is the place where the 4 Nayles of oure Lord weren hidd: for he had 2 in his Hondes, and 2 in his Feet: and of on of theise, the Emperour of Costantynoble made a Brydille to his Hors, to bere him in Bataylle; and thorghe vertue there of, he overcam his Enemyes, and wan alle the Lond of Asye the lesse; that is to seye, Turkye, Ermonye the lasse and the more; and from Surrye to Jerusalem, from Arabye to Persie, from Mesopotayme to the Kyngdom of Halappee, from Egypt the highe and the lowe, and all the othere Kyngdomes, unto the Depe of Ethiope, and into Ynde the lesse, that then was Cristene. And there were in that tyme many gode Holy Men and Holy Heremytes; of whom the Book of Fadres Lyfes spekethe: and thei ben now in Paynemes and Sarazines Honds. But whan God alle myghty wole, righte als the Londes weren lost thorghe Synne of Cristene Men, so schulle thei ben wonnen azen be Cristen men thorghe help of God. And in myddes of that Chirche is a Compas, in the whiche Joseph of Aramathie leyde the Body of oure Lord, whan he had taken him down of the Croys: and there he wassched the Woundes of oure Lord: and that Compas, seye men, is the myddes of the World. And in the Chirche of the Sepulchre, on the Northe syde, is the place where oure Lord was put in Presoun; (for he was in Presoun in many places) and there is a partye of the Cheyne that he was bounden with: and there he appered first to Marie Magdaleyne, whan he was rysen; and sche wende, that he had ben a Gardener. In the Chirche of Seynt Sepulchre was wont to ben Chanouns of the ordre of seynt Augustyn, and hadden a Priour: but the Patriark was here Sovereygne. And withe oute the Dores of the Chirche, on the right syde, as men gon upward 18 Greces, seyde oure Lord to his Moder, *Mulier, ecce filius tuus;* that is to seye, *Woman, lo thi Sone.* And aftre that, he seyde to John his Disciple, *Ecce mater tua;* that is to seyne,

Lo, behold thi Modir: And these wordes he seyde on the Cros. And on theise Greces wente oure Lord, whan he bare the Crosse on his Schuldir. And undir this Grees is a Chapelle; and in that Chapelle syngen Prestes, Yndyenes; that is to seye, Prestes of Ynde; noght aftir oure Lawe, but aftir here: and alle wey thei maken here Sacrement of the Awtier, seyenge, *Pater noster*, and othere Preyeres there with: with the which Preyeres, thei seye the Wordes, that the Sacrement is made of. For thei ne knowe not the Addiciouns, that many Popes han made: but thei synge with gode Devocioun. And there nere, is the place where that oure Lord rested him, whan he was wery, for berynge of the Cros. And zee schulle undirstonde, that before the Chirche of the Sepulcre, is the Cytee more feble than in ony othere partie, for the grete playn that is betwene the Chirche and the Citee. And toward the Est syde, with oute the Walles of the Cytee, is the Vale of Josaphathe, that touchethe to the Walles, as thoughe it were a large Dyche. And anen that Vale of Josaphathe, out of the Cytee, is the Chirche of seynt Stevene,

where he was stoned to Dethe. And there beside, is the gildene Zate, that may not ben opened; be the whiche Zate, oure Lord entrede on Palmesonday, upon an Asse; and the Zate opened azenst him, whan he wolde go unto the Temple: And zit apperen the Steppes of the Asses feet, in 3 places of the Degrees, that ben of fulle harde Ston. And before the Chirche of seynt Sepulcre, toward the Southe, a 200 Paas, is the gret Hospitalle of Seynt John; of the whiche the Hospitleres hadde here foundacioun. And with inne the Palays of the Seke Men of that Hospitalle ben 124 Pileres of Ston: and in the Walles of the Hows, with oute the nombre aboveseyd, there ben 54 Pileres, that beren up the Hows. And fro that Hospitalle, to go toward the Est, is a fulle fayr Chirche, that is clept *Nostre Dame la Graund*. And than is there another Chirche right nyghe, that is clept *Nostre Dame de Latyne*. And there weren Marie Cleophee and Marie Magdaleyne, and teren here Heer, whan oure Lord was peyned in the Cros.

Cap. VIII.

Of the Temple of oure Lord. Of the Crueltee of Kyng Heroud. Of the Mount Syon. Of Probatica Piscina. And of Natatorium Siloe.

AND fro the Chirche of the Sepulcre, toward the Est, at 160 Paas, is *Templum Domini*. It is right a feir Hows, and it is alle round, and highe, and covered with Leed, and it is well paved with white Marble: but the Sarazine wole not suffre no Cris-

tene man ne Jewes to come there in; for thei seyn, that none so foule synfulle men scholde not come in so holy place: but I cam in there, and in othere places, where I wolde; for I hadde Lettres of the Soudan, with his grete Seel; and comounly other Men han but his Signett. In the whiche Lettres he comanded, of his specyalle grace, to all his Subgettes, to lete me seen alle the places, and to enforme me pleynly alle the Mysteries of every place, and to condyte me fro Cytee to Cytee, zif it were nede, and buxomly to resceyve me and my Companye, and for to obeye to alle my requestes resonable, zif thei weren not gretly azen the Royalle power, and dignytee of the Soudan or of his Lawe. And to othere, that asken him grace, suche as han served him, he ne zevethe not but his Signet; the whiche thei make to be born before hem, hangynge on a Spere; and the folk of the Contree don gret worschipe and reverence to his Signett or his Seel, and knelen there to, as lowly as wee don to *Corpus Domini.* And zit men don fulle grettere reverence to his Lettres. For the Admyralle and alle othere Lordes, that thei ben schewed to, before or thei resceyve hem, thei knelen doun, and than thei take hem, and putten hem on here Hedes, and aftre thei kissen hem, and than thei reden hem, knelynge with gret reverence, and than thei offren hem to do alle, that the berere askethe. And in this *Templum Domini* weren somtyme Chanouns Reguleres: and thei hadden an Abbot, to whom thei weren obedient. And in this Temple was Charlemayn, when that the Aungelle broughte him the Prepuce of oure Lord Jesu Crist, of his Circumcisioun: and aftre Kyng Charles leet bryngen it to Parys, in to his Chapelle: and aftre that, he leet brynge it to Peyteres, and aftre that to Chartres. And zee schulle undirstonde, that this is not the Temple that Salomon made: for that Temple dured not, but 1102 Zeer. For Tytus, Vespasianes Sone, Emperour of Rome, had leyd sege aboute Jerusalem, for to discomfyte the Jewes: for thei putten oure Lord to Dethe, with outen Leve of the Emperour. And whan he hadde wonnen the Cytee, he brente the Temple and beet it down, and alle the Cytee, and toke the Jewes, and dide hem to Dethe, 1100000: and the othere he putte in Presoun, and solde hem to Servage, 30 for o Peny: for thei seyde, thei boughte Jesu for 30 Penyes: and he made of hem bettre cheep, whan he zaf 30 for o Peny. And aftre that tyme, Julianus Apostate,

that was Emperour, zaf leve to the Jewes to make
the Temple of Jerusalem : for he hated Cristene
Men; and zit he was cristned, but he forsoke his
Law, and becam a Renegate. And whan the Jewes
hadden made the Temple, com an Erthe quakeng,
and cast it doun (as God wolde) and destroyed alle
that thei had made. And aftre that, Adryan, that
was Emperour of Rome, and of the Lynage of
Troye, made Jerusalem azen, and the Temple, in
the same manere, as Salomon made it. And he
wolde not suffre no Jewes to dwelle there, but only
Cristene men. For alle thoughe it were so, that
hee was not cristned, zet he lovede Cristene men,
more than ony other Nacioun, saf his owne. This
Emperour leet enclose the Chirche of seynt Sepulcre, and walle it, within the Cytee, that before
was with oute the Cytee, long tyme beforn. And
he wolde have chaunged the Name of Jerusalem,
and have cleped it Elya : but that Name lasted not
longe. Also zee schulle undirstonde, that the Sarazines don moche reverence to that Temple; and
thei seyn, that that place is right holy. And whan
thei gon in, thei gon barefote, and knelen many
tymes. And whanne my Felowes and I seyghe that,
whan we comen in, wee diden of oure Schoon, and
camen in barefote, and thoughten that we scholden
don as moche Worschipe and Reverence there to,
as ony of the mysbeleevynge men scholde, and as
gret compunction in Herte to have. This Temple is 64 Cubytes of wydenesse, and als manye in
lengthe; and of heighte it is 120 Cubites : and it
is with inne, alle aboute, made with Pyleres of
Marble : and in the myddel place of the Temple
ben manye highe Stages, of 14 Degrees of heighte,

made with gode Pyleres alle aboute: and this Place the Jewes callen *Sancta Sanctorum;* that is to seye, *holy of halewes.* And in that place comethe no Man, saf only here Prelate, that makethe here Sacrifise. And the folk stonden alle aboute, in diverse Stages, aftre thei ben of Dignytee or of Worschipe; so that thei alle may see the Sacrifice. And in that Temple ben 4 Entrees; and the Zates ben of Cypresse, wel made and curiousely dight. And with in the Est Zate, oure Lorde seyde, *Here is Jerusalem.* And in the Northsyde of that Temple, with in the Zate, there is a Welle; but it rennethe noght; of the whiche Holy Writt spekethe, and seythe, *Vidi Aquam egredientem de Templo;* that is to seyne, *I saughe Watre come out of the Temple.* And on that other syde of the Temple, there is a Roche, that men clepen Moriache: but aftre it was clept Bethel; where the Arke of God, with Relykes of Jewes, weren wont to ben put. That Arke or Hucche, with the Relikes, Tytus ledde with hym to Rome, whan he had scomfyted alle the Jewes. In that Arke weren the 10 Cōmandementes, and of Arones Zerde, and of Moyses Zerde, with the whiche he made the Rede See departen, as it had ben a Walle, on the righte syde and on the left syde, whils that the Peple of Israel passeden the See drye foot: And with that Zerde he smoot the Roche; and the Watre cam out of it: And with that Zerde he dide manye Wondres. And there in was a Vessel of Gold, fulle of Manna, and Clothinges and Ournements and the Tabernacle of Aarō, and a Tabernacle square of Gold, with 12 precyous Stones, and a Boyst of Jasper grene, with 4 Figures, and 8 Names of oure Lord, and 7 Candelstykes of Gold, and 12 Pottes of Gold, and 4 Censeres of Gold, and an Awtier of Gold, and 4 Lyouns of Gold, upon the whiche thei bare Cherubyn of Gold, 12 Spannes long, and the Cercle of Swannes of Hevene, with a Tabernacle of Gold, and a Table of Sylver, and 2 Trompes of Silver, and 7 Barly Loves, and alle the othere Relikes, that weren before the Birthe of oure Lord Jesu Crist. And upon that Roche, was Jacob slepynge, when he saughe the Aungeles gon up and doun, by a Laddre, and he seyd, *Vere Locus iste sanctus est, et ego ignorabam;* that is to seyne, *Forsothe this place is holy, and I wiste it nought.* And there an Aungel helde Jacob stille, and turned his Name, and cleped him Israel. And in that same place, David saughe the Aungelle, that smot the folk with a Swerd, and put it up blody in the Schethe. And in that same Roche, was seynt Symeon, whan he resceyved oure Lord in to the Temple. And in this Roche he sette him, whan the Jewes wolde a stoned him; and a Sterre cam doun, and zaf him light. And upon that Roche, prechede our Lord often tyme to the Peple; and out of that seyd Temple, oure Lord drof the Byggeres and the Selleres. And upon that Roche, oure Lord sette him, whan the Jewes wolde have stoned him; and the Roche cleef in two, and in that clevynge was oure Lord hidd; and there cam doun a Sterre, and zaf Lighte and served him with claretee; and upon that Roche, satt oure Lady, and lerned hire Sawtere: and there our Lord forzaf the Wōman hire Sinnes, that was founden in Avowtrie: and there was oure Lord circumcyded: and there the Aungelle schewede tydynges to Zacharie of the Birthe of

Seynt Baptyst his Sone: and there offred first Melchisedeche Bred and Wyn to oure Lord, in tokene of the Sacrement, that was to comene; and there felle David preyeng to oure Lord, and to the Aungelle, that smot the peple, that he wolde have mercy on him and on the peple; and oure Lord herde his Preyere; and therefore wolde he make the Temple in that place: but oure Lord forbade him, be an Aungelle, for he had don Tresoun, whan he leet sle Urie the worthi Knyght, for to have Bersabee his Wyf; and therfore all the purveyance, that he hadde ordeyned to make the Temple with, he toke it Salomon his Sone; and he made it. And he preyed oure Lord, that alle tho that preyeden to him, in that place, with gode Herte, that he wolde heren here Preyere and graunten it hem, zif thei asked it rightefullyche: and oure Lord graunted it him: and therfore Salomon cleped that Temple, the Temple of Conseille and of Help of God. And with oute the Zate of that Temple is an Awtiere, where Jewes werein wont to offren Dowves and Turtles. And betwene the Temple and that Awtiere was Zacharie slayn. And upon the Pynacle of that Temple was oure Lord brought, for to ben tempted of the Enemye, the Feend. And on the heighte of that Pynacle, the Jewes setten Seynt Jame, and casted him down to the Erthe, that first was Bisschopp of Jerusalē. And at the entree of that Temple, toward the West, is the Zate that is clept *Porta speciosa*.[1] And nyghe besyde that Temple, upon the right syde, is a Chirche covered with Leed, that is clept Salomones Scole. And fro that Temple,

---

[1] Beautiful Gate, Acts iii. 2.

towardes the Southe, right nyghe, is the Temple of Salomon, that is righte fair and wel pollisscht. And in that Temple duellen the Knyghtes of the Temple, that weren wont to be clept Templeres: and that was the foundacioun of here Ordre: so that there duelleden Knyghtes; and in *Templo Domini*, Chanouns Reguleres. Fro that Temple toward the Est, a 120 Paas, in the Cornere of the Cytee, is the Bathe of oure Lord: and in that Bathe was wont to come Watre fro Paradys, and zit it droppethe. And there besyde, is oure Ladyes Bed. And faste by, is the Temple of Seynt Symeon: and with oute the Cloyster of the Temple, toward the Northe, is a fulle faire Chirche of Seynte Anne, oure Ladyes Modre: and there was oure Lady conceyved. And before that Chirche, is a gret Tree, that began to growe the same nyght. And undre that Chirche, in goenge doun be 22 Degrees, lythe Joachym, oure Ladyes fader, in a faire Tombe of Ston: and there besyde, lay somtyme seynt Anne his Wyf; but seynt Helyne leet translate hire to Costantynople. And in that Chirche is a Welle, in manere of a Cisterne, that is clept *Probatica Piscina*, that hathe 5 Entreez. Into that Welle, Aungeles werē wont to come from Hevene, and bathen hem with inne: and what Man that first bathed him, aftre the mevynge of the Watre, was made hool, of what maner Sykenes that he hadde: and there oure Lord heled a Man of the Palasye, that laye 38 Zeer: and oure Lord seyde to him, *Tolle Grabatum tuum & ambula;* that is to seye, *Take thi Bed, and go.* And there besyde, was Pylates Hows. And faste by, is Kyng Heroudes Hows, that leet sle the Innocentes. This Heroude was over moche cursed and cruelle: for first he leet sle his Wif, that he lovede righte welle; and for the passynge Love, that he hadde to hire, whan he saughe hire ded, he felle in a rage, and oute of his Wytt, a gret while; and sithen he cam azen to his Wytt: and aftre he leet sle his two Sones, that he hadde of that Wyf: and aftre that, he leet sle another of his Wyfes, and a Sone, that he hadde with hire: and aftre that, he leet sle his owne Modre: and he wolde have slayn his Brother also, but he dyede sodeynly. And aftre he fell into Seknesse, and whan he felte, that he scholde dye, he sente aftre his Sustre, and aftre alle the Lordes of his Lond; and whan thei were comen, he leet cōmande hem to Prisoun, and than he seyde to his Sustre, he wiste wel, that men of the Contree wolde make no Sorwe for his Dethe; and therfore he made his Sustre swere, that sche scholde lete smyte of alle the Heds of the Lordes, whan he were ded; and than scholde alle the Lond make Sorwe for his Dethe, and else nought: and thus he made his Testement. But his Sustre fulfilled not his Wille: for als sone as he was ded, sche delyvered alle the Lordes out of Presoun, and lete hem gon, eche Lord to his owne; and tolde hem alle the purpos of hire Brothers Ordynance: and so was this cursed Kyng never made Sorwe for, as he supposed for to have ben. And zee schulle undirstonde, that in that tyme there weren 3 Heroudes, of gret Name and Loos for here crueltee. This Heroude, of whiche I have spoken offe, was Heroude Ascalonite: and he that leet beheden seynt John the Baptist, was Heroude

Antypa : and he that leet smyte of seynt James hed, was Heroude Agrippa ; and he putte seynt Peter in Presoun.

Also furthermore, in the Cytee, is the Chirche of Seynt Savyour: And there is the left Arm of John Crisostom, and the more partye of the Hed of seynt Stevene. And on that other syde of the Strete, toward the Southe, as Men gon to Mount Syon, is a Chirche of seynt James, where he was

beheded. And fro that Chirche, a 120 Paas, is the Mount Syon : and there is a faire Chirche of oure Lady, where sche dwelled ; and there sche dyed. And there was wont to ben an Abbot of Chanouns Reguleres. And fro thens, was sche born of the Apostles, unto the Vale of Josaphathe. And there is the Ston, that the Aungelle broughte to oure Lady, fro the Mount of Synay ; and it is of that colour, that the Roche is of seynt Kateryne. And there besyde, is the Zate, where thorghe oure Ladye wente, whan sche was with Childe, whan sche wente to Betheleem. Also at the entree of

the Mount Syon, is a Chapelle; and in that
Chapelle is the Ston gret and large, with the
whiche the Sepulcre was covered with, whan
Josephe of Aramathie had put oure Lord thereinne: the whiche Ston the 3 Maries sawen turnen
upward, whan thei comen to the Sepulcre, the Day
of his Resurrexioun; and there founden an Aungelle, that tolde hem of oure Lordes uprysynge
from Dethe to Lyve. And there also is a Ston, in
a Walle, besyde the Zate, of the Pyleer, that oure
Lord was scourged ate: And there was Annes
Hows, that was Bishop of the Jewes, in that tyme.
And there was oure Lord examyned in the nyght,
and scourged and smytten and vylently entreted.
And in that same place, seynt Peter forsoke oure
Lord thries, or the Cok creew. And there is a party
of the Table, that he made his Souper onne, whan
he made his Maundee, with his Discyples; whan
he zaf hem his Flesche and his Blode, in forme
of Bred and Wyn. And undre that Chapelle, 32
Degrees, is the place, where oure Lord wossche
his Disciples Feet: and zit is the Vesselle, where
the Watre was. And there besyde that same
Vesselle, was seynt Stevene buryed. And there is
the Awtier, where oure Lady herde the Aungeles
synge Messe. And there appered first oure Lord
to his Disciples, after his Resurrexioun, the Zates
enclosed, and seyde to hem, *Pax vobis;* that is to
seye, *Pees to Zou.* And on that Mount, appered
Crist to seynt Thomas the Apostle, and bad him
assaye his Woundes; and there beleeved he first,
and seyde, *Dominus meus & Deus meus;* that is to
seye, *my Lord and my God.* In the same Chirche,
besyde the Awteer, weren alle the Aposteles on

Wytsonday, whan the Holy Gost descended on hem, in lyknesse of Fuyr. And there made oure Lord his Pask, with his Disciples. And there slepte seynt John the Evaungelist, upon the Breeste of oure Lord Jesu Crist, and saughe slepynge many hevenly prevytees.

Mount Syon is with inne the Cytee; and it is a lytille hiere than the other syde of the Cytee: and the Cytee is strongere on that syde, than on that other syde. For at the foot of the Mount Syon, is a faire Castelle and a strong, that the Soudan leet make. In the Mount Syon weren buryed Kyng David and Kyng Salomon, and many othere Kynges, Jewes of Jerusalem. And there is the place, where the Jewes wolden han cast up the body of oure Lady, whan the Apostles beren the Body to ben buryed, in the Vale of Josaphathe. And there is the Place, where Seynt Petir wepte fulle tenderly, aftre that he hadde forsaken oure Lord. And a Stones cast fro that Chapelle, is another Chapelle, where oure Lord was jugged: for that tyme, was there Cayphases Hows. From that Chapelle, to go toward the Est, at 140 Paas, is a deep Cave undre the Roche, that is clept the Galylee of oure Lord; where seynt Petre hidde him, whanne he had forsaken oure Lord. Item, betwene the Mount Syon and the Temple of Salomon, is the place, where oure Lord reysed the Mayden, in hire Fadres Hows. Undre the Mount Syon, toward the Vale of Josaphathe, is a Welle, that is clept *Natatorium Siloe;* and there was oure Lord wasshen, aftre his Bapteme: And there made oure Lord the blynde Man to see. And there was y buryed Ysaye the Prophete. Also streghte from

Natatorie Siloe, is an Ymage of Ston, and of olde auncyen Werk, that Absalon leet make: and because there of, men clepen it the Hond of Absalon. And faste by, is zit the Tree of Eldre, that Judas henge him self upon, for despeyr that

he hadde, whan he solde and betrayed oure Lord. And there besyde, was the Synagoge, where the Bysshoppes of Jewes and the Pharyses camen to gidere, and helden here Conseille. And there caste Judas the 30 Pens before hem, and seyde, that he hadde synned, betrayenge oure Lord. And there nyghe was the Hows of the Apostles, Philippe and Jacob Alphei. And on that other syde of Mount Syon, toward the southe, bezonde the Vale, a Stones cast, is Acheldamache; that is to seye, the Feld of Blood; that was bought for the 30 Pens, that oure Lord was sold fore. And in that Feld ben many Tombes of Cristene Men: for there ben manye Pilgrymes graven. And there ben many Oratories, Chapelles and Heremytages, where Heremytes weren wont to duelle. And toward the Est, an 100 Pas, is the Charnelle of the Hospitalle of seynt John, where men weren wont to putte the Bones of dede men.

Also fro Jerusalem, toward the West, is a fair Chirche, where the Tree of the Cros grew. And 2 Myle fro thens, is a faire Chirche; where oure Lady mette with Elizabethe, whan thei weren bothe with Childe; and seynt John stered in his Modres Wombe, and made reverence to his Creatour, that he saughe not. And undre the Awtier of that Chirche, is the place where seynt John was born. And fro that Chirche, is a Myle to the Castelle of Emaux: and there also oure Lord schewed him to 2 of his Disciples, aftre his Resurrexioun. Also on that other syde, 200 Pas fro Jerusalem, is a Chirche, where was wont to be the Cave of the Lioun: and undre that Chirche, at 30 Degrees of Depnesse, weren entered 12000 Martires, in the tyme of Kyng Cosdroe,[m] that the Lyoun mette with[n] alle in a nyghte, be the wille of God. Also fro Jerusalem 2 Myle, is the Mount Joye, a fulle fair place and a delicyous: and there lythe Samuel the Prophete in a fair Tombe: and men clepen it Mount Joye; for it zevethe joye to Pilgrymes hertes, be cause that there men seen first Jerusalem. Also betwene Jerusalem and the Mount of Olyvete, is the Vale of Josaphathe, undre the Walles of the Cytee, as I have seyd before: and in the myddes of the Vale, is a lytille Ryvere, that men clepen Torrens Cedron; and aboven it, over thwart, lay a Tre, (that the Cros was made offe) that men zeden over onne: and faste by it is a litylle pytt in the Erthe, where the foot of the

[m] Esdre, F.   [n] Collegit, L.; ensemble, F.

Pileer is zit entered; and there was oure Lord first scourged: for he was scourged and vileynsly entreted in many places. Also in the myddel Place of the Vale of Josaphathe, is the Chirche of oure Lady: and it is of 43 Degrees, undre the Erthe, unto the Sepulcre of oure Lady. And oure Lady was of Age, when sche dyed, 72 Zeer. And beside the Sepulcre of oure Lady, is an Awtier, where oure Lord forzaf seynt Petir all his Synnes. And fro thens, toward the West, undre an Awtere, is a Welle, that comethe out of the Ryvere of Paradys. And witethe wel, that that Chirche is fulle lowe in the Erthe; and sum is alle with inne the Erthe. But I suppose wel, that it was not so founded: but for because that Jerusalem hathe often tyme ben destroyed, and the Walles abated and beten doun and tombled in to the Vale, and that thei han ben so filled azen, and the ground enhaunced; and for that skylle, is the Chirche so lowe with in the Erthe: and natheles men seyn there comounly, that the Erthe hathe so ben cloven, sythe the tyme, that oure Lady was there buryed: and zit men seyn there, that it wexethe and growethe every day, with outen dowte. In that Chirche were wont to ben blake Monkes, that hadden hire Abbot. And besyde that Chirche, is a Chapelle, besyde the Roche, that highte Gethesamany: and there was oure Lord kyssed of Judas; and there was he taken of the Jewes; and there laft oure Lord his Disciples, whan he wente to preye before his Passioun, whan he preyed and seyde, *Pater, si fieri potest, transeat a me Calix iste;* that is to seye, *Fadre, zif it may be, do lete this Chalys go fro me.* And whan he

cam azen to his Disciples, he fond hem slepynge.
And in the Roche, with inne the Chapelle, zit
apperen the fyngres of oure Lordes Hond, whan
he putte hem in the Roche, whan the Jewes wolden
have taken him. And fro thens a Stones cast,
toward the Southe, is another Chapelle, where
oure Lord swette droppes of Blood. And there
righte nyghe, is the Tombe of Kyng Josaphathe;
of whom the Vale berethe the name. This Josaphathe was Kyng of that Contree, and was converted by an Heremyte, that was a worthi man,
and dide moche gode. And fro thens a Bowe
drawghte, toward the South, is the Chirche, where
seynt James and Zacharie the Prophete weren
buryed. And above the Vale, is the Mount of
Olyvete: and it is cleped so, for the plentee of
Olyves, that growen there. That Mount is more
highe than the Cytee of Jerusalem is: and therfore
may men, upon that Mount, see manye of the
Stretes of the Cytee. And between that Mount
and the Cytee, is not but the Vale of Josaphathe,
that is not fulle large. And fro that Mount,
steighe oure Lord Jesu Crist to Hevene, upon
Ascencioun day: and zit there schewethe the
schapp of his left Foot, in the Ston. And there
is a Chirche, where was wont to be an Abbot and
Chanouns reguleres. And a lytylle thens, 28 Pas,
is a Chapelle, and there in is the Ston, on the
whiche oure Lord sat, whan he prechede the 8
Blessynges, and seyde thus; *Beati pauperes Spi-
ritu*: And there he taughte his Disciples the *Pater
noster*; and wrote with his finger in a Ston. And
there nyghe is a Chirche of Seynte Marie Egip-
cyane; and there sche lythe in a Tombe. And

fro thens toward the Est, a 3 Bow schote, is Bethfagee; to the whiche oure Lord sente seynt Peter and seynt James, for to feche the Asse, upon Palme Sonday, and rode upon that Asse to Jerusalem. And in comynge doun fro the Mount of Olyvete, toward the Est, is a Castelle, that is cleped Bethanye: and there dwelte Symon leprous, and there herberwed oure Lord; and aftre, he was baptized of the Apostles, and was clept Julian, and was made Bisschoppe: and this is the same Julyan, that men clepe to for gode Herberghgage: for oure Lord herberwed with him, in his Hows. And in that Hous, oure Lord forzaf Marie Magdaleyne hire Synnes; there sche whassched his Feet with hire Teres, and wyped hem with hire Heer. And there served seynt Martha, oure Lord. There oure Lord reysed Lazar fro Dethe to lyve, that was ded 4 dayes and stank, that was brother to Marie Magdaleyne and to Martha. And there duelte also Marie Cleophe. That Castelle is wel a Myle long fro Jerusalem. Also in comynge doun fro the Mount of Olyvete, is the place where oure Lord wepte upon Jerusalem. And there besyde is the place, where oure Lady appered to seynt Thomas the Apostle, aftre hire Assumptioun, and zaf him hire Gyrdylle. And right nyghe is the Ston, where oure Lord often tyme sat upon, whan he prechede: and upon that same schalle he sytte, at the day of Doom; righte as him self seyde.

Also aftre the Mount of Olyvete, is the Mount of Galilee: there assembleden the Apostles, whan Marie Magdaleyne cam, and tolde hem of Cristes uprisynge. And there, betwene the Mount Olyvete and the Mount Galilee, is a Chirche, where the

H

Aungel seyde to oure Lady, of hire Dethe. Also fro Bethanye to Jerico, was somtyme a litylle Cytee: but it is now alle destroyed; and now is there but a litylle Village. That Cytee tok Josue, be myracle of God and cōmandement of the Aungel, and destroyed it and cursed it, and alle hem that bylled it azen. Of that Citee was Zacheus the Dwerf, that clomb up in to the Sycomour Tre, for to see oure Lord; be cause he was so litille, he myghte not seen him for the peple. And of that Cytee was Raab the comoun Wōman, that ascaped allone, with hem of hire lynage; and sche often tyme refressched and fed the Messageres of Israel, and kepte hem from many grete periles of Dethe: and therfore sche hadde gode reward; as Holy Writt seythe: *Qui accipit Prophetam in nomine meo, mercedem Prophetæ accipiet;* that is to seye, *He that takethe a Prophete in my name, he schalle take mede of the Prophete:* and so hadde sche; for sche prophecyed to the Messageres, seyenge, *Novi quod Dominus tradet vobis Terram hanc;* that is to seye, *I wot wel, that oure Lord schal betake zou this Lond:* and so he dide. And aftre Salomon, Naasones Sone, wedded hire; and fro that tyme was sche a worthi Wōman, and served God wel. Also from Betanye gon men to flom Jordan, by a Mountayne, and thorghe Desert; and it is nyghe a day iorneye fro Bethanye, toward the Est, to a gret hille, where oure Lord fasted 40 dayes. Upon that Hille, the enemy of Helle bare oure Lord, and tempted him, and seyde; *Dic ut lapides isti panes fiant;* that is to seye, *Sey, that theise Stones be made Loves.* In that place, upon the hille, was wont to ben a faire

Chirche; but it is alle destroyed, so that there is now but an Hermytage, that a maner of Cristene men holden, that ben cleped Georgyenes: for seynt George converted hem. Upon that hille duelte Abraham a gret while: and therfore men clepen it, Abrahames Gardyn. And betwene the Hille and this Gardyn renneth a lytille Broke of Watre, that was wont to ben byttre; but be the blessyng of Helisee the Prophete, it becam swete and gode to drynke. And at the foot of this Hille, toward the Playn, is a gret Welle, that entrethe in to Flom Jordan. Fro that Hille to Jerico, that I spak of before, is but a Myle, in goynge toward Flom Jordan. Also as men gon to Jerico, sat the blynde man, cryenge, *Jesu, fili David, miserere mei;* that is to seye, *Jesu, Davides sone, have mercy on me:* and anon he hadde his sighte. Also 2 Myle fro Jerico, is Flom Jordan: and an half myle more nyghe, is a faire Chirche of Seynt John the Baptist; where he baptised oure Lord: and there besyde, is the Hous of Jeremye the Prophete.

Cap. IX.

Of the dede See; and of the Flom Jordan. Of the Hed of seynt John the Baptist; and of the Usages of the Samaritanes.

AND fro Jerico, a 3 Myle, is the dede See. Aboute that See growethe moche Alom and of Alkatran.°

° Dalem et Dalketram, L.; De Alym et Dalketran, F.

Betwene Jerico and that See, is the Lond of Dengadde; and there was wont to growe the Bawme: but men make drawe the braunches there of, and berē hem to ben graffed at Babiloyne ;ᵖ and zit men clepen hem Vynes of Gaddy. At a Cost of that See, as men gone from Arabe, is the Mount of the Moabytes; where there is a Cave, that men clepen Karua. Upon that hille, ladde Balak the Sone of Booz, Balaam the Prest, for to curse the Peple of Israel. That dede See departethe the Lond of Yndē and of Arabye: and that See lastethe from Soara unto Arabye. The Watre of that See is fulle bytter and Salt: and ziff the Erthe were made moyst and weet with that Watre, it wolde nevere bere Fruyt. And the Erthe and the Lond chaungeth often his colour. And it castethe out of the Watre a thing that men clepen Aspalt; also gret peces, as the gretnesse of an Hors, every day, and on alle sydes. And fro Jerusalem to that See, is 200 Furlonges. That See is in lengthe 580 Furlonges, and in brede 150 Furlonges: and it is clept the dede See, for it rennethe nought, but is evere unmevable. And nouther manne, best, ne no thing that berethe lif in him, ne may not dyen in that See: and that hathe ben preved manye tymes, be men that han disserved to ben dede, that han ben cast there inne, and left there inne 3 dayes or 4, and thei ne myghte never dye ther inne: for it resceyvethe no thing with inne him, that berethe lif. And no man may drynken of the Watre, for bytternesse. And zif a man caste Iren there in, it wole flete aboven. And zif men caste a Fedre there in, it wole synke to the botme: and

ᵖ Translatum fuit ad Babilonem, L.

theise ben thinges azenst kynde. And also the
Cytees there weren lost, be cause of Synne. And
there besyden growen trees, that beren fulle faire

Apples, and faire of colour to beholde; but whoso
brekethe hem or cuttethe hem in two, he schalle
fynde with in hem Coles and Cyndres; in tokene
that, be Wratthe of God, the Cytees and the Lond
weren brente and sonken in to Helle. Sum men
clepen that See, the Lake Dalfetidee; summe, the
Flom of Develes; and sūme, the Flom that is ever
stynkynge. And in to that See sonken the 5 Cytees,
be Wratthe of God; that is to seyne, Sodom, Gomorre, Aldama, Seboym and Segor, for the abho-
mynable synne of Sodomye, that regned in hem. But
Segor, be the preyer of Lothe, was saved and kept
a gret while: for it was sett upon an hille; and zit
schewethe therof sum party, above the Watre: and
men may see the Walles, when it is fayr Wedre
and cleer. In that Cytee Lothe dwelte, a lytylle
while; and there was he made dronken of his
Doughtres, and lay with hem, and engendred of
hem Moab and Amon. And the cause whi his

Doughtres made him dronken, and for to ly by him, was this; because thei sawghe no man aboute hem, but only here Fadre: and therfore thei trowed, that God had destroyed alle the World, as he hadde don the Cytees; as he hadde don before, be Noes Flood. And therfore thei wolde lye with here Fadre, for to have Issue, and for to replenysschen the World azen with Peple, to restore the World azen be hem: for thei trowed, that ther had ben no mo men in alle the World. And zif here Fadre had not ben dronken, he hadde not y leye with hem. And the hille aboven Segor, men cleped it thanne Edom: and aftre men cleped it Seyr, and aftre Ydumea. Also at the righte syde of that dede See, dwellethe zit the Wife of Lothe, in lyknesse of a salt Ston; for that schee loked behynde hire, whan the Cytees sonken in to Helle. This Lothe was Araammes sone, that was Brother to Abraham. And Sarra Abrahames Wif, and Melcha Nachors Wif, weren Sustren to the seyd Lothe. And the same Sarra was of elde 90 Zeer, when Ysaac hire sone was goten on hire. And Abraham hadde another sone Ysmael, that he gat upon Agar his Chambrere. And when Ysaac his sone was 8 dayes olde, Abraham his Fadre leet him ben circumcyded, and Ysmael with him, that was 14 Zeer old: wherfore the Jewes, that comen of Ysaacces lyne, ben circumcyded the 8 Day; and the Sarrazines, that comen of Ysmaeles lyne, ben circumcyded whan thei ben 14 Zeer of Age.

And zee schulle undirstonde, that with in the dede See rennethe the Flom Jordan, and there it dyethe; for it rennethe no furthermore: and that is a place, that is a Myle fro the Chirche of seynt

John the Baptist, toward the West, a lytille benethe the place, where that Cristene men bathen hem comounly. And a Myle from Flom Jordan, is the Ryvere of Jabothe, the whiche Jacob passed over, whan he cam fro Mesopotayme. This Flom Jordan is no gret Ryvere; but it is plenteous of gode Fissche: and it cometh out of the hille of Lyban be 2 Welles, that ben cleped Jor and Dan: and of tho 2 Welles hath it the name. And it passethe be a Lake, that is clept Maron; and aftre it passethe by the See of Tyberye, and passethe undre the hilles of Gelboe: and there is a fulle faire Vale, bothe on that o syde and on that other of the same Ryvere. And men gon the hilles of Lyban, alle in lengthe, unto the desert of Pharan. And tho hilles departen the kyngdom of Surrye and the Contree of Phenesie. And upon tho hilles growen Trees of Cedre, that ben fulle hye, and thei beren longe Apples, and als grete as a mannes heved. And also this Flom Jordan departeth the Lond of Galilee and the Lond of Ydumye and the Lond of Betron: and that rennethe undre Erthe a gret weye, unto a fayre playn and a gret, that is clept Meldan, in Sarmoyz; that is to seye, Feyre or Markett, in here Langage; be cause that there is often Feyres in that pleyn. And there becomethe the Watre gret and large. And that Playn is the Tombe of Job. And in that Flom Jordan above-seyd, was oure Lord baptized of seynt John; and the voys of God the Fadre was herd seyenge, *Hic est Filius meus dilectus, &c.*; that is to seye, *This is my beloved sone, in the whiche I am well plesed; herethe hym.* And the Holy Gost alyghte upon hym, in lyknesse of a Colver: and so at his Baptizynge, was alle the hool Trynytee. And thorghe that Flom passeden the Children of Israel, alle drye feet: and thei putten Stones there in the myddel place, in tokene of the Myracle, that the Watre withdrowghe him so. Also in that Flom Jordan, Naaman of Syrie bathed him; that was fulle riche, but he was meselle: and there anon he toke his hele. Abouten the Flom Jordan ben manye Chirches, where that manye Cristene men dwelleden. And nyghe therto is the Cytee of Hay, that Josue assayled and toke. Also bezonde the Flom Jordan, is the Vale of Mambre; and that is a fulle fair Vale. Also upon the hille, that I spak of before, where oure Lord fasted 40 dayes, a 2 Myle long from Galilee, is a faire hille and an highe; where the Enemye, the Fend, bare oure Lord, the thridde tyme, to tempte him, and schewede him alle the Regiouns of the World, and seyde, *Hec omnia tibi dabo, si cadens adoraveris me;* that is to seyne, *All this schalle I zeve the, zif thou falle and worschipe me.*

Also fro the dede See, to gon Estward out of the Marches of the Holy Lond, that is clept the Lond of Promyssioun, is a strong Castelle and a fair, in an hille, that is clept Carak, en Sarmoyz; that is to seyne, Ryally. That Castelle let make kyng Baldwyn, (that was Kyng of France) whan he had conquered that Lond; and putte it in to Cristene mennes hondes, for to kepe that Contree. And for that cause, was it clept the Mownt rialle. And undre it there is a Town, that hight Sobache: and there alle abowte dwellen Cristene men, undre Trybute. Fro thens gon Men to Nazarethe, of the whiche oure Lord berethe the Surname. And fro thens, there is 3 Journeyes to Jerusalem: and men gon be the Provynce of Galylee, be Ramatha, be Sothym and be the highe hille of Effraim; where Elchana and Anna, the Modre of Samuelle the Prophete, dwelleden. There was born this Prophete: and aftre his Dethe, he was buryed at Mount Joye, as I have seyd zou before. And than gon men to Sylo; where the Arke of God with the Relikes weren kept longe tyme, undre Ely the Prophete. There made the peple of Ebron Sacrifice to oure Lord: and ther thei zolden up here Avowes: and there spak God first to Samuelle, and schewed him the mutacioun of ordre of Presthode, and the misterie of the Sacrement. And right nyghe, on the left syde, is Gabaon and Rama and Beniamyn; of the whiche Holy Writt spekethe offe. And aftre men gon to Sychem, sumtyme clept Sychar; and that is in the Provynce of Samaritanes; and there is a fulle fair Vale and a fructuouse, and there is a fair Cytee and a gode, that men clepen Neople. And from thens is a jorneye to Jerusalem. And there is the Welle, where oure Lord spak to the Wōman of Samaritan. And there was wont to ben a Chirche; but it is beten doun. Besyde that Welle, Kyng Roboas let make 2 Calveren of Gold, and made hem to ben worschipt, and put that on at Dan, and that other at Betelle. And a Myle fro Sychar, is the Cytee of Deluze. And in that Cytee dwelte Abraham, a certeyn tyme. Sychem is a 10 Myle fro Jerusalem, and it is clept Neople; that is for to seyne, the newe Cytee. And nyghe besyde is the Tombe of Josephe the Sone of Jacob, that governed Egypt: for the Jewes baren his Bones from Egypt, and buryed hem there. And thidre gon the Jewes oftentyme in Pilgrimage, with gret Devocioun. In that Cytee was Dyne Jacobes Doughter ravysscht; for whom hire Bretheren slowen many persones, and diden many harmes to the Cytee. And there besyde, is the hille of Garasoun, where the Samaritanes maken here sacrifice: in that hille wolde Abraham have sacrificed his Sone Ysaac. And

there besyde is the Vale of Dotaym: and there is the Cisterne, where Josephe was cast in of his Bretheren, which thei solden; and that is a 2 Myle fro Sychar. From thens gon men to Samarye, that men clepen now Sebast; and that is the chief Cytee of that Contree: and it sytt betwene the hille of Aygnes, as Jerusalem dothe. ᛫ In that Cytee was the syttinges of the 12 Tribes of Israel:

but the Cytee is not now so gret, as it was wont to be. There was buryed seynt John the Baptist, betwene 2 Prophetes, Helyseus and Abdyan: but he was beheded in the Castelle of Macharyme, besyde the dede See: and aftre he was translated of his Disciples, and buryed at Samarie: and there let Julianus Apostata dyggen him up, and let brennen his Bones; (for he was that time Emperour) and let wyndwe the Askes in the Wynd. But the Fynger, that schewed oure Lord, seyenge, *Ecce Agnus Dei;* that is to seyne, *Lo the Lamb of God:* that nolde nevere brenne, but is alle hol: that Fynger leet seynte Tecle the holy Virgyne be born in to the hille of Sebast; and there maken men gret feste. In that place was wont to ben a faire Chirche; and many othere there weren; but thei ben alle beten doun. There was wont to ben the heed of seynt John Baptist, enclosed in the Walle: but the Emperour Theodosie let drawe it out, and fond it wrapped in a litille Clothe, alle blody; and so he leet it to be born to Costantynoble: and zit at Costantynoble is the hyndre partye of the Heed: and the for partie of the Heed, til undre the Chyn, is at Rome, undre the Chirche of seynt Silvestre, where ben Nonnes of an hundred Ordres:[q] and it is zit alle broylly, as thoughe it were half brent: for the Emperour Julianus aboveseyd, of his cursednesse and malice, let brennen that partie with the other bones; and zit it schewethe: and this thing hathe ben preved, both be Popes and by Emperours. And the Jowes benethe, that holden to the Chyn, and a partie of the Assches, and the Platere, that the Hed was

[q] Moniales Cordularie, L.

leyd in, whan it was smyten of, is at Gene: and the Geneweyes maken of it gret Feste; and so don the Sarazynes also. And sum men seyn, that the Heed of seynt John is at Amyas, in Picardye: and other men seyn, that it is the Heed of seynt John the Bysschop. I wot nere, but God knowethe: but in what wyse than men worschipen it, the blessed seynt John holt him a payd.

From this Cytee of Sebast unto Jerusalem, is 12 Myle. And betwene the Hilles of that Contree, there is a Welle, that 4 Sithes in the Zeer chaungethe his Colour; somtyme grene, somtyme reed, somtyme cleer, and somtyme trouble: and men clepen that Welle Job. And the folk of that

Contree, that men clepen Samaritanes, weren converted and baptized by the Apostles; but thei holden not wel here Doctryne; and alle weys thei holden Lawes by hem self, varyenge from Cristene men, from Sarrazines, Jewes and Paynemes. And the Samaritanes leeven well in o God: and thei

seyn wel, that there is but only o God, that alle formed, and alle schalle deme: and thei holden the Bible aftre the Lettre; and thei usen the Psawtere, as the Jewes don: and thei seyn, that thei ben the righte Sones of God: and among alle other folk, thei seyn that thei ben best beloved of God; and that to hem belongethe the Heritage, that God behighte to hise beloved Children: and thei han also dyverse Clothinge and Schapp, to loken on, than other folk han; for thei wrappen here Hedes in red Linnene Clothe, in difference frō othere. And the Sarazines wrappen here Hedes in white lynnene Clothe. And the Cristene men, that duellen in the Contree, wrappen hem in blew of Ynde; and the Jewes in zelow Clothe. In that Contree duellen manye of the Jewes, payenge Tribute, as Cristene men don. And zif zee wil knowe the Lettres, that the Jewes usen, thei ben suche; and the names ben, as thei clepen hem, written aboven, in manner of here *A. B. C.*

א	ב	ג	ד	ה	ו	ז	ח
Alephe.	Bethe.	Gymel.	Delethe.	He.	Vau.	Zay.	Cy.

ט	י	כ	ל	מ	נ	ס	ע
Thet.	Joht.	Kapho.	Lampd.	Mem.	Num.	Samethe.	Ey.

פ	צ	ק	ר	ש	ת		
Fhee.	Sade.	Cophe.	Resch.	Son.	Tau.	.	

Cap. IX.

Of the Province of Galilee, and where Antecrist schalle be born. Of Nazarethe. Of the Age of oure Lady. Of the Day of Doom; and of the Customes of Jacobites, Surryenes; and of the Usages of Georgyenes.

FROM this Contree of the Samaritanes, that I have spoken of before, gon men to the Playnes of Galilee. And men leven the hilles, on that o partye. And Galilee is on of the Provynces of the Holy Lond: and in that Provynce is the Cytee of Naym and Capharnaum and Chorosaym and Bethsayde. In this Bethseyde was seynt Petre and seynt Andrew borne. And thens, a 4 Myle, is Chorosaym: and 5 Myle fro Chorosaym, is the Cytee of Cedar, where of the Psautre spekethe: *Et habitavi cum habitantibus Cedar;* that is for to seye, *And I have dwelled with the dwellynge men in Cedar.* In Chorosaym schalle Antecrist be born, as sum men seyn; and other men seyn, he schalle be born in Babyloyne: for the Prophete seyth; *De Babilonia Coluber exiet, qui totum mundum devorabit;* that is to seyne, *Out of Babiloyne schal come a Worm, that schal devourē alle the World.* This Antecrist schal be norysscht in Bethsayda, and he schalle regne in Capharnaum: and therfore seythe Holy Writt; *Ve tibi, Chorosaym: ve tibi, Bethsayda: ve tibi, Capharnaum;* that is to seye, *Wo be to the, Chorosaym; wo to the, Bethsayda: wo to the,*

Capharnaum. And alle theise Townes ben in the Lond of Galilee. And also, the Cane of Galilee is 4 Myle fro Nazarethe: of that Cytee was Simon Chananeus, and his Wif Canee; of the whiche the Holy Evaungelist spekethe off: there dide oure Lord the firste Myracle at the Wedyng, whan he turned Watre in to Wyn. And in the ende of Galilee, at the hilles, was the Arke of God taken; and on that other syde is the Mownt Hendor or Hermon. And there aboute gothe the Broke of Cison: and there besyde, Barache, that was Abymeleche Sone, with Delbore the Prophetisse, overcam the Oost of Ydumea, whan Cysera the Kyng was slayn of Gebelle, the Wyf of Aber;[r] and chaced bezonde the Flom Jordan, be Strengthe of Sword, Zeb and Zebee and Salmana; and there he slowghe hem. Also a 5 Myle fro Naym, is the Cytee of Jezreel, that somtyme was clept Zarym; of the whiche Cytee Jexabel the cursed Queen was Lady and Queen, that toke awey the Vyne of Nabaothe, be hire strengthe. Faste by that Cytee, is the Feld Magede, in the whiche the Kyng Joras was slayn of the Kyng of Samarie, and aftre was translated and buryed in the Mount Syon. And a Myle fro Jezrael ben the Hilles of Gelboe, where Saul and Jonathas that weren so faire, dyeden: wherfore David cursed hem, as Holy Writt seythe; *Montes Gelboe, nec Ros nec Pluvia, &c.;* that is to seye, *Zee Hilles of Gelboe, nouther Dew ne Reyn com upon zou.* And a Myle fro the Hilles of Gelboe, toward the Est, is the Cytee of Cyrople, that was clept before Bethsayn.

---

[r] Jael, the wife of Heber.

And upon the Walles of that Cytee was the Hed of Saul honged.

Aftre gon men be the hille, besyde the Pleynes of Galylee, unto Nazarethe, where was wont to ben a gret Cytee and a fair: but now there is not, but a lytille Village, and Houses a brood here and there. And it is not walled; and it sytt in a litille Valeye, and there ben Hilles alle aboute. There was oure Lady born: but sche was goten at Jerusalē. And be cause that oure Lady was born at Nazarethe, therfore bare oure Lord his Surname of that Town. There toke Josephe our Lady to Wyf, whan sche was 14 Zeere of Age: and there Gabrielle grette our Lady, seyenge, *Ave Gratia plena, Dominus tecum;* that is to seyne, *Heyl fulle of Grace, oure Lord is with the.* And this Salutacioun was don in a place of a gret Awteer of a faire Chirche, that was wont to be somtyme: but it is now alle downe: and men han made a litylle Resceyt, besyde a Pylere of that Chirche, for to resceyve the Offrynges of Pilgrymes. And the Sarrazines kepen that place fulle derely, for the profyte that thei han there offe: and thei ben fulle wykked Sarrazines and cruelle, and more dispytous than in ony other place, and han destroyed alle the Chirches. There nyghe is Gabrielles Welle, where oure Lord was wont to bathe him, whan he was zong: and fro that Welle bare he Watre often tyme to his Modre: and in that Welle sche wossche often tyme the Clowtes of hire Sone Jesu Crist. And fro Jerusalem unto thidre, is 3 Journeyes. At Nazarethe was our Lord norisscht. Nazarethe is als meche to seye, as Flour of the

Gardyn: and be gode skylle may it ben clept Flour; for there was norisscht the Flour of Lyf, that was Crist Jesu. And 2 Myle fro Nazarethe, is the Cytee of Sephor, be the Weye, that gothe fro Nazerethe to Acon. And an half Myle fro Nazarethe, is the Lepe of oure Lorde: for the Jewes ladden him upon an highe Roche, for to make him lepe doun, and have slayn him: but Jesu passed amonges hem, and lepte upon another Roche; and zit ben the Steppes of his Feet sene in the Roche, where he allyghte. And therfore seyn sum men, whan thei dreden hem of Thefes, on ony Weye, or of Enemyes; *Jesus autem transiens per medium illorū ibat;* that is to seyne, *Jesus forsothe passynge be the myddes of hem, he wente:* in tokene and mynde, that oure Lord passed thorghe out the Jewes Crueltee, and scaped safly fro hem: so surely mowe men passen the perile of Thefes. And than sey Men 2 Vers of the Psautre, 3 Sithes: *Irruat super eos formido & pavor, in magnitudine Brachii tui, Domine. Fiant inmobiles, quasi Lapis, donec pertranseat populus tuus, Domine; donec pertranseat populus tuus iste, quem possedisti.* And thanne may men passe with outen perile. And zee schulle undirstonde, that oure Lady hadde Child, whan sche was 15 Zeere old: and sche was conversant with hire Sone 33 Zeer and 3 Monethes. And aftre the Passioun of oure Lord, sche lyvede 24 Zeer.

Also fro Nazarethe, men gon to the Mount Thabor; and that is a 4 Myle: and it is a fulle faire Hille, and well highe, where was wont to ben a Toun and many Chirches; but thei ben alle destroyed; but zit there is a place, that men clepen the Scole of God, where he was wont to teche his Disciples, and tolde hem the Prevytees of Hevene. And at the foot of that Hille, Melchisedeche, that was Kyng of Salem, in the turnynge of that Hille, mette Abraham in comynge azen from the Bataylle, whan he had slayn Abymeleche: and this Melchisedeche was bothe Kyng and Prest of Salem, that now is cleped Jerusalem. In that Hille Thabor, oure Lord transfigured him before seynt Petre, seynt John and seynt Jame; and there they sawghe gostly Moyses and Elye the Prophetes besyde hem: and therfore seyde seynt Petre, *Domine, bonum est nos hic esse; faciamus tria Tabernacula;* that is to seye, *Lorde, it is gode for us to ben here; make we here 3 dwellyng places.* And there herd thei a Voys of the Fadir, that seye, *Hic est filius meus dilectus, in quo mihi bene complacui.* And oure Lord defended hem, that thei scholde not telle that Avisioun, til that he were rysen from Dethe to Lyf. In that Hille and in that same place, at the day of Doom, 4 Aungeles, with 4 Trompes, schulle blowen and reysen alle men, that hadden suffred Dethe, sithe that the World was formed, from Dethe to Lyve; and schulle comen in Body and Soule in Juggement; before the face of oure Lord, in the Vale of Josaphathe. And the Doom schalle ben on Estre Day, suche tyme as oure Lord aroos: and the Dom schalle begynne, suche houre as oure Lord descended to Helle and dispoyled it: for at such Houre schal he dispoyle the World, and lede his chosene to Blisse; and the othere schalle be condempne to perpetuelle

Peynes: and thanne schalle every man have aftir his dissert, outher Gode or Evylle; but zif the Mercy of God passe his Rightewisnesse.

Also a Myle from Mount Thabor, is the Mount Heremon; and there was the Cytee of Naym. Before the Zate of that Cytee, reysed oure Lord the Wydewes sone, that had no mo Children. Also 3 Myle fro Nazarethe, is the Castelle Saffra; of the whiche, the Sones of Zebedee and the Sones of Alphee weren. Also a 7 Myle fro Nazarethe, is the Mount Kayn; and undre that is a Welle, and besyde that Welle, Lameche Noees Fadre sloughe Kaym with an Arwe. For this Kaym wente thorghe Breres and Busshes, as a wylde Best; and he had lyved fro the tyme of Adam his Fadir, unto the tyme of Noe; and so he lyvede nyghe to 2000 Zeer. And this Lameche was alle blynd for elde.

Fro Saffra, men gothe to the See of Galylee and to the Cytee of Tyberye, that sytt upon the same See. And alle be it, that men clepen it a See, zit is it nouther See ne Arm of the See: for it is but a Stank of fresche Watir, that is in lengthe 100 Furlonges; and of brede 40 Furlonges; and hathe with in him gret plentee of gode Fissche, and rennethe in to Flom Jordan. The Cytee is not fulle gret, but it hathe gode Bathes with in him. And there, as the Flom Jordan partethe fro the See of Galilee, is a gret Brigge, where men passen from the Lond of Promyssioun, to the Lond of Baazan and the Lond of Gerrasentz, that ben about the Flom Jordan, and the begynnynge of the See of Tyberie. And fro thens may men go to Damask, in 3 dayes, be the Kyngdom of Traconye; the whiche Kyngdom lastethe fro Mount

Heremon to the See of Galilee, or to the See of
Tyberie, or to the See of Jenazarethe; and alle is
o See, and this the Stank that I have told zou; but
it chaungethe thus the name, for the names of the
Cytees that sytten besyde hem. Upon that See,
went oure Lord drye feet; and there he toke up
seynt Petir, when he began to drenche with in the
See, and seyde to him, *Modice Fidei, quare dubi-
tasti?* And aftre his Resurrexioun, oure Lord
appered on that See, to his Disciples, and bad
hem fyssche, and filled alle the Nett fulle of gret
Fisshes. In that See rowed oure Lord often tyme;
and there he called to him, seynt Petir, seynt
Andrew, seynt James and seynt John, the Sones
of Zebedee. In that Cytee of Tyberie, is the
Table, upon the whiche oure Lord eete upon, with
his Disciples, aftre his Resurrexioun; and thei
knewen him in brekynge of Bred, as the Gospelle
seythe; *Et cognoverunt eum in fractione Panis.*
And nyghe that Cytee of Tyberie, is the Hille,
where oure Lord fedde 5 thousand Persones, with

5 barly Loves and 2 Fisshes. In that Cytee, a man cast an brennynge Dart in wratthe aftir oure Lord, and the Hed smot in to the Eerthe, and wax grene, and it growed to a gret Tree; and zit it growethe, and the Bark there of is alle lyk Coles. Also in the Hed of that See of Galilee, toward the Septemtryon, is a strong Castelle and an highe, that highte Saphor: and fast besyde it, is Capharnaum: with in the Lond of Promyssioun, is not so strong a Castelle: and there is a gode Toun benethe, that is clept also Saphor. In that Castel, seynt Anne our Ladyes Modre was born. And there benethe was Centurioes Hous. That Contree is clept the Galilee of Folk,[5] that weren taken to Tribute of Sabulon, and of Neptalym. And in azen comynge fro that Castelle, a 30 Myle, is the Cytee of Dan, that somtyme was clept Belynas, or Cesaire Philippon, that sytt at the foot of the Mount of Lyban, where the Flom Jordan begynnethe. There begynnethe the Lond of Promyssioun, and durethe unto Bersabee, in lengthe, in goynge toward the Northe in to the Southe; and it conteynethe well a 180 Myles: and of brede, that is to seye, fro Jericho unto Jaffe, and that conteynethe a 40 Myle of Lombardye, or of oure Contree, that ben also lytylle Myles. Theise ben not Myles of Gascoyne, ne of the Provynce of Almayne, where ben gret Myles. And wite zee welle, that the Lond of Promyssioun is in Sirye. For the Reme of Syrie durethe fro the Desertes of Arabye, unto Cecyle, and that is Ermonye the grete, that is to seyne, fro the Southe to the Northe: and fro the Est to the West, it durethe fro the grete Desertes of Arabye

[5] Gentiles.

unto the West See. But in that Reme of Syrie, is the Kyngdom of Judee, and many other Provynces, as Palestyne, Galilee, litylle Cilicye, and many othere. In that Contree and other Contrees bezonde, thei han a Custom, whan thei schulle usen Werre, and whan men holden Sege abouten Cytee or Castelle, and thei with innen dur not senden out Messagers with Lettres, frō Lord to Lord, for to aske Sokour, thei maken here Letters and bynden hem to the Nekke of a Colver, and leten

the Colver flee; and the Colveren ben so taughte, that thei fleen with tho Lettres to the verry place, that men wolde sende hem to. For the Colveres ben norysscht in tho Places, where thei ben sent to; and thei senden hem thus, for to beren here Lettres. And the Colveres retournen azen, where as thei ben norisscht; and so thei don comounly.

And zee schulle undirstonde, that amonges the Sarazines, o part and other, duellen many Cristene men, of many maneres and dyverse names; and alle ben baptized, and han dyverse Lawes and

dyverse Customes: but alle beleven in God the
Fadir and the Sone and the Holy Gost: but alle
weys fayle thei, in sōme Articles of oure Feythe.
Some of theise ben clept Jacobytes: for seynt
Jame converted hem, and seynt John baptized
hem. They seyn, that a Man schal maken his
Confessioun only to God, and not to a Man: for
only to him, scholde man zelden him gylty of alle,
that he hathe mys don. Ne God ordeyned not,
ne never devysed, ne the Prophete nouther, that a
man scholde schryven him to another, (as thei
seyn) but only to God: as Moyses writethe in the
Bible, and as David seythe in the Psawtre Boke;
Confitebor tibi, Domine, in toto Corde meo: and,
Delictum meum tibi cognitum feci: And, *Deus meus*

es tu, & confitebor tibi; And, *Quoniam cogitatio
hominis confitebitur tibi;* &c. For thei knowen alle
the Bible, and the Psautere: and therfore allegge
thei so the Lettre: but thei alleggen not the Auctoritees thus in Latyn, but in here Langage, fulle
appertely; and seyn wel, that David and other

Prophetes seyn it. Natheles seynt Austyn and seynt Gregory seyn thus: Augustinus; *Qui scelera sua cogitat, & conversus fuerit, veniam sibi credat.* Gregorius; *Dominus potius mentem quam verba respicit.* And seynt Hillary seythe; *Longorū temporum crimina, in ictu Oculi pereunt, si Cordis nata fuerit compunctio.* And for suche Auctoritees, thei seyn, that only to God schalle a man knouleche his Defautes, zeldynge him self gylty, and cryenge him mercy, and behotynge to him to amende him self. And therfore whan thei wil schryven hem, thei taken Fyre, and sette it besyde hem, and casten therin Poudre of Frank encens; and in the Smoke therof, thei schryven hem to God, and cryen him mercy. But Sothe it is, that this Confessioun was first and kyndely: but seynt Petre the Apostle, and thei that camen aftre him, han ordeynd to make here Confessioun to man; and

be gode resoun: for thei perceyveden wel, that no Syknesse was curable, by gode Medycyne to leye therto, but zif men knewen the nature of the Maladye. And also no man may zeven covenable Medicyne, but zif he knowe the qualitee of the

Dede. For o Synne may be grettere in o man
than in another, and in o place and in o tyme
than in another: and therfore it behovethe him,
that he knowe the kynde of the Dede, and thereupon to zeven him Penance.

There ben othere, that ben clept Surienes;
and thei holden the Beleeve amonges us, and of
hem of Grece. And thei usen alle Berdes, as men
of Grece don: and thei make the Sacrement of
therf Bred: and in here Langage, thei usen Lettres of Sarrazines; but aftre the Misterie of Holy
Chirche, thei usen Lettres of Grece; and thei
maken here Confessioū, right as the Jacobytes
don.

There ben othere, that men clepen Georgyenes,
that seynt George converted; and him thei worschipen, more than ony other Seynt; and to him
thei cryen for help: and thei camen out of the
Reme of George. Theise Folk usen Crounes
schaven. The Clerkes han rounde Crounes, and

the lewed men han Crownes alle square: and thei holden Cristene Lawe, as don thei of Grece; of whom I have spoken of before.

Othere there ben, that men clepen Cristene men of Gyrdynge: for thei ben alle gyrt aboven. And ther ben othere, that men clepen Nestoryenes; and summe Arryenes, sūme Nubyenes, sūme of Grees, sūme of Ynde, and sūme of Prestre Johnes Lond. And alle theise han manye Articles of oure Feythe, and to othere thei ben varyaunt. And of here variance, were to longe to telle; and so I wil leve, as for the tyme, with outen more spekynge of hem.

Cap. XI.

Of the Cytee of Damasce. Of 3 Weyes to Jerusalem; on be Londe and be See; another more be Londe than be See; and the thridde Weye to Jerusalem, alle be Londe.

Now aftre that I have told zou sum partye of Folk, in the Contrees before, now wille I turnen azen to my Weye, for to turnen azen to this half. Thanne whoso wil go fro the Lond of Galilee, of that that I have spoke, for to come azen on this half, men comen azen be Damasce, that is a fulle fayre Cytee, and fulle noble, and fulle of alle Merchandises, and a 3 Journeyes long fro the See, and a 5 Journeyes fro Jerusalem. But upon Camaylles, Mules, Hors, Dromedaries and other Bestes, men caryen here Marchandise thidre: and thidre comethe Marchauntes with Marchandise be See, from Yndee, Persee, Caldee, Ermonye, and of manye othere Kyngdomes. This Cytee founded Helizeus Damascus, that was Zoman and Despenser of Abraham, before that Ysaac was born: for he thoughte for to have ben Abrahames Heir: and he named the Toun aftre his Surname Damasce. And in that place, where Damasc was founded, Kaym sloughe Abel his Brother. And

besyde Damasc is the Mount Seyr. In that Cytee of Damasce, ther is gret plentee of Welles: and with in the Cytee and with oute, ben many fayre Gardynes, and of dyverse frutes. Non other Cytee is not lyche in comparisoun to it, of faire Gardynes, and of faire Desportes. The Cytee is gret and fulle of Peple, and wel walled with double Walles. And there ben manye Phisicyens. And seint Poul him self was there a Phisicyen, for to kepen mennes Bodies in hele, before he was converted; and aftre that, he was Phisicien of Soules. And seynt Luke the Evaungelist was Disciple of seynt Poul, for to lerne Phisik; and many othere. For seynt Poul held thanne Scole of Phisik. And neere besyde Damasce, was he converted: and aftre his Conversioun, he duelte in that Cytee 3 Dayes, with outen sight, and with outen Mete or Drinke. And in tho 3 Dayes he was ravisscht to Hevene, and there he saughe many prevytees of oure Lord. And faste besyde Damasce, is the Castelle of Arkes, that is bothe fair and strong. From Damasce, men comen azen, be oure Lady of Sardenak, that is a 5 Myle on this half Damasce; and it is sytt upon a Roche, and it is a fulle faire place, and it semethe a Castelle; for there was wont to ben a Castelle: but it is now a fulle faire Chirche. And there with inne, ben Monkes and Nonnes Cristene. And there is a Vowt, undre the Chirche, where that Cristene men duellen also: and thei han many gode Vynes. And in the Chirche, behynde the highe Awtere, in the Walle, is a Table of black Wode, on the whiche somtyme was depeynted an Ymage of oure Lady, that turnethe into Flesche; but now the Ymage schewethe but litille: [t] but evermore thorewe the grace of God, that Table droppeth as hyt were of Olyve. And there is a Vessel of Marbre, undre the Table, to resseyve the Oyle, thare of thay yeven unto Pylgrymes: for it heleth of many Sykenesses. And he that kepeth it clanly a yere, aftre that yere, hyt turneth yn to Flesche and Bloode.

By twyne the Cytee of Darke and the Cytee of

[t] Three leaves being lost in the Cotton MS. are transcrib'd from E. 2.

Raphane, ys a Ryvere, that men clepen Sabatorye. For on the Saturday, hyt renneth faste; and alle the Wooke elles, hyt stondeth stylle, and renneth nouzt or lytel. And thare ys a nother Ryvere, that upon the nyzt freseth wondur faste; and uppon the day, ys noon Frost sene. And so gon men by a Cytee, that men clepen Beruche. And thare men gon un to the See, that schal goon un to Cypre. And thay aryve at Porte de Sure or of Tyrye; and thanne un to Cypre. Or elles men mowen gon from the Porte of Tyrye ryzt welle, and com not yn to Cypre; and aryve at som Haven of Grece: and thanne comen men un to theis Countrees, by weyes, that I have spoken of by fore.

Now have I tolde you of Wayes, by the whyche men gon ferrest and longest; as by Babyloyne and Mounte Synay and other places many, thorewe the whyche Londes, men turne azen to the Lande of Promyssyoun. Now wul y telle the ryzt Way to Jerusalem. For som men wyl nouzt passe hyt, som for thay have nouzt Despence of hem, for they have noon Companye, and other many Causes resonables. And thare fore I telle yow schorttely, how a man may goon with lytel costage and schortte tyme. A man that cometh from the Londes of the Weste, he gothe thorewe Fraunce, Borgoyne and Lumbardye, and to Venys and to Geen, or to som other Havene of the Marches, and taketh a Schyppe thare, and gon by See to the Isle of Gryffle;[u] and so aryveth hem yn Grece or in Port Myroche or Valon or Duras, or at som other Havene, and gon to Londe, for to reste

[u] Gresse, L.; Grif, F.

hem; and gon ayen to the See, and aryves in Cypre; and cometh nouzt yn the Ile of Roodes; and aryves at Famegoste, that ys the chefe Havene of Cypre, or elles at Lamatoun. And thenne entreth yn to the Schyp ayen, and by syde the Havene of Tyre, and come nouzt to Lande; and so passeth he by alle the Havens of that Coost, un til he come to Jaffe, that ys the neyest Haven unto Jerusalem: for it is seven and twenty Myle. And from Jaffe, men goon to the Cytee of Rames: and that ys but lytel thenne, and hyt ys a fayre Cytee. And by syde Rames, ys a fayre Churche of oure Lady, whare oure Lord schewede hym to oure Lady, in thys lykenesse, that he tokeneth the Trynyte. And thare fast by, ys a Churche of seynt George, whare that hys Heed was smyten of. And thanne un to the Castel Emaus; and thanne un to Mounte Joye: and from thenne, Pylgrymes mowen fyrste se un to Jerusalem. And thanne un to Mount Modeyn: and thanne unto Jerusalem. And at the Mount Modeyn, lythe the Prophete Machabee. And overe Ramatha, ys the Town of Douke;[x] where of Amos the goude Prophete was.

A nother Way. For alse moche as many men ne may not suffre the Savour of the See, but hadden lever to gon by Londe, they[y] that hyt be more payne; a man schal soo goon un to on of the Havenes of Lumbardye, als Venys or an other: and he schal passe yn to Grece, thorwe Port Moroche, or an other, and so he schal gon un to Constantynople. And he schal so passe the Wature, that ys cleped the Brace of seynt George, that ys an Arm of the See. And frō thens he

[x] Teuke, L. and F.; Tekoa, Amos i. 1.   [y] Though.

schal com un to Pulveralle; and sythen un to the Castelle of Cynople. And from thens schal he gon un to Capadose, that ys a grete Countree, whare that ben many grete Hylles. And he schal gon thorewe Turkye, and unto the Cytee of Nyke, the whyche they wonne from the Emperoure of Constantynople. And hyt ys a fayre Cytee, and wounder wel walled: and thare ys a Ryvere, that men clepen the Laye: and thare men goon by the Alpes of Aryoprynant,[a] and by the Valez of Mallebrynez, and eke the Vale of Ernax; and so un to Anthyoche the lesse, that sytteth on the Rychay.[a] And there aboute ben many goude Hylles and fayre, and many fayre Woodes, and eke Wylde Beestes.

And he that wylle goon by an other way, he mote goon by the Playnes of Romayne, costynge the Romayne See. Uppon that Cost, ys a woundur fayre Castelle, that men clepen Florathe. And whanne that a man ys oute of that ylke Hylles, men passen thenne thorewe a Cytee, that ys called Maryoche and Arteyse, whare that ys a grete Brygge upon the Ryvere of Ferne, that men clepen Fassar:[b] and hyt ys a grete Ryvere, berynge Schyppes. And by syde the Cytee of Damas, ys a Ryvere that cometh from the Mounteyne of Lybane, that men hyt callen Albane. Atte passynge of this Ryvere, seynt Eustache loste hys two Sones, whanne that he hadde lost hys Wyffe. And yt gooth thorewe the Playne of Arthadoe; and so un to the Reed See. And so

[a] Noirmont, L. 1, 2; F. 1, 2. Mormaunt, E. 3, 4.
[a] Super fluvium Reclay, L. and F.
[b] Farfar, L. 1, 2; F. 1, 2.

men moten goon un to the Cytee of Phenne, and so un to the Cytee of Ferne. And Antyoche ys a ful fayre Cytee and wel walled. For hyt ys two Myle longe, and eche Pylere of the Brygge thare ys a goud Toure. And thys ys the beest cytee of the kyngdom of Surrye. And from Antyoche, men moten so forth goon un to the Cytee of Lacuthe; and thanne un to Geble; and thanne un tyl Tourtous: and thare by ys the Lande of Cambre, whare that ys a stronge Castelle, that men clepen Maubeke. And from Tourtouse men goon un to Thryple, uppon the See. And uppon the See, men goon unto Dacres; and thare ben two Weyes un to Jerusalem: Uppon the lyfte way, men goon fyrst un to Damas, by Flome Jordane: uppon the ryzt syde, men goon thorewe the Lande of Flagam, and so un to the Cytee of Cayphas: of the whiche Cayphas was Lord: and som clepeth hyt the Castelle Pellerynez: And from thens ys foure dayes Journeys un to Jerusalem: And they goon thorewe Cesarye Phylyppum and Jaffe and Ramys and Emaux, and so unto Jerusalem.

Now have I told yow som of the Wayes, by the Lande, and eke by Water, how that men mowen goon unto Jerusalem: they^c that hyt be so, that there been many other Wayes, that men goon by, aftur Countrees, that thay comen fram, nevere the lasse thay turne alle un tylle an ende. Yet is thare a way, alle by lande, un to Jerusalem, and pass noon See; that ys from Fraunce or Flaundres: but that Way ys full lange and perylous, of grete Travayle; and thare fore fewe goon

^c Though.

that ylke way. And who so gooth that, he mote goon thorewe Almayn and Pruys; and so un to Tartarye. This Tartarye ys holden of the great Chan, of whom y schal speke more afterwarde. For thydur lasteth hys Lordschup. And the Lordes of Tartarye yeldeth unto the grete Chan Trybute. Thys ys a ful ille Lande, and a sondye, and wel lytel fruyt beryng. For thare groweth lytel goude of Corne or Wyn, ne Benes ne Pese: but Beestes ben thare y nowe, and that ful grete plente. And thare ete thay nougt but Flesche with outen Brede; and thay soupe the Brothe there of: and also thay drynke the mylk. And alle manere of wylde Beestes they eten,[d] Houndes, Cattes, Ratouns, and alle othere wylde Bestes. And thei have no Wode, or elle lytylle. And therfore thei warmen and sethen here Mete with Hors Dong and Cow Dong, and of other Bestes, dryed azenst the Sonne. And Princes and othere eten not, but ones in the day; and that but lytille. And thei ben righte foule folk and of evyl kynde. And in Somer, be alle the Contrees, fallen many Tempestes and many hydouse Thondres and Leytes, and slen meche Peple, and Bestes also, fulle often tyme. And sodeynly is there passynge hete, and sodeynly also passynge cold. And it is the foulest Contree, and the most cursed, and the porest, that men knowen. And here Prince, that governethe that Contree, that thei clepen Batho, duellethe at the Cytee of Orda. And treuly no gode man scholde not duellen in that Contre. For the Lond and the Contree is not worthi Houndes to dwelle inne. It were a

[d] Thus far out of E. z.

K

gode Contree to sowen inne Thristelle and Breres
and Broom and Thornes; and for no other thing
is it not good. Natheless there is gode Londe in
sum place; but it is pure litille, as men seyn. I
have not ben in that Contree, ne be tho Weyes:
but I have ben at other Londes, that marchen to
tho Contrees; and in the Lond of Russye, and in
the Lond of Nyflan, and in the Reme of Crako,
and of Letto, and in the Reme of Daresten, and
in manye other places, that marchen to the Costes:
but I wente never be that weye to Jerusalem;
wherfore I may not wel telle zou the manere. But
zif this matiere plese to ony worthi man, that
hathe gon be that weye, he may telle it, zif him
lyke; to that entent, that tho that wole go by that
weye, and maken here viage be tho Costes, mowen
knowen what weye is there. For no man may
passe be that Weye godely, but in time of Wyntir,
for the perilous Watres, and wykkede Mareyes that
ben in tho Contrees; that no man may passe, but
zif it be strong Frost, and Snowe aboven. For
zif the Snow ne were, men myght not gon upon
the Yse, ne Hors ne Carre nouther. And it
is wel a 3 Journeys of suche Weye, to passe frō
Prusse to the Lond of Sarazin habitable. And
it behovethe to the Cristene men, that schulle
Werre azen hem every Zeer, to bere here Vitaylles
with hem: for thei schulle fynde there no good.
And than most thei let carye here Vitaylle upon
the Yse, with Carres that have no Wheeles, that
thei clepen Scleyes. And als longe as here Vitaylles lasten, thei may abide there, but no longer.
For there schulle thei fynde no Wight, that will
selle hem ony Vitaille or ony thing. And whan

the Spyes seen ony Cristene men comen upon hem, thei rennen to the Townes, and cryen with a lowd voys, Kerra, Kerra, Kerra; and than anon thei armen hem and assemblen hem to gydere.

And zee schulle undirstonde, that it fresethe more strongly in tho Contrees than on this half; and therfore hathe every man Stewes in his Hous, and in tho Stewes thei eten and don here Occupatiouns, alle that thei may. For that is at the Northe parties, that men clepen the Septentrionelle, where it is alle only cold. For the Sonne is but lytille or non toward tho Contreyes: and therfore in the Septentryon, that is verry Northe, is the Lond so cold, that no man may duelle there: and in the contrarye, toward the Southe, it is so hoot, that no man ne may duelle there; because that the Sonne, whan he is upon the Southe, castethe his Bemes alle streghte upon that partye.

Cap. XII.

Of the Customes of Sarasines, and of hire Lawe; and how the Soudan arresond me, Auctour of this Book. And of the begynnynge of Machomete.

Now because that I have spoken of Sarazines and of here Contree, now zif zee wil knowe a party of here Lawe and of here Beleve, I schalle telle zou, aftre that here Book, that is clept Alkaron, tellethe. And sum men clepen that Book Meshaf: and sum men clepen it Harme, aftre the dyverse Langages of the Contree. The whiche Book Machamete toke hem. In the whiche Boke, among other thinges, is writen, as I have often tyme seen and radd, that the Gode schulle gon to Paradys, and the Evele to Helle: and that beleven alle Sarrazines. And zif a Man aske hem, what Paradys thei menen; thei seyn, to Paradys, that is a place of Delytes, where men schulle fynde alle maner of Frutes, in alle Cesouns, and Ryveres rennynge of Mylk and Hony, and of Wyn, and of swete Watre; and that thei schulle have faire Houses and noble, every man aftre his Dissert, made of precyous Stones, and of Gold, and of Sylver; and that every man schalle have 80^e Wyfes, alle Maydenes; and he schalle have ado every day with hem, and zit he schalle fynden hem alle weys Maydenes. Also thei beleeven and spekē gladly of the Virgine Marie and of the Incarnacioun. And thei seyn, that Marye was taughte of the Angel; and that Gabrielle seyde to hire, that sche was forchosen from the begynnynge of the World; and that he schewed to hire the Incarnacioun of Jesu Crist; and that sche conceyved and bare Child, Mayden: and that wytnessethe here Boke. And thei seyn also, that Jesu Crist spak als sone as he was born; and that he was an Holy Prophete and a trewe, in woord and dede, and meke and pytous and rightefulle and with outen ony vyce. And thei seyn also, that whan the Angel schewed the Incarnacioun of Crist unto Marie, sche was zong, and had gret drede. For there was thāne an Enchantour in the Contree, that deled with Wycche craft, that men clepten Taknia, that be his Enchauntementes cowde make him in lyknesse of an Angel, and wente often tymes and lay with Maydenes: and therfore Marie dredde, lest it hadde ben Taknia,

^e 10, E. 1, 2, 4; L. 1.   90, F. 1, 2.

that cam for to desceyve the Maydenes. And
therfore sche conjured the Angel, that he scholde
telle hire, zif it were he or no. And the Angel
answerde and seyde, that sche scholde have no
drede of him: for he was verry Messager of Jesu
Crist. Also here Book seythe, that whan that
sche had childed undre a Palme Tree, sche had
gret schame, that sche hadde a Child; and sche
grette, and seyde, that sche wolde that sche hadde
ben ded. And anon the Child spak to hire and
comforted hire, and seyde, Modir, ne dismaye the
noughte; for God hathe hidd in the his prevytees,
for the salvacioun of the World. And in othere
many places seythe here Alkaron, that Jesu Crist
spak als sone as he was born. And that Book
seythe also, that Jesu was sent from God alle
myghty, for to ben Myrour and Ensample and
Tokne[f] to alle men. And the Alkaron seythe also
of the day of Doom, how God schal come to deme
alle maner of folk; and the Gode he schalle drawen
on his syde, and putte hem in to Blisse; and the
wykkede he schal condempne to the peynes of
Helle. And amonges alle Prophetes, Jesu was
the most excellent and the moste worthi, next
God; and that he made the Gospelles, in the
whiche is gode Doctryne and helefulle, fulle of
Charitee and Sothefastnesse, and trewe prechinge
to hem that beleeven in God; and that he was a
verry Prophete, and more than a Prophete; and
lyved with outen Synne, and zaf syghte to the
Blynde, and helede the Lepres, and reysede dede
men, and steyghe to Hevene. And whan thei
mowe holden the Boke of the Gospelles of oure

[f] Speculum.

Lord writen, and namely, *Missus est Angelus Gabriel;* that Gospel thei seyn, tho that ben lettred, often tymes in here Orisouns, and thei kissen it and worschipen it, with gret devocioun. Thei fasten an hool Monethe in the Zeer, and eten noughte but be nyghte, and thei kepen hem fro here Wyfes alle that Monethe: but the seke men be not constreyned to that Fast. Also this Book spekethe of Jewes; and seythe, that thei ben cursed; for thei wolde not beleven, that Jesu Crist was comen of God; and that thei lyeden falsely on Marie and on hire Sone Jesu Crist, seyenge that thei hadden crucyfyed Jesu the Sone of Marie: for he was nevere crucyfyed, as thei seyn; but that God made him to stye up to him with outen Dethe, and with outen Anoye: but he transfigured his lyknesse in to Judas Scariothe, and him crucyfyeden the Jewes, and wenden that it had ben Jesus: but Jesus steyge to Hevenes alle quyk; and therfore thei seyn, that the Cristene men erren and han no gode knowleche of this, and that thei beleeven folyly and falsly, that Jesu Crist was crucyfyed. And thei seyn zit, that and he had ben crucyfyed, that God had don azen his rightewisnesse, for to suffre Jesu Crist, that was innocent, to ben put upon the Cros, with outen Gylt. And in this Article thei seyn, that wee faylen, and that the gret Rightewisnesse of God ne myghte not suffre so gret a wrong. And in this, faylethe here Feythe. For thei knoulechen wel, that the Werkes of Jesu Crist ben gode, and his Wordes and his Dedes and his Doctryne by his Gospelles, weren trewe, and his Meracles also trewe; and the blessed Virgine Marie is good, and holy Mayden, before and aftre the Birthe of Jesu Crist; and that alle tho, that beleven perfitely in God, schul ben saved. And because that thei gon so nye oure Feythe, thei ben lyghtly converted to Cristene Lawe, whan men prechen hem and schewen hem distynctly the Lawe of Jesu Crist, and tellen hem of the Prophecyes. And also thei seyn, that thei knownen wel, be the Prophecyes, that the Lawe of Machomete schalle faylen, as the Lawe of the Jewes dide; and that the Lawe of Cristine peple schalle laste to the day of Doom. And zif ony man aske hem, what is here Beleeve; thei answeren thus, and in this forme, Wee beleven God Formyour of Hevene and of Erthe and of alle othere things, that he made. And withouten him is no thing made. And we beleven of the day of Doom, and that every man schalle have his Meryte, aftre he hathe disserved. And we beleve it for Sothe, alle that God hathe seyd be the mouthes of his Prophetes. Also Machomet cōmanded in his Alkaron, that every man scholde have 2 Wyfes or 3 or 4; but now thei taken unto 9, and of Lemmanes als manye as he may susteyne. And zif ony of here Wyfes mys beren hem azenst hire Husbonde, he may caste hire out of his House, and departe from him, and take another: but he schalle departe with hire his Godes. Also whan men speken to hem, of the Fadre and of the Sone and of the Holy Gost, thei seyn, that thei ben 3 persones; but not o God. For here Alkaron spekethe not of the Trynyte. But thei seyn wel, that God hathe speche, and elle where he dowmb; and God hathe also a Spirit, thei knowen wel, for elle thei seyn, he were not in lyve. And whan

men speken to hen of the Incarnacioū, how that
be the word of the Angel, God sente his Wysdom
in to Erthe, and enumbred him in the Virgyne
Marie: and be the woord of God, schulle the
Dede bē reysed, at the day of Doom; thei seyn,
that it is Sothe, and that the Woord of God hathe
gret Strengthe. And thei seyn, that whoso knew
not the Woord of God, he scholde not knowe God.
And thei seyn also, that Jesu Crist is the Woord
of God; and so seythe here Alkaron, where it
seythe, that the Angel spak to Marie and seyde,
Marie, God schalle preche the Gospel be the
Woord of his Mowthe, and his name schalle be
clept Jesu Crist. And thei seyn also, that Abraham was Frend to God, and that Moyses was
famileer spekere with God; and Jesu Crist was
the Woord and the Spirit of God; and that Machomete was right Messager of God. And thei
seyn, that of theise 4, Jesu was the most worthi
and the most excellent and the most gret; so that
thei han many gode Articles of oure Feythe, alle
be it that thei have no parfite Lawe and Feythe,
as Cristene men han; and therfore ben thei lightly
converted; and namely, tho that undirstonden the
Scriptures and the Prophecyes. For thei han
Gospelles and the Prophecyes and the Byble,
writen in here Langage. Wherfore thei conne
meche of Holy Wrytt, but thei undirstonde it not,
but aftre the Lettre: and so don the Jewes; for
thei undirstonde not the Lettre gostly, but bodyly:
and therfore ben thei repreved of the wise, that
gostly understonden it. And therfore seythe seynt
Poul; *Litera occidit; Spiritus vivificat.* Also the
Sarazines seyn, that the Jewes ben cursed: for

thei han defouled the Lawe, that God sente hem
be Moyses. And the Cristene ben cursed also, as
thei seyn: for their kepen not the Comandementes
and the Preceptes of the Gospelle, that Jesu Crist
taughte hem. And therfore I schalle telle zou,
what the Soudan tolde me upon a day, in his
Chambre. He leet voyden out of his Chambre
alle manner of men, Lordes and othere: for he
wolde speke with me in Conseille. And there he
askede me, how the Cristene men governed hem
in oure Contree. And I seyde him, Righte wel:
thonked be God. And he seyde me, Treulyche,
nay: for zee Cristene men ne recthen righte
noghte how untrewly to serve God. Ze scholde
zeven ensample to the lewed peple, for to do wel;
and zee zeven hem ensample to don evylle. For
the Comownes, upon festyfulle dayes, whan thei
scholden gon to Chirche to serve God, than gon
thei to Tavernes, and ben there in glotony, alle the
day and alle nyghte, and eten and drynken, as
Bestes that have no resoun, and wite not whan
thei have y now. And also the Cristene men en-
forcen hem, in alle maneres that thei mowen, for
to fighte, and for to desceyven that on that other.
And there with alle thei ben so proude, that thei
knowen not how to ben clothed; now long, now
schort, now streyt, now large, now swerded,
now daggered, and in alle manere gyses. Thei
scholden ben symple, meke and trewe, and
fulle of Almes dede, as Jhesu was, in whom thei
trowe: but thei ben alle the contrarie, and evere
enclyned to the Evylle, and to don evylle. And
thei ben so coveytous, that for a lytylle Sylver,
thei sellen here Doughtres, here Sustres and here

owne Wyfes, to putten hem to Leccherie. And
on with drawethe the Wif of another: and non of
hem holdethe Feythe to another: but thei defoulen
here Lawe, that Jhesu Crist betook hem to kepe, for
here Salvacioun. And thus for here Synnes, han
thei lost alle this Lond, that wee holden. For,
for hire Synnes there God hathe taken hem in to
oure Hondes, noghte only be Strengthe of our self,
but for here Synnes. For wee knowen wel in
verry sothe, that whan zee serve God, God wil
helpe zou: and whan he is with zou, no man may
be azenst you. And that knowe we wel, be oure
Prophecyes, that Cristene men schulle wynnen
azen this Lond out of oure Hondes, whan thei
serven God more devoutly. But als longe als thei
ben of foule and of unclene Lyvynge, (as thei ben
now) wee have no drede of hem, in no kynde: for
here God wil not helpen hem in no wise. And
than I asked him, how he knew the State of Cristene men. And he answered me, that he knew
alle the state of the Comounes also, be his Messangeres, that he sente to alle Londes, in manere as
thei weren Marchauntes of precyous Stones, of
Clothes of Gold and of othere things; for to
knowen the manere of every Contree amonges
Cristene men. And than he leet clepe in alle the
Lordes, that he made voyden first out of his Chambre; and there he schewed me 4, that weren grete
Lordes in the Contree, that tolden me of my Contree, and of many othere Cristene Contrees, als
wel as thei had ben of the same Contree: and thei
spak Frensche righte wel; and the Sowdan also,
where of I had gret Marvaylle. Allas! that it is
gret sclaundre to oure Feythe and to oure Lawe,

whan folk that ben with outen Lawe, schulle repreven us and undernemen us of oure Synnes. And thei that scholden ben converted to Crist and to the Lawe of Jhesu, be oure gode Ensamples and be oure acceptable Lif to God, and so converted to the Lawe of Jhesu Crist, ben thorghe oure Wykkednesse and evylle lyvynge, fer fro us and Straungeres fro the holy and verry Beleeve, schulle thus appelen us and holden us for wykkede Lyveres and cursed. And treuly thei sey sothe. For the Sarazines ben gode and feythfulle. For thei kepen entierly the Cōmaundement of the Holy Book Alkaron, that God sente hem be his Messager Machomet; to the whiche, as thei seyne, seynt Gabrielle the Aungel often tyme tolde the wille of God. And zee schulle undirstonde, that Machamote was born in Arabye, that was first a pore Knave, that kept Cameles, that wenten with Marchantes for Marchandize; and so befelle, that he wente with the Marchandes in to Egipt: and thei weren than Cristene, in tho partyes. And at the Desertes of Arabye, he wente in to a Chapelle, where a Eremyte duelte. And when he entred in to the Chapelle, that was but a lytille and a low thing, and had but a lityl Dore and a low, than the Entree began to wexe so gret and so large and so highe, as thoughe it had ben of a gret Mynstre, or the Zate of a Paleys. And this was the firste Myracle, the Sarazins seyn, that Machomete dide in his Zouthe. Aftre began he for to wexe wyse and riche; and he was a gret Astronomer: and aftre he was Goveronour and Prince of the Lond of Cozrodane; and he governed it fully wisely, in suche manere, that whan the Prince was ded, he toke the Lady to Wyfe, that highte Gadridge. And Machomete felle often in the grete Sikenesse, that men callen the fallynge Evylle: wherfore the Lady was fulle sorry, that evere sche toke him to Husbonde. But Machomete made hire to beleeve, that alle tymes, whan he felle so, Gabriel the Angel cam for to speke with him; and for the gret lighte and brightnesse of the Angelle, he myghte not susteyne him fro fallynge. And therfore the Sarazines seyn, that Gabriel cam often to speke with him. This Machomete regned in Arabye, the Zeer of oure Lord Jhesu Crist 610; and was of the Generacioun of Ysmael, that was Abrahames Sone, that he gat upon Agar his Chamberere. And therfore ther ben Sarazines, that ben clept Ismaelytenes; and sūme Agaryenes, of Agar: and the othere propurly ben clept Sarrazines, of Sarra: and sūme ben clept Moabytes, and sūme Amonytes; fro the 2 Sones of Lothe, Moab and Amon, that he begat on his Doughtres, that weren aftirward grete erthely Princes. And also Machomete loved wel a gode Heremyte, that duelled in the Desertes, a Myle fro Mount Synay, in the Weye that men gon fro Arabye toward Caldee, and toward Ynde, o day journey fro the See, where the Marchauntes of Venyse comen often for Marchandise. And so often wente Machomete to this Heremyte, that alle his men weren wrothe: for he wolde gladly here this Heremyte preche, and make his men wake alle nyghte: and therfore his men thoughten to putte the Heremyte to Dethe: and so it befelle upon a nyght, that Machomete was dronken of gode Wyn, and he felle on slepe; and his men toke Machometes Swerd out

of his Schethe, whils he slepte, and there with thei slowghe this Heremyte; and putten his Swerd alle blody in his Schethe azen. And at morwe, whan he fond the Heremyte ded, he was fulle sory and wrothe, and wolde have don his men to Dethe: but thei alle with on accord seyd, that he him self had slayn him, when he was dronken, and schewed him his Swerd alle blody: and he trowed, that thei hadden seyd sothe. And than he cursed the Wyn, and alle tho that drynken it. And therfore Sarrazines, that be devout, drynken nevere no Wyn: but sūme drynken it prevyly. For zif thei dronken it openly, thei scholde ben repreved. But thei drynken gode Beverage and swete and norysshynge, that is made of Galamelle: and that is that men maken Sugar of, that is of righte gode savour: and it is gode for the Breest. Also it befallethe sumtyme, that Cristene men becomen Sarazines, outher for povertee, or for symplenesse, or elles for here owne wykkednesse. And therfore the Archiflamyn or the Flamyn, as oure Erchebisshopp or Bisshopp, whan he resceyvethe hem, seythe thus, *La ellec, Sila. Machomete rores alla;* that is to seye, *There is no God but on, and Machomete his Messager.*

Cap. XIII.

Of the Londes of Albanye, and of Libye. Of the Wisshinges, for Wacchinge of the Sperkauk; and of Noes Schippe.

Now sithe I have told zou beforn of the Holy Lond, and of that Contree abouten, and of many Weyes for to go to that Lond, and to the Mount Synay, and of Babyloyne the more and the lesse, and to other places, that I have spoken beforn; now is tyme, zif it lyke zou, for to telle zou of the Marches and Iles, and dyverse Bestes, and of dyverse folk bezond theise Marches. For in tho Contrees bezonden, ben many dyverse Contrees, and many grete Kyngdomes; that ben departed be the 4 Flodes, that comen from Paradys terrestre. For Mesopotayme and the Kyngdō of Caldee and Arabye, ben betwene the 2 Ryveres of Tygre and of Eufrates. And the Kyngdom of Mede and of Persye, ben betwene the Ryveres of Nile and of Tigres. And the Kyngdom of Syrie, where of I have spoken beforn, and Palestyne and Phenycie, ben betwene Eufrates and the See Medyterrane: the whiche See durethe in Lengthe, fro Mayrok, upon the See of Spayne, unto the grete See; so that it lastethe bezonde Costantynople

3040 Myles of Lombardye. And toward the See Occyan in Ynde, is the Kyngdom of Shithie, that is alle closed with Hilles. And aftre undre Schithie, and fro the See of Caspie, unto the Flom Thainy, is Amazoyne, that is the Lond of Femynye, where that no man is, but only alle Wommen. And aftre is Albanye, a fulle gret Reme. And it is clept Albanye, because the Folk ben whitere there, than in other Marches there abouten. And in that Contree ben so gret Houndes and so stronge, that thei assaylen Lyouns, and

sleu hem. And thanne aftre is Hircanye, Bactrye, Hiberye, and many other Kyngdomes. And betwene the rede See and the See Occyan, toward the Southe, is the Kyngdom of Ethiope, and of Lybye the hyere. The which Lond of Lybye, (that is to seyne Libye the lowe) that begynnethe at the See of Spayne, fro thens where the Pyleres of Hercules ben, and durethe unto aneyntes Egipt and towards Ethiope. In that Contree of Libye, is the See more highe than the Lond; and it semethe that it wolde covere the Erthe, and natheles zit it passethe not his Markes. And men seen in that Contre a Mountayne, to the whiche no man comethe. In this Lond of Libye, whoso turnethe toward the Est, the Schadewe of him self is on the right syde: and here in oure Contree, the schadwe is on the left syde. In that See of Libye, is no Fissche: for thei mowe not lyve ne dure, for the gret hete of the Sonne; because that the Watre is evermore boyllynge, for the gret hete. And many othere Londes there ben, that it were to long to tellen or to nombren: but of sum parties, I schal speke more pleynly here aftre.

Whoso wil thanne gon toward Tarterie, toward Persie, toward Caldee, and toward Ynde, he most entre the See, at Gene or at Venyse or at sum other Havene, that I have told zou before. And than passe men the See, and arryven at Trapazond, that is a gode Cytee; and it was wont to ben the Havene of Pountz. There is the Havene of Persanes and of Medaynes and of the Marches there bezonde. In that Cytee lythe seynt Athanasie, that was Bisshopp of Alisandre. that made the Psalm *Quicunq; vult*. This Athanasius was a gret Doctour of Dyvynytee: and because that he preched and spak so depely of Dyvynytee and of the Godhede, he was accused to the Pope of Rome, that he was an Heretyk. Wherfore the Pope sente aftre hym, and putte him in Presoun: and whils he was in Presoun, he made that Psalm, and sente it to the Pope, and seyde; that zif he were an Heretyk, that was that Heresie; for that, he seyde, was his Beleeve.

And whan the Pope saughe it, and had examyned it, that it was parfite and gode, and verryly oure Feythe and oure Beleeve, he made him to ben delyvered out of Presoun, and cōmanded that Psalm to ben seyd every day at Pryme: and so he held Athanasie a gode man. But he wolde nevere go to his Bisshopriche azen, because that thei accused him of Heresye. Trapazond was wont to ben holden of the Emperour of Costantynople: but a gret man, that he sente for to kepe the Contree azenst the Turkes, usurped the Lond, and helde it to himself, and cleped him Emperour of Trapazond.

And from thens, men gon thorghe litille Ermonye. And in that Contree is an old Castelle, that stont upon a Roche, the whiche is cleped the Castelle of the Sparrehawk, that is bezonde the Cytee of Layays, beside the Town of Pharsipee, that belongethe to the Lordschipe of Cruk; that is a riche Lorde and a gode Cristene man; where men fynden a Sparehauk upon a Perche righte fair, and righte wel made; and a fayre Lady of Fayrye, that kepethe it. And who that wil wake that Sparhauk, 7 dayes and 7 nyghtes, and as sūme men seyn, 3 dayes and 3 nyghtes, with outen Companye and with outen Sleep, that faire Lady schal zeven him, whan he hathe don, the first Wyssche, that he wil wyssche, of erthely thinges: and that hathe been proved often tymes. And o tyme befelle, that a Kyng of Ermonye, that was a worthi Knyght and doughty man and a noble Prince, woke that Hauk sum tyme: and at the ende of 7 dayes and 7 nyghtes, the Lady cam to him, and bad him wisschen; for he had wel

disserved it. And he answerde, that he was gret Lord y now, and wel in pees, and hadde y nowghe of worldly Ricchesse; and therfore he wolde wisshe non other thing, but the body of that faire Lady, to have it at his wille. And sche answerde him, that he knew not what he asked; and seyde, that he was a Fool, to desire that he myghte not have: for sche seyde, that he scholde not aske, but erthely thing: for sche was non erthely thing, but a gostly thing. And the Kyng seyde, that he ne wolde asken non other thing. And the Lady answerde, Sythe that I may not withdrawe zou fro zoure lewed Corage, I schal zeve zou with outen wysschinge, and to alle hem that schulle com of zou. Sire Kyng, zee schulle have Werre withouten Pees, and alle weys to the 9 Degree, zee schulle ben in Subjeccioun of zoure Enemyes; and zee schulle ben nedy of alle Godes. And nevere sithen, nouther the Kyng of Ermonye, ne the Contree, weren never in Pees, ne thei hadden never sithen plentee of Godes; and thei han ben sithen alle weyes undre Tribute of the Sarrazines. Also the sone of a pore man woke that Hauke, and wisshed that he myghte cheve[g] wel, and to ben happy to Marchandise. And the Lady graunted him. And he becam the most riche and the most famouse Marchaunt, that myghte ben on See or on Erthe. And he becam so riche, that he knew not the 1000 part of that he hadde: and he was wysere, in wisschynge, than was the Kyng. Also a Knyght of the Temple wooke there; and wyssched a Purs evere more fulle of Gold; and the Lady graunted him. But sche seyde him, that he had asked the destruccioun of here Ordre; for the trust and the affiance of that Purs, and for the grete pryde, that thei scholde haven: and so it was. And therfore loke, he kepe him wel, that schalle wake: for zif he slepe, he is lost, that nevere man schalle seen him more. This is not the righte Weye for to go to the parties, that I have nempned before; but for to see the Merveyle, that I have spoken of.

And therfore who so will go right weye, men gon fro Trapazond toward Ermonye the grete, unto a Cytee that is clept Artyroun,[h] that was wont to ben a gode Cytee and a plentyous; but the Turkes han gretly wasted it. There aboute growethe no Wyn ne Fruyt, but litylle or elle non. In this Lond, is the Erthe more highe than in ony other; and that makethe gret cold. And there ben many gode Watres, and gode Welles, that comen undre erthe, fro the Flom of Paradys, that is clept Eufrates, that is a Jorneye besyde that

[g] Chevir, F.   [h] Atpirou, L. 1, 2.

Cytee.[i] And that Ryvere comethe towardes Ynde, undre Erthe, and resortethe in to the Lond of Altazar.[k] And so passe men be this Ermonie, and entren the See of Persie. Fro that Cytee of Artyroun go men to an Hille, that is clept Sabissocolle.[l] And there besyde is another Hille, that men clepen Ararathe: but the Jewes clepen it Taneez;[m] where Noes Schipp rested, and zit is upon that Montayne: and men may seen it a ferr, in cleer Wedre: and that Montayne is wel a 7 Myle highe. And sum men seyn, that thei han seen and touched the Schipp; and put here Fyngres in the parties, where the Feend went out, whan that Noe seyde, *Benedicite*. But thei that seyn suche Wordes, seyn here Wille: for a man may not gon up the Montayne, for gret plentee of Snow, that is alle weyes on that Montayne, nouther Somer ne Wynter: so that no man may gon up there; ne nevere man dide, sithe the tyme of Noe; saf a Monk, that, be the grace of God, broughte on of the Plankes doun; that zit is in the Mynstre, at the foot of the Montayne. And besyde is the Cytee of Dayne, that Noe founded. And faste by is the Cytee of Any, in the whiche were a 1000 Chirches. But upon that Montayne, to gon up, this Monk had gret desir; and so upon a day, he wente up: and whan he was upward the 3 part of the Montayne, he was so wery, that he myghte no ferthere, and so he rested him, and felle o slepe; and whan he awook, he fonde him self liggynge at the foot of the Montayne. And than he preyede devoutly to God, that he wolde

[i] Ab ista Civitate, L.
[k] Aliazar, L. 1, 2.
[l] Sabissabella, L. 1, 2.
[m] Tham, L. 1; Tam, L. 2.

vouche saf to suffre him gon up. And an Angelle cam to him, and seyde, that he scholde gon up; and so he dide. And sithe that tyme never non. Wherfore men scholde not beleeve suche Woordes.

Fro that Montayne go men to the Cytee of Thauriso, that was wont to ben clept Taxis, that is a fulle fair Cytee, and a gret, and on of the beste, that is in the World, for Marchandise: and it is in the Lond of the Emperour of Persie. And men seyn, that the Emperour takethe more gode, in that Cytee, for Custom of Marchandise, than dothe the ricchest Cristene Kyng of alle his Reme, that livethe. For the Tolle and the Custom of his Marchantes is with outen estymacioun to ben nombred. Beside that Cytee, is a Hille of Salt;

and of that Salt, every man takethe what he will, for to salte with, to his nede. There duellen many Cristene men, undir Tribute of Sarrazines. And fro that Cytee, men passen be many Townes and Castelles, in goynge toward Ynde, unto the Cytee

of Sadonye, that is a 10 iourneyes fro Thauriso;
and it is a fulle noble Cytee, and a gret. And
there duellthe the Emperour of Persie, in Somer:
for the Contree is cold y now. And ther ben gode
Ryveres, berynge Schippes. Aftre go men the
Weye toward Ynde, be many iorneyes, and be
many Contreyes, unto the Cytee, that is clept
Cassak, that is a fulle noble Cytee, and a plentyous
of Cornes and Wynes, and of alle other Godes.
This is the Cytee, where the 3 Kynges metten to
gedre, whan thei wenten to sechen oure Lord in
Bethlem, to worschipe him, and to presente him
with Gold, Ensence, and Myrre. And it is from
that Cytee to Bethleem 53 iourneyes. Fro that
Cytee, men gon to another Cytee, that is clept
Bethe, that is a iourneye fro the See, that men
clepen the gravely[n] See. That is the beste Cytee,
that the Emperour of Persie hathe, in alle his
Lond. And thei clepen it there Chardabago; and
others clepen it Vapa. And the Paynemes seyn,
that no Cristene man may not longe duelle, ne
enduren with the lif, in that Cytee: but dyen with
in schort tyme; and no man knowethe not the
cause. Aftre gon men, be many Cytees, and
Townes, and grete Contrees, that it were to longe
to telle, unto the Cytee of Cornaa, that was wont
to be so gret, that the Walles abouten holden 25
Myle aboute. The Walles schewen zit: but it is
not alle enhabited. From Cornaa, go men be
many Londes, and many Cytees and Townes, unto
the Lond of Job: and there endethe the Lond of
the Emperour of Persie.

[n] Arenosum, L.

Cap. XIV.

Of the Lond of Job; and of his Age. Of the Aray of men of Caldee. Of the Lond where Wommen duellen, with outen companye of men. Of the knouleche and vertues of the verray Dyamant.

AFTRE the departynge fro Cornaa, men entren in to the lond of Job, that is a fulle fair Contree, and a plentyous of alle Godes. And men clepen that Lond, the Lond of Sweze. In that Lond, is the Cytee of Theman.[a] Job was a Payneem, and he was Are of Gosre his Sone,[b] and held that Lond, as Prynce of that Contree; and he was so riche, that he knew not the hundred part of his Godes. And alle thoughe he were a Payneem, natheles he served wel God, aftre his Lawe: and oure Lord toke his Service to his plesance. And whan he felle in poverte, he was 78 Zeer of Age. And aftre, whan God had preved his pacyence, and that it was so gret, he broughte him azen to richesse, and to hiere Estate than he was before. And aftre that he was Kyng of Ydumye, aftre Kyng Esau. And whan he was Kyng, he was clept Jobab. And in that Kyngdom, he lyvede aftre 170 Zere:[c] and so he was of Age, whan he dyede, 248 Zeer. In that Lond of Job, there nys no defaute of no thing, that is nedefulle to mannes

---

[a] Hemon, L. 1, 2; Thomar, E.
[b] Cofraas son, E. 4; Cosraa ys sone, E. 2, 3 : Are de Gofra, L. 1, 2.
[c] 140 Years, Job, xlii. 16.

body. There ben Hilles, where men geten gret plentee of Manna, in gretter habundance, than in ony other Contree. This Manna is clept Bred of Aungeles; and it is a white thing, that is fulle swete and righte delicyous, and more swete than Hony or Sugre; and it comethe of the dew of Hevene, that fallethe upon the Herbes, in that Contree; and it congelethe and becomethe alle white and swete: and men putten it in Medicynes for riche men, to make the Wombe lax, and to purge evylle Blode: for it clensethe the Blode, and puttethe out Malencolye. This Lond of Job marchethe to the Kyngdom of Caldee. This Lond of Caldee is fulle gret: and the Langage of that Contree is more gret in sownynge, that it is in other parties bezonde the See. Men passen to go bezonde, be the Tour of Babiloyne the grete; of the whiche I have told zou before, where that alle the Langages weren first chaunged. And that is a 4 Jorneyes fro Caldee. In that Reme, ben faire men, and thei gon fulle nobely arrayed in Clothes

of Gold, or frayed and apparayled with grete Perles and precyous Stones, fulle nobely : and the Wŏmen ben righte foule and evylle arrayed; and thei gon alle bare fote, and clothed in evylle Garnementes, large and wyde, but thei ben schorte to the Knees; and longe Sleves doun to the feet, lyche a Monkes Frokke; and here Sleves ben hongyng aboute here Schuldres : and thei ben blake Women, foule and hidouse; and treuly as foule as thei ben, als evele thei ben. In that Kyngdom of Caldee, in a Cytee, that is clept Hur, duelled Thare, Abrahames Fadre: and there was Abraham born : and that was in that tyme, that Nunus was Kyng of Babiloyne, of Arabye and of Egypt. This Nunus made the Cytee of Nynyvee, the whiche that Noe had begonne before: and be cause that Nunus performed it, he cleped it Nynyvee, aftre his owne name. There lythe Thobye the Prophete, of whom Holy Writt spekethe offe. And fro that Cytee of Hur, Abrahā departed, be the cōmandement of God, fro thens, aftre the Dethe of his Fadre; and ladde with him Sarra his Wif and Lothe his brotheres sone, because that he hadde no Child. And thei wenten to duelle in the Lond of Chanaan, in a place, that is clept Sychem. And this Lothe was he, that was saved, whan Sodom and Gomorre and the othere Cytees weren brent and sonken doun to Helle; where that the dede See is now, as I have told zou before. In that lond of Caldee, thei han here propre Langages, and here propre Lettres.

Besyde the Lond of Caldee, is the Lond of Amazoyne. And in that Reme is alle Wŏmen, and no man; noght, as sūme men seyn, that men

mowe not lyve there, but for because that the
Wōmen will not suffre no men amonges hem, to
ben here Sovereynes. For sum tyme, ther was a
Kyng in that Contrey; and men maryed, as in
other contreyes: and so befelle, that the Kyng
had Werre, with hem of Sithie; the whiche Kyng
highte Colopeus, that was slayn in Bataylle, and
alle the gode Blood of his Reme. And whan the
Queen and alle the othere noble Ladyes sawen,
that thei weren alle Wydewes, and that alle the
rialle Blood was lost, thei armed hem, and as
Creatures out of Wytt, thei slowen alle the men
of the Contrey, that weren laft. For thei woldē,
that alle the Wōmen weren Wydewes, as the
Queen and thei weren. And fro that tyme hider-
wardes, thei nevere wolden suffren man to dwelle
amonges hem, lenger than 7 dayes and 7 nyghtes;
ne that no Child that were Male, scholde duelle
amonges hem, lenger than he were noryscht; and
thanne sente to his Fader. And whan thei wil
have ony companye of man, than thei drawen
hem towardes the Londes marchynge next to hē:
and than thei have Loves, that usen hem; and thei
duellen with hem an 8 dayes or 10; and thanne
gon hom azen. And zif thei have ony knave
Child, thei kepen it a certeyn tyme, and than
senden it to the Fadir, whan he can gon allone,
and eten be him self; or elle thei sleen it: and zif
it be a femele, thei don away that on Pappe, with
an hote Hiren: and zif it be a Womman of gret
Lynage, thei don awey the left Pappe, that thei
may the better beren a Scheeld: and zif it be a
Woman of symple Blood, thei don awey the rygt
Pappe, for to scheten with Bowe Turkeys: for thei

schote well with Bowes. In that Lond thei have a Queen, that governethe alle that Lond: and alle thei ben obeyssant to hire. And alweys thei maken here Queen by Eleccioun, that is most worthy in

Armes. For thei ben right gode Werryoures, and wyse, noble and worthi. And thei gon often tyme in sowd, to help of other Kynges, in here Werres, for Gold and Sylver, as othere Sowdyoures don: and thei meyntenen hem self right vygouresly. This Lord of Amazoyne is an Yle, alle envirouned with the See, saf in 2 places, where ben 2 entrees. And bezond that Watir, duellen the men, that ben here Paramoures and hire Loves, where thei gon to solacen hem, whan thei wole. Besyde Amazoyne, is the Lond of Tarmegyte, that is a gret Contree and a fulle delectable: and for the godnesse of the Contree, Kyng Alisandre leet first make there the Cytee of Alisandre; and zit he made 12 Cytees of the same name: but that Cytee is now clept Celsite. And fro that other Cost of Caldee, to ward the Southe, is Ethiope, a

gret Contree, that strecchethe to the ende of
Egypt. Ethiope is departed in 2 princypalle
parties; and that is, in the Est partie and in the
Meridionelle partie: the whiche partie meridionelle is clept Moretane. And the folk of that
Contree ben blake y now, and more blake than in
the tother partie; and thei ben clept Mowres. In
that partie is a Welle, that in the day it is so cold,
that no man may drynke there offe; and in the
nyght it so hoot, that no man may suffre his
hond there in. And bezonde that partie, toward
the Southe, to passe by the See Occean, is a gret
Lond and a gret Contrey: but men may not duelle
there, for the fervent brennynge of the Sonne; so
is it passynge hoot in that Contrey. In Ethiope
alle the Ryveres and alle the Watres ben trouble,
and thei ben somdelle salte, for the gret hete that
is there. And the folk of that Contree ben lyghtly

dronken, and han but litille appetyt to mete: And thei han comounly the Flux of the Wombe: and thei lyven not longe. In Ethiope ben many dyverse folk: and Ethiope is clept Cusis. In that Contree ben folk, that han but o foot: and thei gon so fast, that it is marvaylle: and the foot is so large, that it schadewethe alle the Body azen the Sonne, whanne thei wole lye and reste hem.[d] In Ethiope, whan the Children ben zonge and lytille, thei ben alle zelowe: and whan that thei wexen of Age, that zalownesse turnethe to ben alle blak. In Ethiope is the Cytee of Saba; and the Lond, of the whiche on of the 3 Kynges, that presented oure Lord in Bethleem, was Kyng offe.

Fro Ethiope men gon to Ynde, be manye dyverse Contreyes. And men clepen the highe Ynde, Emlak. And Ynde is devyded in 3 princypalle parties; that is, the more, that is a fulle hoot Contree; and Ynde the lesse, that is a fulle atempree Contrey, that strecchethe to the Lond of Mede: and the 3 part toward the Septentrion, is fulle cold; so that for pure cold and contynuelle Frost, the Watre becomethe Cristalle. And upon tho Roches of Cristalle, growen the gode Dyamandes,[e] that ben of trouble Colour. Zalow Cristalle drawethe Colour lyke Oylle. And thei ben so harde, that no man may pollysche hem: and men clepen hem Dyamandes in that Contree, and Hamese in another Contree. Othere Dya-

---

[d] See Pliny's Natural History, lib. vii. c. 2, q. Item hominum genus, qui Monoscelli vocarentur, singulis cruribus, miræ pernicitatis ad saltum; eosdemq; Sciopodas vocari, quod in majori æstu, humi jacentes resupini, umbrâ se pedum protegant.

[e] See Pliny, in his 37th Book and 4th Chap.

mandes men fynden in Arabye, that ben not so
gode; and thei ben more broun and more tendre.
And other Dyamandes also men fynden in the Ile
of Cipre, that ben zit more tendre; and hem men
may wel pollische. And in the Lond of Macedoyne
men fynden Dyamaundes also. But the beste and
the most precyouse ben in Ynde. And men fynden
many tymes harde Dyamandes in a Masse, that
comethe out of Gold, whan men puren it and
fynen it out of the Myne; whan men breken that
Masse in smale peces. And sum tyme it happenethe, that men fynden sūme as grete as a pese,
and sūme lasse; and thei ben als harde as tho
of Ynde. And alle be it that men fynden gode
Dyamandes in Ynde, zit natheles men fynden hem
more comounly upon the Roches in the See, and
upon Hilles where the Myne of Gold is. And
thei growen many to gedre, on lytille, another
gret. And ther ben sūme of the gretness of a
Bene, and sūme als grete as an Haselle Note.
And thei ben square and poynted of here owne
kynde, bothe aboven and benethen, with outen
worchinge of mannes hond. And thei growen to
gedre, male and femele. And thei ben norysscht
with the Dew of Hevene. And thei engendren
comounly, and bryngen forthe smale Children,
that multiplyen and growen alle the Zeer. I have
often tymes assayed, that zif a man kepe hem
with a litylle of the Roche, and wete hem with
May Dew ofte sithes, thei schulle growe everyche
Zeer; and the smale wole wexen grete. For righte
as the fyn Perl congelethe and wexethe gret of the
Dew of Hevene, righte so dothe the verray Dyamand: and righte as the Perl of his owne kynde

takethe Roundnesse, righte so the Dyamand, be vertu of God, takethe squarenesse. And men schalle bere the Dyamaund on his left syde: for it is of grettere vertue thanne, than on the righte syde. For the strengthe of here growynge is toward the Northe, that is the left syde of the World; and the left parte of man is, whan he turnethe his Face toward the Est. And zif zou lyke to knowe the Vertues of the Dyamand, (as men may fynde in the Lipidarye, that many men knowen noght) I schalle telle zou: as thei bezonde the See seyn and affermen, of whom alle Science and alle Philosophie comethe from. He that berethe the Diamand upon him, it zevethe him hardynesse and manhode, and it kepethe the Lemes of his Body hole. It zevethe him victorye of his Enemyes, in Plee and in Werre; zif his cause be rightefulle: and it kepethe him that berethe it, in gode Wytt: and it kepethe him fro Strif and Riot, fro Sorwes and frō Enchauntementes and from Fantasyes and illusiouns of wykked Spirites. And zif ony cursed Wycche or Enchauntour wolde bewycche him, that berethe the Dyamand; alle that Sorwe and myschance schalle turne to him self, thorghe Vertu of that Ston. And also no wylde Best dar assaylle the man, that berethe it on him. Also the Dyamand scholde ben zoven frely, with outen coveytynge and with outen byggynge: and than it is of grettere vertu. And it makethe a man more strong and more sad azenst his Enemyes. And it helethe him that is lunatyk, and hem that the Fend pursuethe or travaylethe. And zif Venym or Poysoun be broughte in presence of the Dyamand, anon it begynnethe to wexe moyst and for to swete. There ben also Dyamandes in Ynde, that ben clept Violastres; (for here colour is liche Vyolet, or more browne than the Violettes) that ben fulle harde and fulle precyous: but zit sum men love not hem so wel as the othere: but in sothe to me, I wolde loven hem als moche as the othere; for I have seen hem assayed. Also there is an other maner of Dyamandes, that ben als white as Cristalle; but thei ben a litylle more trouble: and thei ben gode and of gret vertue, and alle thei ben square and poynted of here owne kynde. And sūme ben 6 squared, sūme 4 squared, and sūme 3, as nature schapethe hem. And therfore whan grete Lordes and Knyghtes gon to seche Worschipe in Armes, thei beren gladly the Dyamaund upon hem.

I schal speke a litille more of the Dyamandes, alle thoughe I tarye my matere for a tyme, to the ende that thei that knowen hem not, be not disceyved be Gabberes,[f] that gon be the Contree, that sellen hem. For whoso wil bye the Dyamand, it is nedefulle to him, that he knowe hem; be cause that men counterfeten hem often of Cristalle, that is zalow; and of Saphires of cytryne colour, that is zalow also; and of the Saphire Loupe, and of many other Stones. But I telle zou, theise contrefetes ben not so harde; and also the poyntes wil breken lightly, and men may easily pollische hem. But sūme Werkmen, for malice, will not pollische hem, to that entent, to maken men beleve, that thei may not ben pollischt. But men may assay hē in this manere; First schere

[f] Barratours, F.

with hem or write with hem in saphires, in Cristalle or in other precious Stones. Aftre that men taken the Ademand, that is the Schipmannes Ston, that drawethe the Nedle to him, and men leyn the Dyamand upon the Ademand, and leyn the Nedle before the Ademand; and zif the Dyamand be gode and vertuous, the Ademand drawethe not the Nedle to him, whils the Dyamand is there present. And this is the preef, that thei bezonde the See maken. Natheles it befallethe often tyme, that the gode Dyamande lesethe his vertue, be syñe and for Incontynence of him, that berethe it: and thanne it is nedfulle to make it to recoveren his vertu azen, or elle it is of litille value.

Cap. XV.

Of the Customs of Yles abouten Ynde. Of the difference betwix Ydoles and Simulacres. Of 3 maner growing of Peper upon a Tree. Of the Welle, that chaungethe his odour, every hour of the day; and that is Mervaylle.

IN Ynde ben fulle manye dyverse Contrees : and it is cleped Ynde, for a Flom, that rennethe thorghe out the Contree, that is clept Ynde. In that Flōme men fynden Eles of 30 Fote long and more.[a] And the folk that duellen nyghe that Watre, ben of evylle colour, grene and zalow. In Ynde and abouten Ynde, ben mo than 5000 Iles, gode and grete, that men duellen in, with outen tho that ben inhabitable, and with outen othere

[a] Pliny, lib. ix. c. 3.

smale Iles. In every Ile, is gret plentee of Cytees and of Townes and of folk, with outen nombre.[a] For men of Ynde han this condicioun of kynde, that thei nevere gon out of here owne Contree; and therfore is ther gret multitude of peple: but thei ben not sterynge ne mevable, be cause that thei ben in the firste Clymat, that is of Saturne. And Saturne is sloughe and litille mevynge: for he taryethe to make his turn be the 12 Signes, 30 Zeer; and the Mone passethe thorghe the 12 Signes in o Monethe. And for be cause that Saturne is of so late sterynge, therfore the folk of that Contree, that ben undre his Clymat, han of kynde no wille for to meve ne stere to seche strange places. And in oure Contree is alle the contrarie. For wee ben in the seventhe Clymat, that is of the Mone. And the Mone is of lyghtly mevynge; and the Mone is Planete of Weye: and for that skylle, it zevethe us wille of kynde, for to meve lyghtly, and for to go dyverse weyes, and to sechen strange thinges and other dyversitees of the World. For the Mone envyrounethe the Erthe more hastyly than ony othere Planete.

Also men gon thorghe Ynde be many dyverse Contrees, to the grete See Occean. And aftre men fynden there an Ile, that is clept Crues:[b] and thidre comen Marchantes of Venyse and Gene and of other Marches, for to byen Marchandyses. But there is so grete hete in tho Marches, and namely in that Ile, that for the grete distresse of the hete, mennes Ballokkes hangen doun to here

[a] Pliny, lib. vi. c. 17. b.
[b] Hermes, E. 1, 2, 3, 4; Crynes, F. 1, 2; Grynes, 1, 2; Ormens, L. 3; Ormuz, L. 4.

knees, for the gret dissolucioun of the Body. And men of that Contree, that knowen the manere, lat bynde hem up, or elle myghte thei not lyve; and anoynt hem with Oynementes made therfore, to holde hem up. In that Contree and in Ethiope and in many other Contrees, the folk lyggen alle naked in Ryveres and Watres, men and wommen to gedre, fro undurne of the day, tille it be passed the noon.ᶜ And thei lyen alle in the Watre, saf

the visage, for the gret hete that there is. And the Wōmen haven no schame of the men; but lyen alle to gidre, syde to syde, tille the hete be past. There may men see many foule figure assembled, and namely nyghe the gode Townes. In that Ile ben Schippes with outen Nayles of Iren or Bonds, for the Roches of the Ademandes: for thei ben alle fulle there aboute, in that See, that it is merveyle to speken of. And zif a Schipp passed be tho Marches, that hadde outher Iren Bondes or Iren Nayles, anon he scholde ben

ᶜ A diei hora tertia usq; ad nonam. L.

perisscht. For the Ademand, of his kynde, drawethe the Iren to him: and so wolde it drawe to him the Schipp, because of the Iren: that he scholde never departen fro it, ne never go thens.

Fro that Ile, men gon be See to another Ile, that is clept Chana, where is gret plentee of Corn and Wyn: and it was wont to ben a gret Ile, and a gret Havene and a good; but the See hathe gretly wasted it and overcomen it. The Kyng of that Contree was wont to ben so strong and so myghty, that he helde Werre azenst King Alisandre. The folk of that Contree han a dyvers Lawe: for sūme of hem, worschipe the Sonne, sūme the Mone, sūme the Fuyr, sūme Trees, sūme Serpentes, or the first thing that thei meeten at morwen: and sūme worschipen Symulacres, and sūme Ydoles. But betwene Symulacres and Ydoles, is a gret difference. For Symulacres ben Ymages made aftre lyknesse of Men or of Wōmen, or of the Sonne or of the Mone, or of ony Best, or of ony kyndely thing: and Ydoles, is an Ymage made of lewed wille of man, that man may not fynden among kyndely thinges; as an Ymage, that hathe 4 Hedes, on of a Man, another of an Hors, or of an Ox, or of sum other Best, that no man hathe seyn aftre kyndely disposicioun. And thei that worschipen Symulacres, thei worschipen hem for sum worthi man, that was sum tyme, as Hercules and many othere, that diden many marvayles in here tyme. For thei seyn wel, that thei be not Goddes: for thei knowen wel, that there is a God of kynde, that made alle thinges; the whiche is in Hevene. But thei knowen wel, that this may not do the Marvayles that he made, but zif it had ben

be the specyalle zifte of God: and therfore thei
seyn, that he was wel with God. And for be
cause that he was so wel with God, therfore thei
worschipe him. And so seyn thei of the Sonne;
be cause that he chaungethe the tyme and zevethe
hete and norisschethe alle thinges upon Erthe; and
for it is of so gret profite, thei knowe wel, that that
myghte not be, but that God lovethe it more than
ony other thing. And for that skylle, God hath
zoven it more gret vertue in the World: therfore it
is gode resoun, as thei seyn, to don it Worschipe
and Reverence. And so seyn thei, that maken
here resounes, of othere Planetes; and of the Fuyr
also, because it is so profitable. And of Ydoles,
thei seyn also, that the Ox is the moste holy Best,
that is in Erthe, and most pacyent and more profitable than ony other. For he dothe good y now,
and he dothe non evylle. And thei knowen wel,
that it may not be with outen specyalle grace of
God: and therfore maken thei here God, of an
Ox the on part, and the other halfondelle of a
Man: because that man is the most noble creature

in Erthe; and also for he hathe Lordschipe aboven
alle Bestes: therfore make thei the halfendel of
Ydole of a man upwardes, and the tother half of
an Ox dounwardes: And of Serpentes and of other
Bestes, and dyverse thinges, that thei worschipen,
that thei meten first at Morwe. And thei worschipen also specyally alle tho that thei han gode
meetynge of; and whan thei speden wel in here
iorneye, aftre here meetynge; and namely suche
as thei han preved and assayed be experience of
longe tyme. For thei seyn, that thilke gode
meetynge ne may not come, but of the grace of
God. And therfore thei maken Ymages lyche
to tho thinges, that thei han beleeve inne, for
to beholden hem and worschipen hem first at
morwe, or thei meeten ony contrarious thinges.
And there ben also sum Cristene men, that seyn,
that sūme Bestes han gode meetynge, that is to
seye, for to meete with hem first at morwe; and
sūme Bestes wykked meetynge: and that thei han
preved ofte tyme, that the Hare hathe fulle evylle
meetynge, and Swyn, and many othere Bestes.
And the Sparhauk and other Foules of Raveyne,
whan thei fleen aftre here praye, and take it
before men of Armes, it is a gode Signe: and zif
he fayle of takynge his praye, it is an evylle
sygne. And also to suche folk, it is an evylle
meetynge of Ravenes. In theise thinges and in
suche othere, ther ben many folk, that beleeven;
because it happenethe so often tyme to falle, aftre
here fantasyes. And also there ben men y nowe,
that han no beleve in hem. And sithe that Cristene men han suche beleeve, that ben enformed
and taughte alle day, be holy doctryne, where inne
thei schold beleeve, it is no marvaylle thanne, that

the Paynemes, that han no gode Doctryne, but only of here nature, beleeven more largely, for here symplenesse. And treuly I have seen of Paynemes and Sarazines, that men clepen Augurynes, that whan wee ryden in Armes in dyverse Contrees, upon oure Enemyes, be the flyenge of Foules, thei wolde telle us the prenosticaciouns of thinges that felle aftre: and so thei diden fulle often tymes, and profreden here hedes to wedde, but zif it wolde falle as thei seyden. But natheles ther fore scholde noght a man putten his beleeve in suche thinges: but always han fulle trust and beleeve in God oure Sōvereyn Lord. This Ile of Chana, the Sarazines han wōnen and holden. In that Ile ben many Lyouns, and many othere wylde Bestes. And there ben Rattes in that Ile, als grete as Houndes here: and men taken hem with grete Mastyfes: for Cattes may not take hem. In this Ile and many othere, men berye not no dede men: for the hete is there so gret, that in a litylle tyme the Flesche wil consume fro the Bones.

Fro thens men gon be See toward Ynde the more, to a Cytee that men clepen Sarche,[d] that is a fair Cytee and a gode: and there duellen many Cristene men of gode Feythe: and there ben manye religious men, and namely of Mendynantes. Aftre gon men be See, to the Lond of Lomb. In that Lond growethe the Peper, in the Forest that men clepen Combar; and it growethe no where elle in alle the World, but in that Forest: and that dureth wel an 18 iourneyes in lengthe. In the Forest ben 2 gode Cytees; that on highte

---

[d] Sarthye, E. 1; Sarchys, E. 4; Sachee, F. 1; Zarchee, F. 2, L. 2; Barchen, L. 1; Zarke, L. 3, 4.

Fladrine, and that other Zinglantz. And in every of hem, duellen Cristene men, and Jewes, gret plentee. For it is a gode Contree and a plentefous: but there is over meche passynge hete. And zee schulle undirstonde, that the Peper growethe, in maner as dothe a wylde Vyne, that is planted faste by the trees of that Wode, for to susteynen it by, as dothe the Vyne. And the Fruyt therof hangethe in manere as Reysynges. And the Tree is so thikke charged, that it semethe that it wolde breke: and whan it is ripe, it is alle grene as it were Ivy Beryes; and than men kytten hem, as men don the Vynes, and than thei putten it upon an Owven, and there it waxethe blak and crisp. And there is 3 maner of Peper, all upon o Tree; long Peper, blak Peper, and white Peper. The long Peper men clepen Sorbotyn; and the blak Peper is clept Fulfulle, and the white Peper is clept Bano. The long Peper comethe first, whan the Lef begynnethe to come; and it is lyche the Chattes of Haselle, that comethe before the Lef, and it hangethe lowe. And aftre comethe the blake with the Lef, in manere of Clustres of Reysinges, alle grene: and whan men han gadred it, than comethe the white, that is somdelle lasse than the blake; and of that men bryngen but litille in to this Contree; for thei bezonden with holden it for hem self, be cause it is bettere and more attempree in kynde, than the blake: and therfore is ther not so gret plentee as of the blake. In that Contree ben manye manere of Serpentes and of other Vermyn, for the gret hete of the Contree and of the Peper. And sūme men seyn, that whan thei will gadre the Peper, thei maken Fuyr, and brennen aboute, to make the Serpentes and the Cokedrilles to flee. But save here grace of alle that seyn so. For zif thei brenten abouten the Trees, that beren, the Peper scholden ben brent, and it wolde dryen up alle the vertue, as of ony other thing: and than thei diden hemself moche harm; and thei scholde nevere quenchen the Fuyr. But thus thei don; thei anoynten here Hondes and here Feet with a juyce made of Snayles and of othere thinges, made therfore; of the whiche the Serpentes and the venymous Bestes haten and dreden the Savour: and that makethe hem flee before hem, because of the smelle; and than thei gadren it seurly ynow.

Also toward the heed of that Forest, is the Cytee of Polombe. And above the Cytee is a grete Mountayne, that also is clept Polombe: and of that Mount, the Cytee hathe his name. And at the Foot of that Mount, is a fayr Welle and a gret, that hathe odour and savour of alle Spices; and at every hour of the day, he chaungethe his odour and his savour dyversely. And whoso drynkethe 3 tymes fasting of that Watre of that Welle, he is hool of alle maner sykenesse, that he hathe. And thei that duellen there and drynken often of that Welle, thei nevere han Sekenesse, and thei semen alle weys zonge. I have dronken there of 3 or 4 sithes; and zit, methinkethe, I fare the better. Sum men clepen it the Welle of Zouthe: for thei that often drynken there of, semen alle weys Zongly, and lyven with outen Sykenesse. And men seyn, that that Welle comethe out of Paradys: and therfore it is so vertuous. Be alle that Contree growethe gode

Gyngevere : and therfore thidre gon the Marchauntes for Spicerye. In that Lond Men worschipen the Ox, for his symplenesse and for his mekenesse, and for the profite that comethe of him. And thei seyn, that he is the holyest Best in Erthe. For hem semethe, that whoso evere be meke and pacyent, he is holy and profitable : for thanne thei seyn, he hathe alle vertues in him. Thei maken the Ox to laboure 6 zeer or 7, and than thei ete him. And the Kyng of the Contree hathe alle wey an Ox with him : and he that kepethe him, hathe every day grete fees, and kepethe every day his Dong and his Uryne in 2 Vesselles of Gold, and bryngen it before here Prelate, that thei clepen Archiprotopapaton ; and he berethe it before the Kyng, and makethe there over a gret blessynge ; and than the Kyng wetethe his Hondes there, in that thei clepen Gaul, and anyntethe his front and his Brest : and aftre he frotethe him with the Dong and with the Uryne with gret reverence, for to ben fulfilt of vertues of the Ox, and made holy be the vertue of that holy thing, that nought is worthe. And whan the Kyng hathe don, thanne don the Lordes ; and aftre hem here Mynystres and other men, zif thei may have ony remenant. In that Contree thei maken Ydoles, half Man, half Ox ; and in tho Ydoles, eville Spirites speken and zeven answere to men, of what is asked hem. Before theise Ydoles, men sleen here Children many tymes, and spryngen the Blood upon the Ydoles ; and so thei maken here Sacrifise. And whan ony man dyethe in the Contree, thei brennen his Body in name of Penance, to that entent, that he suffre no peyne in Erthe, to ben eten of Wormes. And zif his Wif have no Child, thei brenne hire with him; and seyn, that it is resoun, that sche make him companye in that other World, as sche did in this. But and sche have Children with him, thei leten hire lyve with hem, to brynge hem up, zif sche wole. And zif that sche love more to lyve with here Children, than for to dye with hire Husbonde, men holden hire for fals and cursed: ne schee schalle never ben loved ne trusted of the peple. And zif the Wōman dye before the Husbonde, men brennen him with hire, zif that he wole; and zif he wil not, no man constreynethe him thereto; but he may wedde another tyme with outen blame and repreef. In that Contree growen manye stronge Vynes: and the Wōmen drynken Wyn, and men not: and the Wōmen schaven hire Berdes, and the men not.

Cap. XVI.

Of the Domes made be seynt Thomas. Of Devocyoun and Sacrifice made to Ydoles there, in the Cytee of Calamye; and of the processioun in goynge aboute the Cytee.

FROM that Contree men passen be many Marches, toward a Contree, a 10 iourneyes thens, that is clept Mabaron: and it is a gret Kyngdom, and it hathe many faire Cytees and Townes. In that Kyngdom lithe the body of seynt Thomas the Apostle, in Flesche and Bon, in a faire Tombe, in the Cytee of Calamye : for there he was martyred and buryed. But men of Assirie beeren his Bodye in to Mesopatayme, in to the Cytee of Edisse: and aftre, he was broughte thidre azen. And the Arm and the Hond, (that he putte in oure Lordes syde, whan he appered to him, aftre his Resurrexioun, and seyde to him, *Noli esse in credulus, set fidelis*) is zit lyggynge in a Vesselle with outen the Tombe. And be that Hond thei

maken alle here Juggementes, in the Contree, whoso hathe righte or wrong. For whan ther is ony dissentioun betwene 2 partyes, and every of hem meyntenethe his Cause, and seyth, that his Cause is rightfulle, and that other seythe the contrarye, thanne bothe partyes writen here Causes in 2 Billes, and putten hem in the Hond of seynt Thomas; and anon he castethe awey the Bille of the wrong Cause, and holdethe stille the Bille with the righte Cause. And therfore men comen from fer Contrees to have Juggement of doutable

Causes: and other Juggement usen thei non there. Also the Chirche, where seynt Thomas lythe, is bothe gret and fair, and alle fulle of grete Simulacres: and tho ben grete Ymages, that thei clepen here Goddes; of the whiche, the leste is als gret as 2 men. And amonges theise othere, there is a gret Ymage, more than ony of the othere, that is alle covered with fyn Gold and precyous Stones and riche Perles: and that Ydole is the God of false Cristene, that han reneyed hire Feythe. And it syttethe in a Chayere of Gold, fulle nobely arrayed; and he hathe aboute his Necke large Gyrdles, wroughte of Gold and precyous Stones and Perles. And this Chirche is fulle richely wroughte, and alle over gylt with inne. And to that Ydole gon men on Pylgrimage, als comounly and with als gret Devocioun, as Cristene men gon to seynt James, or other holy Pilgrimages. And many folk that comen fro fer Londes, to seche that Ydole, for the gret devocyoun that thei han, thei loken nevere upward, but evere more down to the Erthe, for drede to see ony thing aboute hem, that scholde lette hem of here Devocyoun. And sũme ther ben, that gon on Pilgrimage to this Ydole, that beren Knyfes in hire Hondes, that ben made fulle kene and scharpe; and alle weyes, as thei gon, thei smyten hem self in here Armes and in here Legges and in here Thyes, with many hydouse Woundes; and so thei scheden here Blood, for love of that Ydole. And thei seyn that he is blessed and holy, that dyethe so for love of his God. And othere there ben, that leden hire Children, for to sle, to make Sacrifise to that

Ydole: and aftre thei han slayn hem, thei spryngen the Blood upon the Ydole. And sūme ther ben, that comē fro ferr, and in goynge toward this Ydole, at every thrydde pas, that thei gon fro here Hows, thei knelen; and so contynuen tille thei come thidre: and whan thei comen there, thei taken Ensense and other aromatyk thinges of noble Smelle, and sensen the Ydole, as we wolde don here Goddes precyouse Body. And so comen folk to worschipe this Ydole, sum fro an hundred Myle, and sūme fro many mo. And before the Mynstre of this Ydole, is a Vyvere,[a] in maner of

a gret Lake, fulle of Watre: and there in Pilgrymes casten Gold and Sylver, Perles and precyous Stones, with outen nombre, in stede of Offrynges. And whan the Mynystres of that Chirche neden to maken ony reparacyoun of the Chirche or of ony of the Ydoles, thei taken Gold and Silver, Perles and precyous Stones out of the Vyvere, to quyten the Costages of suche thing as thei maken or re-

---

[a] Viver, F.; that is, a Fish Pool.

paren; so that no thing is fawty, but anon it schalle ben amended. And zee schulle undirstonde, that whan grete Festes and Solempnytees of that Ydole, as the Dedicacioun of the Chirche, and the thronynge of the Ydole bethe, alle the Contree aboute meten there to gidere; and thei setten this Ydole upon a Chare with gret reverence, wel arrayed with Clothes of Gold, of riche Clothes of Tartarye, of Camacaa, and other precyous Clothes; and thei leden him aboute the Cytee with gret solempnytee. And before the Chare, gon first in processioun alle the Maydenes of the Contree, 2 and 2 to gidere, fulle ordynatly. And aftre tho Maydenes, gon the Pilgrymes. And sūme of hem falle doun undre the Wheles of the Chare, and lat the

Chare gon over hem; so that thei ben dede anon. And sūme han here Armes or here Lymes alle to broken, and sōme the sydes: and alle this don thei for love of hire God, in gret Devocioun. And he thinkethe, that the more peyne and the more tribulacioun, that thei suffren for love of here

God, the more ioye thei schulle have in another World. And schortly to seye zou; thei suffren so grete peynes and so harde martyrdomes, for love of here Ydole, that a Cristene man, I trowe, durst not taken upon him the tenthe part of the peyne, for love of oure Lord Jhesu Crist. And aftre, I seye zou, before the Chare, gon alle the Mynstrelles of the Contrey, with outen nombre, with dyverse Instrumentes; and thei maken alle the melodye, that thei cone. And whan thei han gon alle aboute the Cytee, thanne thei returnen azen to the Mynstre, and putten the Ydole azen in to his place. And thanne, for the love and in worschipe of that Ydole, and for the reverence of the Feste, thei slen himself, a 200 or 300 persones, with scharpe Knyfes, of the whiche thei bryngen the bodyes before the Ydole; and than thei seyn, that tho ben Seyntes, because that thei slowen hemself of here owne gode wille, for love of here Ydole. And as men here, that hadde an holy Seynt of his kyn, wolde thinke, that it were to hem an highe worschipe, right so hem thinkethe there. And as men here devoutly wolde writen holy Seyntes Lyfes and here Myracles, and sewen for here Canonizaciouns, righte so don thei there, for hem that sleen hem self wilfully, for love of here Ydole; and seyn, that thei ben gloriouse Martyres and Seyntes, and putten hem in here Wrytynges and in here Letanyes, and avaunten hem gretly on to another of here holy Kynnesmen, that so become Seyntes; and seyn, I have mo holy Seyntes in my Kynrede, than thou in thin. And the Custome also there is this, that whan thei that han such Devocioun and entent, for to sle him self, for love of his God, thei senden for alle here Frendes, and han gret plentee of mynstrelle, and thei gon before the Ydole ledynge him, that wil sle himself for such devocioun, betwene hem with gret reverence. And he alle naked hath a ful scharp Knyf in his hond, and he cuttethe a gret pece of his Flesche and castethe it in the face of his Ydole, seyenge his Orysounes, recōmendynge him to his God: and than he smytethe himself, and makethe grete Woundes and depe here and there, tille he falle doun ded. And than his Frendes presenten his Body to the Ydole; and than thei seyn, syngynge, Holy God, behold what thi trewe Servant hath don for the; he hathe forsaken his Wif and his Children and his Ricchesse and alle the Godes of the Worlde and his owne Lyf, for the love of the, and to make the Sacrifise of his Flesche and of his Blode. Wherfore, Holy God, putte him among thi beste belovede Seyntes in thi Blisse of Paradys: for he hathe well disserved it. And than thei maken a gret Fuyr, and brennen the Body: and thanne everyche of his Frendes taken a quantyte of the Assches, and kepen hem in stede of Relykes, and seyn, that it is a holy thing. And thei have no drede of no perile, whils thei han tho holy Assches upon hem. And thei putten his name in here Letanyes, as a Seynt.

Cap. XVII.

Of the evylle Customs used in the Yle of Lamary: and how the Erthe and the See ben of round Forme and schapp, be pref of the Sterre, that is clept Antartyk, that is fix in the Southe.

FRO that Contree go men be the See Occean, and be many dyverse Yles, and be many Contrees, that were to longe for to telle of. And a 52 iorneyes fro this Lond, that I have spoken of, there is another Lond, that is fulle gret, that men clepen Lamary. In that Lond is fulle gret Hete: and the Custom there is such, that men and wōmen gon alle naked. And thei scornen, whan thei

seen ony strange Folk goynge clothed. And thei seyn, that God made Adam and Eve alle naked; and that no man scholde schame, that is of kyndely nature. And thei seyn, that thei that ben clothed ben folk of another World, or thei ben folk, that trowen not in God. And thei seyn, that thei beleeven in God, that formede the World, and that made Adam and Eve, and alle other thinges. And thei wedden there no Wyfes: for all the Wōmen there ben cōmoun, and thei forsake no man. And thei seyn, thei synnen, zif thei refusen ony man: and so God cōmaunded to Adam and Eve, and to alle that comen of him, whan he seyde, *Crescite & multiplicamini, & replete Terram.* And therfore may no man in that Contree seyn, This is my Wyf: ne no Wōman may seye, This is myn Husbonde. And whan thei han Children, thei may zeven hem to what man thei wole, that hathe companyed with hem. And also alle the Lond is comoun: for alle that a man holdethe o zeer, another man hathe it another zeer. And every man takethe what part that him lykethe. And also alle the Godes of the Lond ben comoun, Cornes and alle other thinges: for no thing there is clept in clos, ne no thing there is undur Lok; and every man there takethe what he wole, with outen ony contradiccioun : and als riche is o man there, as is another. But in that Contree, there is a cursed Custom: for thei eten more gladly mannes Flesche, than ony other Flesche: and zit is that Contree habundant of Flesche, of Fissche, of Cornes, of Gold and Sylver, and of alle other Godes. Thidre gon Marchauntes, and bryngen with hem Children, to selle to hem of the Contree, and thei byzen hem: and zif thei ben fatte, thei eten hem anon; and zif thei ben lene, thei feden hem, tille thei ben fatte, and thanne thei eten hem: and thei seyn, that it is the best Flesche and the swettest of alle the World. In that Lond, ne in many othere bezonde that, no man may see the Sterre transmontane, that is clept the Sterre of the See, that is unmevable, and that is toward the Northe, that we clepen the Lode Sterre. But men seen another Sterre, the contrarie to him, that is toward the Southe, that is clept Antartyk. And right as the Schip men taken here Avys here, and governe hem be the Lode Sterre, right so don Schip men bezonde the parties, be the Sterre of the Southe, the whiche Sterre apperethe not to us. And this Sterre, that is toward the Northe, that wee clepen the Lode Sterre, ne apperethe not to hem. For whiche cause, men may wel perceyve, that the Lond and the See ben of rownde schapp and forme. For the partie of the Firmament schewethe in o Contree, that schewethe not in another Contree. And men may well preven be experience and sotyle compassement of Wytt, that zif a man fond passages be Schippes, that wolde go to serchen the World, men myghte go be Schippe alle aboute the World, and aboven and benethen. The whiche thing I prove thus, aftre that I have seyn. For I have ben toward the parties of Braban, and beholden the Astrolabre,[a] that the Sterre that is clept the Transmontayne, is 53 Degrees highe. And more forthere in Almayne and Bewme,[b] it hathe 58 Degrees. And more forthe toward the parties septemtrioneles, it is 62 Degrees of heghte, and certeyn Mynutes. For I my self have mesured it by the Astrolabre. Now schulle ze knowe, that

---

[a] In our Author's time, Astronomers had attain'd but very little accuracy in taking Observations.   [b] Bohemia.

azen the Transmontayne, is the tother Sterre, that is clept Antartyke; as I have seyd before. And tho 2 Sterres ne meeven nevere. And be hem turnethe alle the Firmament, righte as dothe a Wheel, that turnethe be his Axille Tree: so that tho Sterres beren the Firmament in 2 egalle parties; so that it hathe als mochel aboven, as it hathe benethen. Aftre this, I have gon toward the parties meridionales, that is toward the Southe: and I have founden, that in Lybye, men seen first the Sterre Antartyk. And so fer I have gon more forthe in tho Contrees, that I have founde that Sterre more highe; so that toward the highe Lybye, it is 18 Degrees of heghte, and certeyn Minutes (of the whiche, 60 Minutes maken a Degree). Aftre goynge be See and be Londe, toward this Contree, of that I have spoke, and to other Yles and Londes bezonde that Contree, I have founden the Sterre Antartyk of 33 Degrees of heghte, and mo mynutes. And zif I hadde had Companye and Schippynge, for to go more bezonde, I trowe wel in certeyn, that wee scholde have seen alle the roundnesse of the Firmament alle aboute. For as I have seyd zou be forn, the half of the Firmament is betwene tho 2 Sterres: the whiche halfondelle I have seyn. And of the tother halfondelle, I have seyn toward the North, undre the Transmontane 62 Degrees and 10 Mynutes; and toward the partie meridionalle, I have seen undre the Antartyk 33 Degrees and 16 Mynutes: and thanne the halfondelle of the Firmament in alle, ne holdethe not but 180 Degrees. And of tho 180, I have seen 62 on that o part, and 33 on that other part, that ben 95 Degrees, and

nyghe the halfondelle of a Degree; and so there
ne faylethe but that I have seen alle the Firmament, saf 84 Degrees and the halfondelle of a
Degree; and that is not the fourthe part of the
Firmament. For the 4 partie of the roundnesse
of the Firmament holt 90 Degrees: so there
faylethe but 5 Degrees and an half, of the fourthe
partie. And also I have seen the 3 parties of alle
the roundnesse of the Firmament, and more zit 5
Degrees and an half. Be the whiche I seye zou
certeynly, that men may envirowne alle the Erthe
of alle the World, as wel undre as aboven, and
turnen azen to his Contree, that hadde Companye
and Schippynge and Conduyt: and alle weyes he
scholde fynde Men, Londes, and Yles, als wel as in
this Contree. For zee wyten welle, that thei that
ben toward the Antartyk, thei ben streghte, feet
azen feet of hem, that dwellen undre the transmontane; als wel as wee and thei that dwellyn
undre us, ben feet azenst feet. For alle the parties
of See and of Lond han here appositees, habi-
tables or trepassables, and thei of this half and
bezond half. And wytethe wel, that aftre that,
that I may parceyve and comprehende, the Londes
of Pestre John, Emperour of Ynde, ben undre us.
For in goynge from Scotland or from Englond
toward Jerusalem, men gon upward alweys. For
oure Lond is in the lowe partie of the Erthe,
toward the West: and the Lond of Prestre John
is the lowe partie of the Erthe, toward the Est:
and thei han there the day, whan wee have the
nyghte, and also highe to the contrarie, thei han
the nyghte, whan wee han the Day. For the
Erthe and the See ben of round forme and schapp,

as I have seyd beforn. And that that men gon upward to o Cost, men gon dounward to another Cost. Also zee have herd me seye,[b] that Jerusalem is in the myddes of the World; and that may men preven and schewen there, be a Spere, that is pighte in to the Erthe, upon the hour of mydday, whan it is Equenoxium, that schewethe no schadwe on no syde. And that it scholde ben in the myddes of the World, David wytnessethe it in the Psautre, where he seythe, *Deus operatus est salutē in medio Terre.*[c] Thanne thei that parten fro the parties of the West, for to go toward Jerusalem, als many iorneyes as thei gon upward for to go thidre, in als many iorneyes may thei gon fro Jerusalem, unto other Confynyes of the Superficialtie of the Erthe bezonde. And whan men gon bezonde tho iourneyes, toward Ynde and to the foreyn Yles, alle is envyronynge the roundnesse of the Erthe and of the See, undre oure Contrees on this half. And therfore hathe it befallen many tymes of o thing, that I have herd cownted, whan I was zong; how a worthi man departed somtyme from oure Contrees, for to go serche the World. And so he passed Ynde, and the Yles bezonde Ynde, where ben mo than 5000 Yles: and so longe he wente be See and Lond, and so enviround the World be many seysons, that he fond an Yle, where he herde speke his owne Langage, callynge on Oxen in the Plowghe, suche Wordes as men speken to Bestes in his owne Contree: whereof he hadde gret Mervayle: for he knewe not how it myghte be. But I seye, that he had gon so longe, be Londe and be See, that he had envyround alle the Erthe, that he was comen azen envirounynge, that is to

[b] P. 79.   [c] Psalm lxxiv. 12.

seye, goynge aboute, unto his owne Marches, zif he wolde have passed forthe, til he had founden his Contree and his owne knouleche. But he turned azen from thens, from whens he was come fro; and so he loste moche peynefulle labour, as him self seyde, a gret while aftre, that he was comen hom. For it befelle aftre, that he wente in to Norweye; and there Tempest of the See toke him; and he arryved in an Yle; and whan he was in that Yle, he knew wel, that it was the Yle, where he had herd speke his owne Langage before, and the callynge of the Oxen at the Plowghe: and that was possible thinge. But how it semethe to symple men unlerned, that men ne mowe not go undre the Erthe, and also that men scholde falle toward the Hevene, from undre! But that may not be, upon lesse, than wee mowe falle toward Hevene, fro the Erthe, where wee ben. For fro what partie of the Erthe, that men duelle, outher aboven or benethen, it semethe alweys to hem that duellen, that thei gon more righte than ony other folk. And righte as it semethe to us, that thei ben undre us, righte so it semethe hem, that wee ben undre hem. For zif a man myghte falle fro the Erthe unto the Firmament; be grettere resoun, the Erthe and the See, that ben so grete and so hevy, scholde fallen to the Firmament: but that may not be: and therfore seithe oure Lord God, *Non timeas me, qui suspendi Terrā ex nichilo?*[c] And alle be it that it be possible thing, that men may so envyronne alle the World, natheles of a 1000 persones, on ne myghte not happen to returnen in to his Contree. For, for the gretnesse of the Erthe and of the See, men may go be a 1000 and

[c] Job xxvi. 7.

a 1000 other weyes, that no man cowde redye him perfitely toward the parties that he cam fro, but zif it were be aventure and happ, or be the grace of God. For the Erthe is fulle large and fulle gret, and holt in roundnesse and aboute envyroun, be aboven and be benethen 20425 Myles, aftre the opynyoun of the olde wise Astronomeres. And here Seyenges I repreve noughte. But aftre my lytylle wytt, it semethe me, savynge here reverence, that it is more. And for to have bettere understondynge, I seye thus, Be ther ymagyned a Figure, that hathe a gret Compas; and aboute the poynt of the gret Compas, that is clept the Centre, be made another litille Compas: than aftre, be the gret Compas devised be Lines in manye parties; and that alle the Lynes meeten at the Centre; so that in as many parties, as the grete Compas schal be departed, in als manye schalle be departed the litille, that is aboute the Centre, alle be it that the spaces ben lesse. Now thanne, be the gret compas represented for the firmament, and the litille compas represented for the Erthe. Now thanne the Firmament is devysed, be Astronomeres, in 12 Signes; and every Signe is devysed in 30 Degrees, that is 360 Degrees, that the Firmament hathe aboven. Also, be the Erthe devysed in als many parties, as the Firmament; and lat every partye answere to a Degree of the Firmament: and wytethe it wel, that aftre the Auctoures of Astronomye, 700 Furlonges of Erthe answeren to a Degree of the Firmament; and tho ben 87 Miles and 4 Furlonges. Now be that here multiplyed by 360 sithes; and than thei ben 31500 Myles, every of 8 Furlonges, aftre Myles of oure Contree. So moche hathe the

Erthe in roundnesse, and of heghte enviroun, aftre myn opynyoun and myn undirstondynge. And zee schulle undirstonde, that aftre the opynyonn of olde wise Philosophres and Astronomeres, oure Contree ne Irelond ne Wales ne Scotlond ne Norweye ne the other Yles costynge to hem, ne ben not in the superficyalte cownted aboven the Erthe; as it schewethe be alle the Bokes of Astronomye. For the Superficialtee of the Erthe is departed in 7 parties, for the 7 Planetes: and tho parties ben clept Clymates. And oure parties be not of the 7 Clymates: for thei ben descendynge toward the West. And also these Yles of Ynde, which beth evene azenst us, beth noght reckned in the Climates: for thei ben azenst us, that ben in the lowe Contree. And the 7 Clymates strecchen hem envyrounynge the World.

Cap. XVIII.

Of the Palays of the Kyng of the Yle of Java. Of the Trees, that beren Mele, Hony, Wyn and Venym; and of othere Mervayilles and Customes, used in the Yles marchinge thereabouten.

BESYDE that Yle that I have spoken of, there is another Yle, that is clept Sumobor, that is a gret Yle: and the Kyng thereof is righte myghty. The folk of that Yle maken hem alweys to ben marked in the visage with an hote Yren, bothe men and wōmen, for gret noblesse, for to ben knowen from other folk. For thei holden hem self most noble and most worthi of alle the World. And thei han Werre alle weys with the folk that gon alle naked. And faste besyde is an-

other Yle, that is clept Betemga,[a] that is a gode Yle and a plentyfous. And many other Yles ben there about; where there ben many of dyverse folk: of the whiche it were to longe to speke of alle.

But fast besyde that Yle, for to passe be See, is a gret Yle and a gret Contree, that men clepen Java: and it is nyghe 2000 Myle in circuyt. And the Kyng of that Contree is a fulle gret Lord and a ryche and a myghty, and hathe undre him 7 other Kynges of 7 other Yles abouten hym. This Yle is fulle wel inhabyted, and fulle wel manned. There growen alle maner of Spicerie, more plentyfous liche than in ony other Contree; as of Gyngevere, Clowegylofres, Canelle, Zedewalle, Notemuges and Maces. And wytethe wel, that the

[a] Betheyna, F. 2.

Notemuge berethe the Maces. For righte as the Note of the Haselle hathe an Husk with outen, that the Note is closed in, til it be ripe, and aftre fallethe out; righte so it is of the Notemuge and of the Maces. Manye other Spices and many other Godes growen in that Yle. For of alle thing is there plenty, saf only of Wyn: but there is Gold and Silver gret plentee. And the Kyng of that Contree hathe a Paleys fulle noble and fulle marveyllous, and more riche than ony in the World. For alle the Degrez to gon up in to Halles and Chambres, ben on of Gold, another of Sylver. And also the Pavmentes of Halles and Chambres ben alle square, on of Gold and another of Sylver: and alle the Walles with inne ben covered with Gold and Sylver, in fyn Plates: and in tho Plates ben Stories and Batayles of Knyghtes enleved. And the Crounes and the Cercles abouten here Hedes ben made of precious Stones and riche Perles and grete. And the Halles and the Chambres of the Palays ben alle covered with inne with Gold and Sylver: so that no man wolde trowe the richesse of that Palays, but he had seen it. And witethe wel, that the Kyng of that Yle is so myghty, that he hathe many tymes overcomen the grete Cane of Cathay in Bataylle, that is the most gret Emperour that is undre the Firmament, outher bezonde the See or on this half. For thei han had often tyme Werre betwene hem, be cause that the grete Cane wolde constreynen him to holden his lond of him: but that other at alle tymes defendethe him wel azenst him.

Aftre that Yle, in goynge be See, men fynden another Yle, gode and gret, that men clepen

Pathen, that is a gret Kyngdom, fulle of faire Cytees and fulle of Townes. In that Lond growen Trees, that beren Mele, wherof men maken gode Bred and white, and of gode savour; and it semethe as it were of Whete, but it is not allynges of suche Savour. And there ben other Trees, that beren Hony, gode and swete; and other Trees, that beren Venym; azenst the whiche there is no Medicyne but on; and that is to taken here propre Leves, and stampe hem and tempere hem with Watre, and then drynke it: and elle he schalle dye; for Triacle will not avaylle, ne non other Medicyne. Of this Venym, the Jewes had let seche of on of here Frendes, for to enpoysone alle Cristiantee, as I have herd hem seye in here Confessioun, before here dyenge. But thanked be alle myghty God, thei fayleden of hire purpos: but alle weys thei maken gret mortalitee of poeple. And other Trees there ben also, that beren Wyn of noble sentement. And zif zou like to here how the Mele comethe out of the Trees, I shalle seye zou. Men hewen the Trees with an Hachet, alle aboute the fote of the Tree, tille that the Bark be parted in many parties; and than comethe out ther of a thikke Lykour, the whiche thei resceyven in Vesselles, and dryen it at the hete of the Sonne; and than thei han it to a Mylle to grynde; and it becomethe faire Mele and white. And the Hony and the Wyn and the Venym ben drawen out of other Trees, in the same manere, and put in Vesselles for to kepe. In that Yle is a ded See, that is a Lake, that hathe no Ground. And zif ony thing falle in to that Lake, it schalle nevere comen up azen. In that Lake growen Reedes, that ben

Cannes, that thei clepen Thaby, that ben 30 Fadme long.[b] And of theise Canes, men maken faire Houses. And ther ben other Canes, that ben not so longe, that growen nere the Lond, and han so longe Rotes, that duren wel a 4 quartres[c] of a Furlong or more; and at the Knottes of tho Rotes, men fynden precious Stones, that han gret vertues: And he that berethe ony of hem upon him, Yren ne Steel ne may not hurt him, ne drawe no Blood upon him: and therfore thei that han tho Stones upon hem, fighten fulle hardyly, bothe on See and Lond: for men may not harmen hem on no partye. And therfore thei that knowen the manere, and schulle fighten with hem, thei schoten to hem Arwes and Quarrelles with outen Yren or Steel; and so thei hurten hem and sleen hem. And also of tho Cānes, thei maken Houses and Schippes and other thinges; as wee han here, makynge Houses and Schippes of Oke or of ony other Trees. And deme no man, that I seye it, but for a Truffulle: for I have seen of the Cannes with myn owne Eyzen, fulle many tymes, lyggynge upon the Ryvere of that Lake: of the whiche, 20 of oure Felowes ne myghten not liften up ne beren on to the Erthe.

Aftre this Yle, men gon be See to another Yle, that is clept Calonak: and it is a fair Lond and a plentifous of Godes. And the Kyng of that Contrey hath als many Wyfes as he wole: for he makethe serche alle the Contree, to geten him the fairest Maydens that may ben founde, and makethe

[b] Plin. lib. vii. c. 2. Arundines vero [in India] tantæ proceritatis, ut singula internodia alveo navigabili ternos interdum homines ferant.   [c] Fourth.

hem to ben broughte before him; and he takethe on o nyght, and another another nyght, and so forthe contynuelle sewyng; so that he hath a 1000 Wyfes or mo. And he liggethe never but o nyght with on of hem, and another nyght with another, but zif that on happene to ben more lusty to his plesance than another. And therfore the Kyng getethe fully many Children; sum tyme an 100, sum tyme an 200, and sum tyme mo. And he hathe also into a 14000 Olifauntz or mo, that he makethe for to ben brought up amonges his Vileynes, be alle his Townes. For in cas that he had ony Werre azenst any other Kyng aboute him, thanne he makethe certeyn men of Armes for to gon up in to the Castelles of Tree, made for the Werre, that craftily ben sett up on the Olifantes

Bakkes, for to fyghten azen hire Enemyes: and so don other Kynges there aboute. For the maner of Werre is not there, as it is here or in

other Contrees; ne the Ordynance of Werre nouther. And men clepen the Olifantes, Warkes.

And in that Yle there is a gret Marvayle, more to speke of than in ony other partie of the World. For alle manere of Fissches, that ben there in the See abouten hem, comen ones in the Zeer, eche manere of dyverse Fissches, on maner of kynde aftre other; and thei casten hem self to the See Banke of that Yle, so gret plentee and multitude, that no man may unnethe See but Fissche; and there thei abyden 3 dayes: and every man of the Contree takethe of hem, als many as him lykethe: And aftre, that maner of Fissche, after the thridde day, departethe and gothe into the See. And aftre hem, comen another multitude of Fyssche of another kynde, and don in the same maner as the firste diden other 3 dayes. And aftre hem, another; tille alle the dyverse maner of Fissches han ben there, and that men han taken of hem, that

hem lykethe. And no man knowethe the cause wherfore it may ben. But thei of the Contree seyn, that it is for to do reverence to here Kyng, that is the most worthi Kyng, that is in the

World, as thei seyn; because that he fulfillethe the Cōmandement, that God bad to Adā and Eve, whan God seyde, *Crescite & multiplicamini & replete Terram*. And for because that he multipliethe so the World with Children, therfore God sendethe him so the Fissches of dyverse kyndes, of alle that ben in the See, to taken at his wille, for him and alle his peple. And therfore alle the Fissches of the See comen, to maken him homage, as the most noble and excellent Kyng of the World, and that is best beloved with God, als thei seyn. I knowe not the resoun, whi it is: but God knowethe. But this, me semethe, is the moste marveylle, that evere I saughe. For this mervaylle is azenst kynde, and not with kynde, that the Fissches, that han fredom to enviroun alle the Costes of the See, at here owne list, comen of hire owne wille to profren hem to the dethe, with outen constreynynge of man: and therfore I am syker, that this may not ben, with outen a gret tokene.

There ben also in that Contree a kynde of Snayles, that ben so grete, that many persones may loggen hem in here Schelles, as men wolde done in a litylle Hous. And other Snayles there ben, that ben fulle grete, but not so huge as the other. And of theise Snayles, and of gret white Wormes, that han blake Hedes, that ben als grete as a mannes thighe, and sōme lesse, as grete Wormes that men fynden there in Wodes, men maken Vyaunde Rialle, for the Kyng and for other grete Lordes. And zif a man, that is maryed, dye in that Contree, men buryen his Wif with him alle quyk. For men seyn there, that it is resoun, that sche make him companye in that other World, as sche did in this.

From that Contree, men gon be the See Occean, be an Yle that is clept Caffolos. Men of that Contree, whan here Frendes ben seke, thei hangen hem upon Trees; and seyn, that it is

bettre, that Briddes, that ben Angeles of God, eten hem, than the foule Wormes of the Erthe.

From that Yle men gon to another Yle, where the folk ben of fulle cursed kynde: for thei norysschen grete Dogges, and techen hem to strangle here Frendes, whan thei ben syke: for thei wil noughte, that thei dyen of kyndely Dethe: for thei seyn, that thei scholde suffren to gret peyne, zif thei abyden to dyen be hem self, as Nature wolde: and whan thei ben thus en-strangled, thei eten here Flesche, in stede of Venysoun.

Aftreward men gon be many Yles be See, unto an Yle, that men clepen Milke: and there is a fulle cursed peple : for thei delyten in ne thing more, than for to fighten and to sle men. And thei drynken gladlyest mannes Blood, the whiche thei

clepen Dieu. And the mo men that a man may slee, the more worschipe he hathe amonges hem. And zif 2 persones ben at debate, and peraventure ben accorded be here Frendes or be sum of here Alliance, it behovethe that every of hem, that schulle ben accorded, drynke of otheres Blood : and elle the Accord ne the Alliance is noghte worthe, ne it schalle not be ne repref to him to breke the Alliance and the Acord, but zif every of hem drynke of otheres Blood.

And from that Yle, men gon be See, from Yle to Yle, unto an Yle, that is clept Tracoda ; where the folk of that Contree ben as Bestes and unresonable, and duellen in Caves, that thei maken in the Erthe ; for thei have no wytt to maken hem Houses. And whan thei seen ony man passynge thorghe here Contrees, thei hyden hem in here Caves. And thei eten Flesche of Serpentes ; and thei eten but litille, and thei speken nought; but thei hissen, as Serpentes don. And thei sette no

prys be no richesse, but only of a precyous Ston, that is amonges hem, that is of 60 coloures. And for the name of the Yle, thei clepen it Tracodon. And thei loven more that Ston, than onything elle: and zit thei knowe not the vertue there of: but thei coveyten it and loven it only for the beautee.

Aftre that Yle, men gon be the See Occean, be many Yles, unto an Yle, that is clept Nacumera; that is a gret Yle and good and fayr: and it is in kompas aboute, more than a 1000 Myle. And alle the men and wōmen of that Yle han Houndes Hedes: and thei ben clept Cynocephali:[c] and thei ben fulle resonable and of gode undirstondynge, saf that thei worschipen an Ox for here God. And also everyche of hem berethe an Ox of Gold or of Sylver in his forhed, in tokene that thei loven wel here God. And thei gon alle naked, saf a litylle Clout, that thei coveren with here Knees

[c] Cynamolgi, Pliny, lib. vi. c. 30.

and hire Membres. Thei ben grete folk and wel fyghtynge; and thei han a gret Targe, that coverethe alle the Body, and a Spere in here hond to fighte with. And zif thei taken ony man in Bataylle, anon thei eten him. The Kyng of that Yle is fulle riche and fulle myghty, and righte devout aftre his Lawe: and he hathe abouten his Nekke 300 Perles oryent, gode and grete, and knotted, as Pater Nostres here of Amber. And in maner as wee seyn oure Pater Noster and oure Ave Maria, cowntyng the Pater Nosters, right so this Kyng seythe every day devoutly 300 Preyeres to his God, or that he ete: and he berethe also aboute his Nekke a Rubye oryent, noble and fyn, that is a Fote of lengthe, and fyve fyngres large. And whan thei chesen here Kyng, thei taken him that Rubye, to beren in his Hond, and so thei leden him rydynge alle abouten the Cytee. And fro thens fromward, thei ben alle obeyssant to him. And that Rubye he schalle bere alle wey aboute his Nekke: for zif he hadde not that Rubye upon him, men wolde not holden him for Kyng. The grete Cane of Cathay hathe gretly coveted that Rubye; but he myghte never han it, for Werre ne for no maner of Godes. This Kyng is so rightfulle and of equytee in his Doomes, that men may go sykerlyche thorghe out alle his Contree, and bere with him what him list, that no man schalle ben hardy to robben hem: and zif he were, the Kyng wolde iustifyed anon.

Fro this Lond men gon to another Yle, that is clept Silha: and it is welle a 800 Myles aboute. In that Lond is fulle mochelle waste; for it is fulle of Serpentes, of Dragouns and of Cokadrilles; that no man dar duelle there. Theise Cocodrilles ben Serpentes, zalowe and rayed aboven, and han 4 Feet and schorte Thyes and grete Nayles, as Clees or Talouns: and there ben sōme that han 5 Fadme

in lengthe, and sūme of 6 and of 8, and of 10: and whan thei gon be places, that ben gravelly, it semethe as thoughe men hadde drawen a gret

Tree thorghe the gravelly place. And there ben
also many wylde Bestes, and namelyche of Oly-
launtes. In that Yle is a gret Mountayne; and
in mydd place of the Mount, is a gret Lake in a
fulle faire Pleyne, and there is gret plentee of
Watre. And thei of the Contree seyn, that Adam
and Eve wepten upon that Mount an 100 Zeer,
whan thei weren dryven out of Paradys. And
that Watre, thei seyn, is of here Teres: for so
moche Watre thei wepten, that made the forseyde
Lake. And in the botme of that Lake, men
fynden many precious Stones and grete Perles.
In that Lake growen many Reedes and grete
Cannes: and there with inne ben many Cocodrilles and Serpentes and grete watre Leches.
And the Kyng of that Contree, ones every zeer,
zevethe leve to pore men to gon in to the
Lake, to gadre hem precyous Stones and Perles,
be weye of Alemesse, for the love of God, that
made Adam. And alle the Zeer, men fynde y
nowe. And for the Vermyn, that is with inne,
thei anoynte here Armes and here Thyes and
Legges with an Oynement, made of a thing that is
clept Lymons, that is a manere of Fruyt, lyche
smale Pesen: and thanne have thei no drede of no
Cocodrilles, ne of non other venymous Vermyn.
This Watre rennethe, flowynge and ebbynge, be a
syde of the Mountayne: and in that Ryver men
fynden precious Stones and perles, gret Plentee.
And men of that Yle seyn comounly, that the
Serpentes and the wilde Bestes of that Contree ne
will not don non harm, ne touchen with evylle,
no strange man, that entrethe into that Contree, but only to men that ben born of the same

Contree. In that Contree and othere there abouten, there ben wylde Gees, that han 2 Hedes:

and there ben Lyouns alle white, and als grete as Oxen, and many other dyverse Bestes, and foules also, that be not seyn amonges us. And witethe wel, that in that Contree and in other Yles there abouten, the See is so highe, that it semethe as though it henge at the Clowdes, and that it wolde covere alle the World: and that is gret Mervaylle, that it myghte be so, saf only the wille of God, that the Eyr susteynethe it. And therfore seyth David in the Psautere, *Mirabiles elationes Maris*.

Cap. XIX.

How men knowen be the Ydole, zif the sike schalle dye or non. Of folk of dyverse schap and merveylously disfigured: And of the Monkes, that zeven hire releef to Babewynes, Apes and Marmesettes and to other Bestes.

FROM that Yle, in goynge be See, toward the Southe, is another gret Yle, that is clept Dondun. In that Yle ben folk of dyverse kyndes; so that the Fadre etethe the Sone, the Sone the Fadre, the Husbonde the Wif, and the Wif the Husbonde. And zif it so befalle, that the Fadre or Modre or ony of here Frendes ben seke, anon the Son gothe to the Prest of here Law, and preyethe him to aske the Ydole, zif his Fadre or Modre or Frend schalle dye on that evylle or non. And than the Prest and the Sone gone to gydere before the Ydole, and knelen fulle devoutly, and asken of the Ydole here demande. And zif the Devylle, that is with inne, answere, that he schalle lyve, thei kepen him wel: and zif he seye, that he schalle dye, than the Prest gothe with the Sone, with the Wif of him that is seeke, and thei putten here hondes upon his mouthe, and stoppen his Brethe, and so thei sleen him. And aftre that, thei choppen alle the Body in smale peces, and preyen alle his Frendes to comen and eten of him, that is ded: and thei senden for alle the Mynstralle of the Contree, and maken a solempne Feste. And

whan thei han eten the Flessche, thei taken the Bones, and buryen hem, and syngen and maken gret melodye. And alle tho that ben of his kyn, or pretenden hem to ben his Frendes, and thei come not to that Feste, thei ben repreved for evere and schamed, and maken gret doel; for nevere aftre schulle thei ben holden as Frendes. And thei seyn also, that men eten here Flesche, for to delyveren hem out of peyne. For zif the Wormes of the Erthe eten hem, the Soule scholde suffre gret peyne, as thei seyn; and namely, whan the Flesche is tendre and megre, thanne seyn here Frendes, that thei don gret Synne, to leten hem have so long langure, to suffre so moche peyne, with oute resoun. And whan thei fynde the Flessche fatte, than thei seyn, that it is wel don, to senden him sone to Paradys; and that thei have not suffred him to longe to endure in peyne. The Kyng of this Yle is a ful gret Lord and a

myghty; and hathe undre him 54 grete Yles, that
zeven Tribute to him : and in everyche of theise
Yles, is a Kyng crowned, and alle ben obeyssant
to that Kyng. And he hathe in tho Yles many
dyverse folk. In on of theise Yles ben folk of
gret Stature, as Geauntes; and thei ben hidouse
for to loke upon; and thei han but on eye,[a]

and that is in the myddylle of the Front; and
thei eten no thing but raw Flessche and raw
Fyssche.

And in another Yle, toward the Southe, duellen
folk of foule Stature and of cursed kynde,[b] that
han no Hedes: and here Eyen ben in here
Scholdres.[b]

[a] Pliny, lib. vi. c. 30 ; and lib. vii. c. 2 : Produntur Arimaspi,
uno oculo in Fronte mediâ insignes.

[b] Pliny, lib. vii. c. 2 : Rursusq; ab his, Occidentem versus,
quosdam sine Cervice, Oculos in Humeris habentes. And lib.
v. c. 8 : Blemmyis traduntur capita abesse, ore et oculis pectori
affixis.

And in another Yle ben folk, that han the face all platt, alle pleyn, with outen Nese^c and with

^c Pliny, lib. vii. c. 2 : Gentem inter Nomadas Indos, Narium loco, foramina tantum habentem.

outen Mouthe :ᵈ but thei han 2 smale holes alle rounde, in stede of hire Eyen : and hire Mouthe is platt also, with outen Lippes.

And in another Yle ben folk of foul fasceon and Schapp, that han the Lippe above the Mouthe so gret, that whan thei slepen in the Sonne, thei keveren alle the face with that Lippe.ᵉ

And in another Yle, ther ben litylle folk, as Dwerghes ;ᶠ and thei ben to so meche as the Pygmeyes, and thei han no Mouthe, but in stede of hire Mouthe, thei han a lytylle round hole: and whan thei schulle eten or drynken, thei taken thorghe a Pipe or a Penne or suche a thing, and sowken it in : for thei han no Tonge ; and therfore thei speke not, but thei maken a maner of hissynge, as a Neddre dothe, and thei maken Signes on to another, as Monkes don ; be the whiche, every of hem undirstondethe other.

And in another Yle ben folk, that han gret Eres and longe, that hangen doun to here Knees.ᵍ

And in another Yle ben folk, that han Hors Feet ;ʰ and thei ben stronge and myghty and swift renneres : for thei taken wylde Bestes with rennyng, and eten hem.

ᵈ Plin. lib. vii. c. 2 : Ad extremos fines Indiæ, ab Oriente, circa fontem Gangis, Astomorum gentem sine ore.

ᵉ Strabo describes such a People, call'd Amyctyræ.

ᶠ Plin. lib. vii. c. 2 : Supra hos, extrema in parte Montium, Spithamæi Pygmæi narrantur, ternas Spithamas longitudine; hoc est, ternos Dodrantes non excedentes.

ᵍ Plin. lib. iv. c. 13 : Fenesiorum aliæ [Insulæ Ponti] in quibus nuda alioquin corpora prægrandes ipsorum Aures tota contegant. Lib. vii. c. 2 : Alios Auribus totos contegi. Strabo calls them ἐνωτόκοιτοι. Isidore calls them Panωtii.

ʰ Plin. lib. iv. c. 13 : Aliæ, in quibus equinis pedibus homines nascantur, Hippopodes appellati.

And in another Yle ben folk, that gon upon hire Hondes and hire Feet, as Bestes:[i] and thei ben alle skynned and fedred, and thei wolde lepen als lightly in to Trees, and fro Tree to Tree, as it were Squyrelles or Apes.

And in another Yle ben folk that ben bothe Man and Wōman:[k] and thei han kynde of that on and of that other; and thei han but o Pappe on the o syde, and on that other non: and thei han Membres of Generacioun of Man and Wōman; and thei usen bothe, whan hem list, ones that on, and another tyme that other: and thei geten Children, whan thei usen the membre of Man; and thei bere Children, whan thei usen the membre of Wōman.

And in another Yle ben folk, that gon alle weyes upon here Knees,[l] ful merveylously; and at every pas that thei gon, it semethe that thei wolde falle: and thei han in every Foot, 8 Toes.

Many other dyverse folk of dyverse natures ben there in other Yles abouten, of the whiche it were to longe to telle: and therfore I passe over schortly.

From theise Yles, in passynge be the See Occean toward the Est, be many iourneyes, men

[i] Plin. lib. v. c. 8: Himantopodes loripedes quidam, quibus serpendo ingredi natura est. And lib. vii. c. 2: Sunt et Satyri subsolanis Indorum montibus, tum quadrupedes tum recte currentes, humanâ effigie.

[k] Ibid. Supra Nasamonas confinesque illis Machlyas, Androgynas esse utriusq; naturæ, inter se vicibus coeuntes, Calliphanes tradit.

[l] Ibid. In quadam convalle magna Imai montis, regio est, quæ vocatur Abarimon, in qua sylvestres vivunt homines, aversis post crura plantis.

fynden a gret Contree and a gret Kyngdom, that men clepen Mancy: and that is in Ynde the more: and it is the beste Lond, and on of the fairest, that may be in alle the World, and the most delectable, and the most plentifous of alle Godes, that is in power of man. In that Lond duellen many Cristene men and Sarrazynes: for it is a gode Contree and a gret. And there ben there inne mo than 2000 grete Cytees aud riche, with outen other grete Townes. And there is more plentee of peple there, than in ony other partie of Ynde; for the bountee of the Contree. In that Contree is no nedy man, ne none that gothe on beggynge. And thei ben fulle faire folk: but thei ben all pale. And the men han thynne Berdes and fewe Heres; but thei ben longe: but unethe hathe ony man passynge 50 Heres in his Berd; and on Heer sitt here, another there, as the Berd of a Lyberd or of a Catt. In that Lond ben many fairere Wōmen, than in ony other Contree bezonde the See: and therfore men clepen that Lond Albanye; because that the folk ben whyte. And the chief Cytee of that Contree is clept Latoryn; and it is a iourneye from the See: and it is moche more than Parys. In that Cytee is a gret Ryvere, berynge Schippes, that gon to alle the Costes in the See. No Cytee of the World is so wel stored of Schippes, as is that. And alle tho of the Cytee and of the Contree worschipen Ydoles. In that Contree ben double sithes more briddes than ben here.[m] There ben white Gees, rede aboute the Nekke, and thei han a gret Crest, as a Cokkes Comb upon hire Hedes: and thei ben

[m] Volucres in duplo sunt majores, L.

meche more there, than thei ben here; and men byen hem there alle quykke, right gret chepe. And there is gret plentee of Neddres, of whom men maken grete Festes, and eten hem at grete sollempnytees. And he that makethe there a Feste, be it nevere so costifous, and he have no Neddres, he hathe no thanke for his travaylle.

Many gode Cytees there ben in that Contree, and men han gret plentee and gret chep of alle Wynes and Vitailles. In that Contree ben manye Chirches of religious men, and of here Lawe: and in tho Chiches been Ydoles, als grete as Geauntes. And to theise Ydoles thei zeven to ete, at grete festyfulle dayes, in this manere. Thei bryngen before hem mete alle soden, als hoot as thei comen fro the Fuyr, and thei leten the smoke gon up towardes the Ydoles; and than thei seyn, that the Ydoles han eten; and than the religious men eten the mete aftrewardes. In that Contree been white Hennes withouten Fetheres: but thei beren white Wolle, as Scheep don here. In that

Contree, Wommen that ben unmaryed, thei han Tokenes on hire Hedes, lyche Coronales, to ben knowen for unmaryed. Also in that Contree, ther ben Bestes, taughte of men to gon in to Watres, in to Ryveres and in to depe Stankes, for to take Fysche: the whiche Best is but lytille, and men clepen hem Loyres. And whan men casten hem in to the Watre, anon thei bringē up gret Fissches, als manye as men wold. And zif men wil have mo, thei cast hem in azen, and thei bryngen up als many as men list to have.

And fro that Cytee, passynge many iourneyes, is another Cytee, on of the grettest of the World, that men clepen Cassay;[n] that is to seyne, the Cytee of Hevene. That Cytee is wel a 50 Myle aboute, and it is strongliche enhabyted with peple, in so moche that in on House men maken 10 Housholdes. In that Cytee ben 12 princypalle Zates; and before every Zate, a 3 Myle or a 4 Myle in lengthe, is a gret Toun, or a gret Cytee. That Cytee sytt upon a gret Lake on the See; as dothe Venyse. And in that Cytee ben mo than 12000 Brigges: and upon every Brigge, ben stronge Toures and gode; in the whiche duellen the Wardeynes, for to kepen the Cytee fro the gret Cane. And on that o part of the Cytee, rennethe a gret Ryvere alle along the Cytee. And there duellen Cristene men, and many Marchauntes and other folk of dyverse Nacyouns: be cause that the Lond is so gode and so plentifous. And there growethe fulle gode Wyn, that men clepen Bigon, that is fulle myghty and gentylle in drynkynge. This is a Cytee ryalle, where the

[n] Lasaye, L. 1, 2; Cansay, L. 3; Casye, L. 4.

P

Kyng of Mancy was wont to duelle: and there duellen many religious men, as it were of the ordre of Freres: for thei ben Mendyfauntes.

From that Cytee, men gon be Watre, solacynge and disportynge hem, tille thei come to an Abbey of Monkes, that is faste bye, that ben gode religious men, after here Feythe and Lawe. In that Abbeye is a gret Gardyn and a fair, where ben many Trees of dyverse manere of Frutes: and in this Gardyn, is a lytille Hille, fulle of delectable Trees. In that Hille and in that Gardyn, ben many dyverse Bestes, as of Apes, Marmozettes, Babewynes, and many other dyverse Bestes. And every day, whan the Covent of this Abbeye hathe eten, the Awmener let bere the releef to the Gardyn, and he smytethe on the Gardyn Zate with a Clyket of Sylver, that he holdethe in his hond, and anon alle the Bestes of the Hille and of dyverse places of the Gardyn, comen out, a 3000 or a 4000; and thei comen in gyse of pore men: and men zeven hem the releef, in faire Vesselles of Sylver, clene over gylt. And whan thei han eten, the Monk smytethe eft sones on the Gardyn Zate with the Clyket; and than anon alle the Bestes retornen azen to here places, that thei come fro. And thei seyn, that theise Bestes ben Soules of worthi men, that resemblen in lyknesse of the Bestes, that ben faire: and therfore thei zeve hem mete, for the love of God. And the other Bestes that ben foule, they seyn, ben Soules of pore men and of rude Comouns. And thus thei beleeven, and no man may putte hem out of this opynyoun. Theise Bestes aboveseyd, thei let taken, whan thei ben zonge, and norisschen hem so with Almesse; als manye, as thei may fynde. And I asked hem, zif it had not ben better, to have zoven that releef to pore men, rathere than to the Bestes. And thei answerde me and seyde, that thei hadde no pore men amonges hem, in that Contree: and thoughe it had ben so, that pore men had ben among hem, zit were it gretter Almesse, to zeven it to tho Soules, that don there here Penance. Many other Marveylles ben in that Cytee and in the Contree there aboute, that were to long to telle zou.

Fro that Cytee, go men be the Contree a 6 iourneyes, to another Cytee, that men clepen Chilenfo:° of the whiche Cytee, the Walles ben 20 Myle aboute. In that Cytee ben 60 Brigges of Ston, so faire, that no man may see fairere. In that Cytee was the firste Sege of the Kyng of Mancy: for it is a fair Cytee, and plenteevous of alle Godes.

Aftre passe men overthwart a gret Ryvere, that men clepen Dalay: and that is the grettest Ryvere of Fressche Water, that is in the World. For there, as it is most narow, it is more than 4 Myle of brede. And thanne entren men azen in to the Lond of the grete Chane. That Ryvere gothe thorghe the Lond of Pigmaus: where that the folk ben of litylle Stature, that ben but 3 Span long :ᵖ and thei ben right faire and gentylle, aftre

° Cheloso, L. 1; Chesolo, L. 2; Tylenso, L. 3, 4; Chybens, E. 1, 2, 3, 4.

ᵖ Plin. vii. 2: Supra hos, [circa Fontem Gangis] extremâ in parte Montium, Spithamæi Pygmæi narrantur, ternas Spithamas longitudine, hoc est, ternos dodrantes non excedentes—Quos à Gruibus infestari Homerus quoque prodidit. Fama est insi-

here quantytees, bothe the Men and the Wommen. And thei maryen hem, whan thei ben half Zere of Age, and geten Children. And thei lyven not, but 6 Zeer or 7 at the moste. And he that lyvethe 8 Zeer, men holden him there righte passynge old. Theise men ben the beste worcheres of Gold, Sylver, Cotoun, Sylk, and of alle suche thinges, of ony other, that be in the World. And thei han often tymes Werre with the Briddes of the Contree, that thei taken and

eten. This litylle folk nouther labouren in Londes ne in Vynes. But thei han grete men amonges hem, of oure Stature, that tylen the Lond, and labouren amonges the Vynes for hem. And of tho men of oure Stature, han thei als grete skorne

dentes arietum caprarumque dorsis, armatos sagittis, Veris tempore, universo agmine ad mare descendere, et ova pullosque earum alitum consumere.

and wondre, as we wolde have among us of
Geauntes, zif thei weren amonges us. There is
a gode Cytee, amonges othere, where there is
duellynge gret plentee of tho lytylle folk: And it
is a gret Cytee and a fair; and the men ben grete,
that duellen amonges hem: but whan thei geten
ony Children, thei ben als litylle as the Pygmeyes:
and therfore thei ben alle, for the moste part, alle
Pygmeyes; for the Nature of the Lond is suche.
The grete Cane let kepe this Cytee fulle wel: for
it is his. And alle be it, that the Pygmeyes ben
lytylle, zit thei ben fulle resonable, aftre here
Age, and connen bothen Wytt and gode and
malice, y now.^q

Fro that Cytee, gon men be the Contree, be
many Cytees and many Townes, unto a Cytee,
that men clepen Jamchay: and it is a noble Cytee
and a riche, and of gret profite to the Lord: and
thidre go men to sechen Marchandise of alle
manere of thing. That Cytee is fulle moche
worthe zerly to the Lord of the Contree. For he
hathe every Zere to rente of that Cytee (as thei
of the Cytee seyn) 50000 Cumantz of Floreyns of
Gold: for thei cownten there alle be Cumanz: and
every Cumant is 10000 Floryns of Gold. Now
may men wel rekene, how moche that it amount-
ethe. The Kyng of that Contree is fulle myghty:
and zit he is undre the grete Cane. And the gret
Cane hathe undre him 12 such Provynces. In
that Contree, in the gode Townes, is a gode
Custom. For whoso wille make a Feste to ony of
his Frendes, there ben certeyn Innes in every gode
Toun; and he that wil make the Feste, wil seye

^q Sciunt sufficientur Bonum et Malum, L.

to the Hostellere, Arraye for me, to morwe, a gode Dyner, for so many folk; and tellethe him the nombre; and devysethe him the Viaundes: and he seythe also, Thus moche I will dispende, and no more. And anon the Hostellere arrayethe for him, so faire and so wel and so honestly, that ther schalle lakke no thing. And it schalle be don sunnere, and with lasse cost, than and a man made it in his owne Hous.

And a 5 Myle fro that Cytee, toward the Hed of the Ryvere of Dalay, is another Cytee, that men clepen Menke. In that Cytee is strong Navye of Schippes; and alle ben white as Snow, of the kynde of the Trees, that thei ben made offe. And thei ben fulle grete Schippes, and faire, and wel ordeyned, and made with Halles and Chambres, and other eysementes, as thoughe it were on the Lond.

Fro thens go men be many Townes and many Cytees, thorghe the Contree, unto a Cytee, that men clepen Lanteryne: and it is an 8 iourneyes from the Cytee aboveseyd. This Cytee sitt upon a faire Ryvere, gret and brood, that men clepen Caramaron. This Ryvere passethe thorghe out Cathay: and it dothe often tyme harm, and that fulle gret, whan it is over gret.

Cap. XX.

Of the grete Chane of Chatay. Of the Rialtee of his Palays, and how he sitt at Mete; and of the grete nombre of Officeres, that serven hym.

CHATAY is a gret Contree and a fair, noble and riche, and fulle of Marchauntes. Thidre gon Marchaundes alle Zeres, for to sechen Spices and alle manere of Marchandises, more comounly than in ony other partye. And zee schulle undirstonde, that Marchaundes, that comen fro Gene or fro Venyse or fro Romanye, or other partyes of Lombardye, thei gon be See and be Londe 11 Monethes, or 12, or more sum tyme, or thei may come to the Yle of Cathay, that is the princypalle Regyoun of alle partyes bezonde; and it is of the grete Cane.

Fro Cathay go men toward the Est, be many iorneyes: and than men fynden a gode Cytee, betwene theise othere, that men clepen Sugarmago.[a] That Cytee is on of the beste stored of Sylk and other Marchandises, that is in the World. Aftre go men zit to another old Cytee, toward the Est: and it is in the Provynce of Cathay. And besyde that Cytee, the men of Tartarye han let make another Cytee, that is clept Caydon; and it hathe 12 Zates: and betwene the two Zates, there is alle weys a gret Myle; so that the 2 Cytees, that is to seyne, the olde and the newe, han in circuyt more than 20 Myle. In this Cytee is the Sege of

[a] Thus the French: but the Latin MSS. have it, Eugarmago.

the grete Cane in a fulle gret Palays, and the most passynge fair in alle the World: of the whiche the Walles ben in circuyt more than 2 Myle: and within the Walles, it is alle fulle of other Palays. And in the Gardyn of the grete Palays, there is a gret Hille, upon the whiche there is another Palays: and it is the most fair and the most riche, that ony man may devyse. And all aboute the Palays and the Hille, ben many Trees, berynge many dyverse Frutes. And allè aboute that Hille, ben Dyches grete and depe: and besyde hem, ben grete Vyneres, on that o part and on that other. And there is a fulle fair Brigge to passe over the Dyches. And in theise Vyneres, ben so many wylde Gees and Gandres and wylde Dokes and Swannes and Heirouns, that it is with outen nombre. And alle aboute theise Dyches and Vyneres, is the grete Gardyn, fulle of wylde Bestes; so that, whan the gret Cane wil have ony Desport on that, to taken ony of the wylde Bestes or of the Foules, he wil lete chace hem and taken hem at the Wyndowes, with outen goynge out of his Chambre. This Palays, where his Sege is, is bothe gret and passynge fair. And with in the Palays, in the Halle, there ben 24 Pyleres of fyn Gold: and alle the Walles ben covered with inne, of rede Skynnes of Bestes, that men clepen Panteres; that ben faire Bestes, and well smellyng: so that for the swete odour of tho Skynnes, non evylle Ayr may entre in to the Palays. Tho Skynnes ben als rede as Blode; and thei schynen so brighte azen the Sonne, that unethes no man may beholden hem. And many folk worschipen tho Bestes, whan thei meeten hem first at Morwe, for here gret vertue and for the gode smelle that thei han: and tho Skynnes thei preysen more than thoughe thei were Plate of fyn Gold. And in the myddes of this Palays is the Mountour[a] for the grete Cane, that is alle wrought of Gold and of precyous Stones and grete Perles: and at 4 Corneres of the Mountour, been 4 Serpentes of Gold: and alle aboute ther is y made large Nettes of Sylk, and Gold and grete Perles hangynge alle aboute the Mountour. And undre the Mountour, ben Condytes of Beverage, that thei drynken in the Emperours Court. And besyde the Condytes, ben many Vesselles of Gold, be the whiche, thei that ben of Houshold, drynken at the Condyt. And the Halle of the Palays is fulle nobelyche arrayed, and fulle merveylleousely atyred on all partyes, in alle thinges, that men apparayle with ony Halle. And first, at the chief of the Halle, is the Emperours Throne, fulle highe, where he syttethe at the Mete: and that is of fyn precyouse Stones, bordured alle aboute with pured Gold and precyous Stones and grete Perles. And the Grees, that he gothe up to the Table, ben of precyous Stones, medled with Gold. And at the left syde of the Emperoures Sege, is the Sege of his firste Wif, o degree lowere than the Emperour: and it is of Jaspere, bordured with Gold and preciouse Stones. And the Sege of his seconde Wif is also another Sege, more lowere than his firste Wif: and it is also of Jaspere, bordured with Gold, as that other is. And the Sege of the thridde Wif is also more lowe, be a Degree, than the seconde Wif. For he hathe alweys 3 Wifes with him,

[a] Ascensorium, L.; Mountaynette, F.

where that evere he be. And aftre his Wyfes, on the same syde, sytten the Ladyes of his Lynage, zit lowere, aftre that thei ben of Estate. And alle tho that ben maryed, han a Countrefete, made lyche a mannes foot, upon here Hedes, a cubyte long, alle wrought with grete Perles, fyne and oryent, and aboven, made with Pecokes Fedres and of other schynynge Fedres; and that stont upon here Hedes, lyke a Crest, in tokene that thei ben undre mannes fote and undre subiectioun of Man. And thei that ben unmaryed, han none suche. And aftre, at the right syde of the Emperour, first syttethe his eldest Sone, that schalle regne aftre him: and he syttethe also o Degree lowere than the Emperour, in suche manere of Seges, as don the Emperesses. And aftre him, sytten other grete Lordes of his Lynage, every of hem a Degree lowere than other, as thei ben of Estate. And the Emperour hathe his Table allone be him self, that is of Gold and of precious Stones, or of Cristalle, bordured with Gold, and fulle of precious Stones or of Amatystes or of Lignū Aloes, that comethe out of Paradys, or of Ivory, bounden or bordured with Gold. And everyche of his Wyfes hathe also hire Table be hire self. And his eldest Sone, and the other Lordes also, and the Ladyes, and alle that sitten with the Emperour, han Tables allone be hem self, fulle riche. And there nys no Table, but that it is worthe an huge Tresour of Gode. And undre the Emperoures Table, sitten 4 Clerkes, that writen alle, that the Emperour seythe, be it good, be it evylle. For alle that he seythe, moste ben holden: for he may not chaungen his Word, ne revoke it. At grete solempne Festes, before the Emperoures Table, men bryngen grete Tables of Gold, and there on ben Pecokes of Gold, and many other maner of dyverse foules, alle of Gold, and richely wrought and enameled; and men maken hem dauncen and syngen, clappynge here Wenges to gydere, and maken gret noyse: and where it be by Craft or be Nygromancye, I wot nere; but it is a gode sight to beholde, and a fair: and it is gret marvayle how it may be. But I have the lasse marvaylle, be cause that thei ben the moste sotyle men in alle Sciences and in alle Craftes, that ben in the World. For of sotyltee and of Malice and of fercastynge, thei passen alle men undre Hevene. And therfore thei seyn hem self, that thei seen with 2 Eyen; and the Cristene men see but with on: be cause that thei ben more sotylle than thei. For alle other Naciouns, thei seyn, ben but blynde in conynge and worchynge, in comparisoun to hem. I did gret besynesse, for to have lerned that Craft: but the Maistre tolde me, that he had made a vow to his God, to teche it to no Creature, but only to his eldeste Sone. Also above the Emperours Table and the othere Tables, and aboven a gret partie in the Halle, is a Vyne, made of fyn Gold: and it spredethe alle aboute the Halle; and it hath many Clustres of Grapes, somme white, sōme grene, sūme zalowe and sōme rede and sōme blake, alle of precious Stones: the white ben of Cristalle and of Berylle and of Iris; the zalowe ben of Topazes; the rede ben of Rubies, and of Grenaz and of Alabraundynes; the grene ben of Emeraudes, of Perydos and of Crisolytes; and the blake ben of Onichez and

Garantez. And thei ben alle so propurlyche made, that it semethe a verry Vyne, berynge kyndely Grapes. And before the Emperoures Table, stonden grete Lordes, and riche Barouns and othere, that serven the Emperour at the Mete. And no man is so hardy, to speke a word, but zif the Emperour speke to him; but zif it be Mynstrelles, that syngen Songes, and tellen Gestes or other desportes, to solace with the Emperour. And alle the Vesselle, that men ben served with, in the Halle or in Chambres, ben of precious Stones; and specially at grete Tables; outher of Jaspre or of Cristalle or of Amatystez or of fyn Gold. And the Cuppes ben of Emeraudez and of Saphires or of Topazes, of Perydoz, and of many other precyouse Stones. Vesselle of Sylver is there non: for thei telle no prys there of, to make no Vesselle offe: but thei maken ther of Grecynges and Pileres and Pawmentes, to Halles and Chambres. And before the Halle Dore, stonden manye Barounes, and Knyghtes clene armed, to kepe that no man entre, but zif it be the wille or the Cōmandement of the Emperour, or but zif thei ben Servauntes or Mynstralle of the Houshold: and other non is not so hardy, to neighen nye the Halle Dore.

And zee schulle undirstonde, that my Felawes and I, with oure Zomen, we serveden this Emperour, and weren his Soudyoures, 15 Monethes, azenst the Kyng of Mancy, that held Werre azenst him. And the cause was, for we hadden gret lust to see his Noblesse and the Estat of his Court and alle his Governance, to wite zif it were suche, as wee herde seye, that it was. And treuly, we fond it more noble and more excellent and ricchere and more marveyllous, than ever we herde speke offe; in so moche, that we wolde never han leved it, had wee not seen it. For I trowe, that no man wolde beleve the Noblesse, the ricchesse, ne the multytude of folk that ben in his Court, but he had seen it. For it is not there, as it is here. For the Lordes here han folk of certeyn nombre, als thei may suffise : but the grete Chane hathe every day folke at his Costages and Expenses, as with outen nombre. But the Ordynance, ne the expenses in mete and drynk, ne the honestee ne the clennesse, is not so arrayed there, as it is here: for alle the Comouns there eten withouten Clothe upon here knees; and thei eten alle maner of Flessche, and litylle of Bred. And aftre Mete, thei wypen here Hondes upon here Skyrtes : and thei eten not but ones a day. But the Estat of Lordes is fulle gret and riche and noble. And alle be it, that sum men wil not trow me; but holden it for Fable, to telle hem the Noblesse of his persone and of his Estate and of his Court and of the gret multytude of folk, that he holt, natheles I schalle seye zou, a partye of him and of his folk, aftre that I have seen, the manere and the ordynance, fulle many a tyme. And whoso that wole, may leve me, zif he wille ; and who so wille not, may chuse. For I wot wel, zif ony man hathe ben in tho Contrees bezonde, thoughe he have not ben in the place, where the grete Chane duellethe, he schalle here speke of him so meche merveylouse thing, that he schalle not trowe it lightly : and treuly, no more did I my self, til I saughe it. And tho that han ben in tho Contrees and in the gret Canes Houshold, knowen wel, that I seye sothe. And therfore I wille not spare, for hem that knowe not, ne beleve not, but that that thei seen, for to telle zou a partie of him and of his estate, that he holt, whan he gothe from Contree to Contree, and whan he makethe solempne Festes.

Cap. XXI.

Wherefore he is clept the grete Chane. Of the Style of his Lettres, and of the Superscripcioun abowten his grete Sealle, and his pryvee Sealle.

FIRST I schalle seye zou, whi he was clept the gret Chane. Zee schulle undirstonde, that alle the World was destroyed be Noes Flood, saf only Noe and his Wif and his Children. Noe had 3 Sones, Sem, Cham and Japhethe. This Cham was he that saughe his Fadres prevy membres naked, whan he slepte, and scorned hem and schewed hem with his finger, to his Brethren, in scornynge wise: and ther fore he was cursed of God. And Japhethe turned his face away, and covered hem. Theise 3 Bretheren had Cesoun in alle the Lond: and this Cham, for his crueltee, toke the gretter and the beste partie, toward the Est, that is clept Asye: and Sem toke Affryk: and Japhethe toke Europe. And therfore is alle the Erthe departed in theise 3 parties, be theise 3 Bretheren. Cham was the grettest, and the most myghty: and of him camen mo generaciouns, than of the othere. And of his Sone Chuse, was engendred Nembrothe the Geaunt, that was the firste Kyng, that ever was in the World: and he began the foundacioū of the Tour of Babyloyne. And that tyme, the Fendes of Helle camen many tymes, and leyen with the Wōmen of his Generacioun, and engendered on hem dyverse folk, as Monstres, and folk disfigured, sūme with outen Hedes, sūme with gret Eres, sūme with on Eye, sūme Geauntes, sūm with Hors feet,[a] and many

other dyverse schapp, azenst kynde. And of that Generacioun of Cham, ben comen the Paynemes, and dyverse folk, that ben in Yles of the See, be alle Ynde. And for als moche as he was the moste myghty, and no man myghte withstonde

[a] Pliny, lib. iv. c. 13: Aliæ [Insulæ Ponti] in quibus equinis pedibus homines nascantur, Hippopodes appellati.

him, he cleped himself the Sone of God, and Sovereyn of alle the World. And for this Cham, this Emperour clepeth him Cham and Sovereyn of alle the World. And of the Generacioun of Sem, ben comen the Sarrazines. And of the Generacioun of Japhethe, is comen the peple of Israel. And thoughe that wee duellen in Europe, this is the opynyoun, that the Syryenes and the Samaritanes han amonges hem; and that thei told me, before that I wente toward Ynde: but I fond it otherwise. Natheles the Sothe is this, that Tartarynes and thei that duellen in the grete Asye, thei camen of Cham. But the Emperour of Cathay clepeth him not Cham, but Can: and I schalle telle zou how. It is but lityle more but 8 score Zeer, that alle Tartarye was in subiectioun and in servage to othere nacyouns abouten: for thei weren but bestyalle folk, and diden no thing but kepten Bestes, and lad hem to Pastures. But among hem, thei hadden 7 princypalle Nacyouns, that weren Soveraynes of hem alle: of the whiche, the firste Nacyoun or Lynage was clept Tartar; and that is the most noble and the moste preysed. The seconde Lynage is clept Tanghot; the thridde Eurache; the 4 Valair; the 5 Semoche; the 6 Megly; the 7 Coboghe. Now befelle it so, that of the firste Lynage, succeeded an old worthi man, that was not riche, that hadde to name Changuys. This man lay upon a nyght in his Bed, and he sawghe in a Visioun, that there cam before him a Knyght armed alle in white, and he satt upon a white Hors, and seyd to him, Can, slepest thou? The inmortalle God hathe sent me to the; and it is his Wille, that thou go to the 7 Lynages, and seye to hem, that thou schalt ben here Emperour. For thou schalt conquere the Londs and the Contrees, that ben abouten: and thei that marchen upon zou, schulle ben undre zoure Subieccioun, as zee han ben undre hires: for that is Goddes Wille inmortalle. And whan he cam at morwe, Changuys roos, and wente to the 7 Lynages, and tolde hem how the white Knyght had seyd. And thei scorned him, and seyden, that he was a fool; and so he departed fro hem alle aschamed. And the nyght sewynge, this white Knyght cam to the 7 Lynages, and commaunded hem, on Goddes behalve inmortalle, that thei scholde make this Changuys here Emperour; and thei scholde ben out of subieccioun; and thei scholde holden alle other Regiounes aboute hem in here servage, as thei had ben to hem beforn. And on the Morwe, thei chosen him to ben here Emperour: and thei setten him upon a blak Fertre; and aftre that, thei liften him up with gret solempnytee, and thei setten him in a Chayer of Gold, and diden hym alle maner of Reverence; and thei cleped him Chan, as the white Knyght called him. And whan he was thus chosen, he wolde assayen, zif he myghte trust in hem or non, and whether thei wolde ben obeyssant to him or non. And thanne he made many Statutes and Ordynances, that thei clepen *Ysya Chan*. The first Statute was, that thei scholde beleeven and obeyen in God inmortalle, that is allemyghty, that wolde casten hem out of servage; and at alle tymes clepe to him for help, in tyme of nede. The tother Statute was, that alle maner of men that myghte beren Armes, scholden ben nombred: and to every 10 scholde ben a Maystre, and to every 100 a Maystre, and to every 1000 a Maystre, and to every 10000 a Maystre. Aftre he cōmanded to the Princypales of the 7 Lynages, that thei scholde leven and forsaken alle that thei hadden in Godes and Heritage; and fro thens forthe to holden hem payd, of that that he wolde zeve hem of his Grace. And thei diden so anon. Aftre he cōmanded to the Princypales of the 7 Lynages, that every of hem scholde brynge his eldest Sone before him, and with here owne handes smyten of here Hedes, with outen taryenge. And anon his Cōmandement was performed. And whan the Chane saghe, that thei made non obstacle to performen his Cōmandement, thanne he thoughte wel, that he myghte trusten in hem, and cōmanded hem anon to make hem redy, and to sewen his Banere. And aftre this, Chane putt in subieccioun alle the Londes aboute him. Aftreward it befelle upon a day, that the Cane rood with a fewe Meynee, for to beholde the strengthe of the Contree, that he had wonnen: and so befelle, that a gret multytude of his Enemyes metten with hem; and for to zeven gode ensample of hardynesse to his peeple, he was the firste that faughte, and in the myddes of his Enemyes encountred; and there he was cast from his Hors, and his Hors slayn. And whan his folk saughe him at the Erthe, thei weren alle abasscht, and wenden he had ben ded, and flowen everych one; and hire Enemyes aftre, and chaced hem: but thei wiste not, that the Emperour was there. And whan thei weren comen azen fro the Chace, thei wenten and soughten the Wodes, zif ony of hem had ben hid in the thikke of the Wodes: and manye thei founden and slowen hem anon. So it happend, that as thei wenten serchinge, toward the place that the Emperour was, thei saughe an Owle sittynge upon a Tree aboven hym; and than thei seyden amonges hem, that there was no man, be cause that thei saughe that Brid there: and so thei wenten hire wey; and thus escaped the Emperour from Dethe. And thanne he wente prevylly, alle be nyghte, tille he cam to his folk, that weren fulle glad of his comynge, and maden grete thankynges to God inmortalle, and to that Bryd, be whom here Lord was saved. And therfore princypally aboven alle Foules of World, thei worschipen the Owle: and whan thei han ony of here Fedres, thei kepen hem fulle precyously, in stede of Relykes, and beren hem upon here Hedes with gret reverence: and thei holden hem self blessed, and saf from alle periles, while that thei han hem upon hem; and therfore thei beren here Fedres upon here Hedes. Aftre alle this the Cane ordeyned him, and assembled his peple, and wente upon hem that hadden assayled hym before, and destroyed hem, and put hem in subieccioun and servage. And whan he had wonnē and putt alle the Londes and Contrees, on this half the Mount Belyan, in subieccioun, the whyte Knyght cam to him azen in his sleep, and seyde to him, Chan, the Wille of God inmortalle is, that thou passe the Mount Belyan; and thou schalt wynne the Lond, and thou schalt putten many Nacyouns in subieccioun: and for thou schalt fynde no gode passage for to go toward that Contree, go to the Mount Belyan, that is upon the See, and knele there 9 tymes toward the Est, in the Worschipe of God inmortalle; and he schal schewe the Weye to passe by. And the Chane dide so. And anon the See, that touched and was fast to the Mount, began to withdrawe him, and schewed fair weye of 9 fote brede large; and so he passed with his folk, and wan the Lond of Cathay, that is the grettest Kyngdom of the World. And for the 9 Knelynges, and for the 9 fote of Weye, the Chane and alle the men of Tartarye han the nombre of 9 in gret reverence. And therfore who that wole make the Chane ony present, be it of Hors, be it of Bryddes, or of Arwes, or Bowes, or of Frute, or of ony other thing, alweys he most make it of the nombre of 9. And so thanne ben the presentes of grettere plesance to him, and more benygnely he wil resceyven hem, than though he were presented with an 100 or 200. For hym semethe the nombre of 9 so holy, be cause the Messagre of God inmortalle devised it. Also whan the Chane of Cathay hadde wonnen the Contree of Cathay, and put in subieccioun and undre fote many Contrees abouten, he felle seek. And whan he felte wel, that he scholde dye, he seyde to his 12 Sones, that everyche of hem scholde brynge him on of his Arewes; and so thei diden anon. And thanne he cōmanded, that men scholde bynden hem to gedre, in 3 places; and than he toke hem to his eldest Sone, and bad him breke hem alle to gedre. And he enforced hem with alle his myght to breken hem: but he ne myghte not. And than the Chane bad his seconde sone to breke hem; and so schortly to alle, eche aftre other: but non of hem myght breke hem. And than he bad the Zongest Sone dissevere everyche from other, and breken everyche be him self: and so he dide. And than seyde the Chane to his eldest Sone, and to alle the othere, Wherfore myght zee not breke hem? And thei answereden, that thei myght not, be cause that thei weren bounden to gydre. And wherfore, quothe he, hathe zoure litylle zongest Brother broken hem? Because, quothe thei, that thei weren departed eche from other. And thanne seyde the Chane, My Sones, quoth he, treuly thus wil it faren be zou. For als longe as zee ben bounden to gedere, in 3 places, that is to seyne, in Love, in Trouthe and in gode Accord, no man schalle ben of powere to greve zou: but and zee ben dissevered fro theise 3 places, that zoure on helpe not zoure other, zee schulle be destroyed and brought to nought: and zif eche of zou love other, and helpe othere, zee schulle be Lordes and Sovereynes of alle othere. And whan he hadde made his Ordynances, he dyed. And thanne after hym, regned Ecchecha[a] Cane his eldest Sone. And his othere Bretheren wenten to wynnen hem many Contrees and Kyngdomes, unto the Lond of Pruysse and of Rossye, and made hem to ben cleped Chane: but thei weren alle obeyssant to hire eldre Brother; and therfore was he clept grete Chane. Aftre Ecchecha, regned Guyo[b] Chane: And aftre him, Mango[c] Chan, that was a gode Cristene man, and baptized, and zaf Let-

[a] Chicoto, E. 1; Cythato, E. 2; Cithote, E. 3; Cythoco, E. 4; Eccocha, F. 1; Ethocha, F. 2; Octochan, L. 1, 2; Ochoto, L. 3, 4.

[b] Cuno, L. 1, 2; Guican, L. 3, 4.

[c] Magnus, L. 1, 2.

tres of perpetuelle pes to alle Cristene men, and sente his Brother Halaon with gret multytude of folk, for to wynnen the Holy Lond, and for to put it in to Cristene mennes hondes, and for to destroye Machametes Lawe, and for to take the Calyphee of Baldak, that was Emperour and Lord of alle the Sarazines. And whan this Calyphee was taken, men fownden him of so highe worschipe,[d] that in alle the remenant of the World, ne myghte a man fynde a more reverent man, ne highere in worschipe. And then Halaon made him come before him, and seyde to hym: Why, quoth he, haddest thow not taken with the mo Sowdyoures, and men y nowe, for a lytille quantytee of thresour, for to defende the and thi Contree, that art so habundant of Tresore and so high in alle worschipe? And the Calyphee answerd him, For he wel trowede, that he hadde y nowe of his owne propre men. And than seyde Halaon, Thou were as a God of the Sarazines: and it is convenyent to a God, to ete no Mete, that is mortalle; and therfore thou schalt not ete, but precyous Stones, riche Perles, and Tresour, that thou lovest so moche. And then he cōmanded him to Presoun, and alle his Tresoure aboute him; and so he dyed for Hungre, and Threst. And than aftre this, Halaon wan alle the Lond of Promyssioun, and putte it in to Cristene mennes hondes. But the grete Chane his Brother dyede; and that was gret sorwe and losse to alle Cristene men.

Aftre Mango Chan, regned Coblya Chan, that

[d] Invenerunt maximam copiam Thesauri apud eum, L.

was also a Cristene man: and he regnede 42 Zeere. He founded the grete Cytee Izonge[e] in Cathay, that is a gret del more than Rome.

The tother gret Chane, that cam aftre him, becam a Payneme, and alle the other aftre him.

The Kyngdom of Cathay is the grettest Reme of the World. And also the gret Chan is the most myghty Emperour of the World, and the grettest Lord undre the Firmament; and so he clepethe him in his Lettres, right thus, *Chan, filius Dei excelsi, omnium universā Terram colentium sūmus Imperator, & Dominus omnium Dominantium*. And the Lettre of his grete Seel, writen abouten, is this, *Deus in Celo, Chan super Terram, ejus fortitudo. Omnium hominum Imperatoris sigillum*. And the Superscripcioun aboute his litylle Seel is this, *Dei Fortitudo omnium hominum. Imperatoris Sigillum*. And alle be it that thei be not cristned, zit natheles the Emperour and alle the Tarterynes beleeven in God inmortalle. And whan thei wille manacen ony man, thanne thei seyn, God knowethe wel, that I schalle do the suche a thing, and tellethe his Manace. And thus have zee herd, whi he is clept the grete Chane.

[e] Jonger, L. 1, 2; Jong, L. 3, 4. F.

Cap. XXII.

Of the governance of the grete Chanes Court, and whan he makethe solempne Festes. Of his Philosophres. And of his Array, whan he ridethe be the Contre.

Now schalle I telle zou the Governance of the Court of the grete Chane, whan he makethe solempne Festes: and that is princypally 4 tymes in the Zeer. The firste Feste is of his Byrthe: that other is of his presentacioun in here Temple, that thei clepen here Moseache,[a] where thei maken a manere of Circumcisioun: and the tother 2 Festes ben of his Ydoles. The firste Feste of the Ydole is, whan he is first put in to hire Temple and throned. The tother Feste is, whan the Ydole begynnethe first to speke or to worche Myracles. Mo ben there not of solempne Festes, but zif he marye ony of his Children. Now undirstondethe, that at every of theise Festes, he hathe gret multytude of peple, well ordeyned and wel arrayed, be thousandes, be hundredes and be tenthes. And every man knowethe wel, what servyse he schalle do. And every man zevethe so gode hede and so gode attendance to his servyse, that no man fyndethe no defaute. And there ben first ordeyned 4000 Baronnes myghty and riche, for to governe and to make ordynance for the Feste, and for to

[a] Moyseac, L. 1, 2; Mosseak, F. 2.

serve the Emperour. And theise solempne Festes ben made with outen, in Hales and Tentes made of Clothes of Gold and of Tartaries, fulle nobely. And alle tho Barouns han Crounes of Gold upon hire Hedes, fulle noble and riche, fulle of precious Stones and grete Perles oryent. And thei ben alle clothed in Clothes of Gold or of Tartaries or of Camokas, so richely and so perfytly, that no man in the World can amenden it, ne better devisen it. And alle tho Robes ben orfrayed alle abouten, and dubbed fulle of precious Stones and of grete oryent Perles, fulle richely. And thei may wel do so: for Clothes of Gold and of Sylk ben gretter chep there a gret del, than ben Clothes of Wolle. And theise 4000 Barouns ben devised in 4 Companyes: and every thousand is clothed in Clothes alle of o colour; and that so wel arrayed and so richely, that it is marveyle to beholde. The firste thousand, that is of Dukes, of Erles, of Marquyses and of Amyralles, alle clothed in Clothes of Gold, with Tysseux of grene Silk, and bordured with Gold, fulle of preciouse Stones, in maner as I have seyd before. The secounde thousand is alle clothed in Clothes dyapred of red Silk, alle wroughte with Gold, and the Orfrayes sett fulle of gret Perl and precious Stones, fulle nobely wroughte. The 3 thousand is clothed in Clothes of Silk, of Purpre or of Ynde. And the 4 thousand is in Clothes of zalow. And alle hire Clothes ben so nobely and so richely wroughte with Gold and precious Stones and riche Perles, that zif a man of this Contree hadde but only on of hire Robes, he myghte wel seye, that he scholde nevere be pore. For the Gold and the precious Stones and the grete oryent Perles ben of gretter value, on this half the See, than thei ben bezond the See, in tho Contrees. And whan thei ben thus apparaylled, thei gon 2 and 2 togedre, fulle ordynatly before the Emperour, with outen speche of ony Woord, saf only enclynynge to him. And everyche of hem berethe a Tablett of Jaspere or of Ivory or of Cristalle; and the Mynstralle goynge before hem, sownyng here Instrumentes of dyverse melodye. And whan the firste thousand is thus passed, and hathe made his Mostre, he withdrawethe him on that o syde. And than entrethe that other secunde thousand, and dothe right so, in the same manere of array and contenance, as did the firste; and aftre the thridde, and than the fourthe; and non of hem seythe not o Word. And at o syde of the Emperours Table, sitten many Philosofres, that ben preved for wise men, in many dyverse Scyences; as of Astronomye, Nigromancye, Geomancye, Pyromancye, Ydromancye, of Augurye and of many other Scyences. And everyche of hem han before hem Astrolabres of Gold; sum Speres, sūme the Brayn Panne of a ded man, sūme Vesselles of Gold fulle of Gravelle or Sond, sūme Vesselles of Gold fulle of Coles brennynge, sūme Vesselle of Gold fulle of Watre and of Wyn and of Oyle, and sūme Oriloges of Gold, mad ful nobely and richely wroughte, and many other maner of Instrumentes aftre hire Sciences. And at certeyn houres, whan hem thinkethe time, thei seyn to certeyn Officeres, that stonden before hem, ordeynd for the tyme, to fulfille hire cōmaundementes, Makethe Pees. And than seyn the Officeres, Now Pees lystenethe.

And aftre that, seyth another of the Philosophres, Every man do Reverence, and enclyne to the Emperour, that is Goddes Sone and Soverayn Lord of alle the World; for now is tyme. And thanne every man bowethe his Hed toward the Erthe. And thanne cōmandethe the same Philosophre azen, Stondethe up. And thei don so. And at another hour, seythe another Philosophre, Puttethe zoure litille fynger in zoure Eres. And anon thei don so. And at another hour, seythe another Philosophre, Puttethe zoure Honde before zoure Mouthe. And anon thei don so. And at another hour, seithe another Philosophre, Puttethe zoure Honde upon zoure Hede. And aftre that, he byddethe hem to don here hond a wey; and thei don so. And so from hour to hour, thei cōmanden certeyn thinges. And thei seyn, that tho thinges han dyverse significaciouns. And I asked hem prevyly, what tho thinges betokened. And on of the Maistres told me, that the bowynge of the Hed at that hour betokened this, that alle tho that boweden here Hedes, scholden evere more aftre ben obeyssant and trewe to the Emperour; and nevere for ziftes, ne for promys in no kynde, ben fals ne Traytour unto him for gode ne evylle. And the puttynge of the litylle fynger in the Ere, betokenethe, as thei seyn, that none of hem ne schalle not here speke no contrarious thing to the Emperour, but that he schalle telle it anon to his Conseille, or discovere it to sum men that wille make relacioun to the Emperour; thoughe he were his Fadre or Brother or Sone. And so forthe of alle other thinges, that is don be the Philosophres, thei tolde me the Causes of many dyverse thinges. And trustethe righte wel in certeyn, that no man dothe no thing to the Emperour, that belongethe unto him, nouther Clothinge, ne Bred, ne Wyn, ne Bathe, ne non other thing, that longethe to hym, but at certeyn houres, that his Philosophres wille devysen. And zif there falle Werre in ony syde to the Emperour, anon the Philosophres comen, and seyn here avys aftre her calculaciouns, and conseylen the Emperour of here avys, be here sciences; so that the Emperour dothe no thing with outen here conseille. And whan the Philosophres han don and perfourmed here Cōmandementes, thanne the Mynstralle begynnen to don here Mynstralcye, everyche in hire Instrumentes, eche aftre other, with alle the melodye, that thei can devyse. And whan thei han done a gode while, on of the Officeres of the Emperour gothe up on an highe Stage wroughte fulle curyously, and cryethe and seythe with lowde voys, Makethe Pees. And than every man is stille. And thanne anon aftre, alle the Lordes, that ben of the Emperoures Lynage, nobely arrayed in riche Clothes of Gold, and ryally apparayled on white Stedes, als manye as may wel sewen hem at that tyme, ben redy to maken here presentes to the Emperour. And than seythe the Styward of the Court to the Lordes be name, N. of N. and nempnethe first the most enoble and the worthieste be name, and seythe, Be zee redy with suche a nombre of white Hors, for to serve the Emperour, zoure Sovereyn Lord. And to another Lord, he seythe, N. of N. be zee redy with suche a nombre, to serve zoure sovereyn Lord. And to another, right so. And to alle the Lordes of the Emperoures Lynage, eche aftre other, as thei ben of Estate. And whan thei ben alle cleped, thei entren eche after other, and presentenen the white Hors to the Emperour; and than gon hire wey. And than aftre, alle the other Barouns every of hem zeven hem presentes, or Juelle, or sum other thing, aftre that thei ben of Estate. And than aftre hem, alle the Prelates of hire Lawe, and religiouse men and other; and every man zevethe him sum thing. And whan that alle men han thus presented the Emperour, the grettest of dignytee of the Prelates zevethe hem a Blessynge, seyenge an Orisoun of hire Lawe. And than begynnen the Mynstrelle to maken hire Mynstralcye, in dyverse Instrumentes, with alle the melodye that thei can devyse. And whan thei han don hire craft, than thei bryngen before the Emperour, Lyouns, Libardes and other dyverse Bestes; and Egles and Veutours, and other dyverse Foules; and Fissches, and Serpentes; for to don him reverence. And than comen Jogulours and Enchauntoures, that don many marvaylles: for thei maken to come in the Ayr, the Sonne and the Mone, be semynge, to every mannes sight. And aftre thei maken the nyght so derk, that no man may see no thing. And aftre thei maken the Day to come azen, fair and plesant with bright Sonne, to every mannes sight. And than thei bryngen in Daunces of the faireste Damyselles of the World, and richest arrayed. And aftre thei maken to comen in, other Damyselles, bryngynge Coupes of Gold, fulle of Mylk of dyverse Bestes, and zeven drynke to Lordes and to Ladyes. And than thei make

Knyghtes to jousten in Armes fulle lustyly; and thei rennen to gidre a gret randoum; and thei frusschen to gidere fulle fiercely; and thei breken here speres so rudely, that the Tronchouns flen in sprotes and peces alle aboute the Halle. And than thei make to come in huntyng, for the Hert and for the Boor, with Houndes rennynge with open Mouthe. And many other thinges thei don, be craft of hire Enchauntementes; that it is marveyle for to see. And suche pleyes of desport thei make, til the takynge up of the Boordes.

This gret Chan hathe fulle gret peple for to serve him, as I have told zou before. For he hathe of Mynstralles the Nombre of 13 Cumanez: but thei abyde not alle weys with hym. For alle the Mynstrelle that comen before hym, of what nacyoun that thei ben of, thei ben withholden with him, as of his Houshold, and entred in his Bokes, as for his owne men. And aftre that, where that evere thei gon, ever more thei cleymen for Mynstralle of the grete Chane: and undre that tytle, alle Kynges and Lordes, cherisschen hem the more with Ziftes and alle thing. And therefore he hathe so gret multytude of hem. And he hathe of certeyn men, as thoughe thei were Zomen, that kepen Bryddes, as Ostrycches, Gerfacouns, Sparehaukes, Faukons gentyls, Lanyeres, Sacres, Sacrettes, Papyngayes wel spekynge, and Briddes syngynge. And also of wylde Bestes, as of Olifauntz, tame and othere, Babewynes, Apes, Marmesettes, and othere dyverse Bestes; the mountance of 15 Cumanez of Zomen. And of Phisicyens Cristene, he hathe 200. And of Leches, that ben Cristene, he hathe 210. And of Leches and Phisicyens, that ben Sarrazines 20 : but he trustethe more in the Cristene Leches, than in the Sarazines. And his other comoun Houshold is with outen nombre: and thei alle han alle necessaries, and alle that hem nedethe, of the Emperoures Court. And he hathe in his Court many Barouns, as Servytoures, that ben Cristene and converted to gode Feythe, be the prechynge of religiouse Cristen men, that duellen with him : but there ben manye mo, that wil not, that men knowen that thei ben Cristene.

This Emperour may dispenden als moche as he wile, with outen estymacioun. For he despendethe not, ne makethe no Money, but of Lether emprented, or of Papyre. And of that Moneye, is som of gretter Prys, and som of lasse prys, aftre the dyversitee of his Statutes. And whan that Money hathe ronne so longe, that it begynnethe to waste, than men beren it to the Emperoures Tresorye: and than thei taken newe Money for the olde. And that Money gothe thorghe out alle the Contree, and thorghe out alle his Provynces. For there and bezonde hem, thei make no Money nouther of Gold nor of Sylver. And therfore he may despende y now, and outrageously. And of Gold and Sylver, that men beren in his Contree, he makethe Cylours, Pyleres and Paumentes in his Palays, and other dyverse thinges, what him lykethe. This Emperour hathe in his Chambre, in on of the Pyleres of Gold, a Rubye and a Charboncle of half a fote long, that in the nyght zevethe so gret clartee and schynynge, that it is als light as day. And he hathe many other precyous

Stones, and many other Rubyes and Charboncles: but tho ben the grettest and the moste precyous.

This Emperour duellethe in Somer in a Cytee, that is toward the Northe, that is cleped Saduz: and there is cold y now. And in Wyntre, he duellethe in a Cytee, that is clept Camaaleche: and that is an hote Contree. But the Contree, where he duellethe in most comounly, is in Gaydo or in Jong, that is a gode Contree and a tempree, aftre that the Contree is there: but to men of this Contree, it were to passyng hoot. And whan this Emperour wille ryde from o Contree to another, he ordeynethe 4 Hostes of his folk; of the whiche, the firste Hoost gothe before him, a dayes journeye. For that Hoost schalle ben logged the nyght, where the Emperour schalle lygge upon the Morwe. And there schalle every man have alle maner of Vytaylle and necessaryes, that ben nedefulle, of the Emperoures costages. And in this firste Hoost is the nombre of poeple 50 Cumaunez; what of Hors, what of Fote: of the whiche, every Cumanez amounten to 10000, as I have told zou before. And another Hoost gothe in the right syde of the Emperour, nygh half a iourneye fro him. And another gothe on the left syde of him, in the same wise. And in every Hoost, is as moche multytude of peple, as in the first Hoost. And thanne aftre comethe the 4 Hoost, that is moche more than ony of the othere, and that gothe behynden him, the mountance of a Bowe draught. And every Hoost hathe his iourneyes ordeyned in certeyn places, where thei schulle be logged at nyght: and there thei schulle have alle, that hem nedethe. And zif it befalle, that ony of the Hoost dye, anon thei putten another in his place; so that the nombre schal evere more ben hool. And zee schulle undirstonde, that the Emperour, in his propre persone, rydethe not as othere gret Lordes don bezonde; but zif him liste to go prevyly with fewe men, for to ben unknowen. And elle he rytt in a Charett with 4 Wheles, upon the whiche is made a faire Chambre; and it is made of a certeyn Wode, that comethe out of Paradys terrestre, that men clepen Lignum Aloes, that the Flodes of Paradys bryngen out at dyverse cesouns, as I have told zou here beforn. And this Chambre is fulle wel smellynge, be cause of the Wode, that it is made offe. And alle this Chambre is covered with inne of Plate of fyn Gold, dubbed with precious Stones and grete Perles. And 4 Olifauntz and 4 grete Destreres[b] alle white, and covered with riche covertoures ledynge the Chariot. And 4 or 5 or 6 of the grettest Lordes ryden aboute this Charyot, fulle richely arrayed and fulle nobely; so that no man schalle neyghe the Charyot, but only tho Lordes, but zif that the Emperour calle ony man to him, that him list to speke with alle. And above the Chambre of this Chariot, that the Emperour sittethe inne, ben sett upon a Perche 4 or 5 or 6 Gerfacouns;[c] to that entent, that whan the Emperour seethe ony wylde foul, that he may take it at his owne list, and have the desport and the pley of the flight; first with on, and aftre with another:

[b] Dextrarii, L.; Dromadayrs, F. 2; Stedes, E. 1, 2, 3; Oxen, E. 4.
[c] Griffones, L.

and so he takethe his desport passynge be the Contree. And no man rydethe before him, of his Companye; but alle aftre him. And no man dar not come nyghe the Chariot, by a Bowe draught, but tho Lordes only, that ben aboute him: and alle the Hoost cometh fayrely aftre him, in gret multitude. And also suche another Charyot, with suche Hoostes, ordeynd and arrayd, gon with the Empresse, upon another syde, everyche be him self, with 4 Hoostes, right as the Emperour dide; but not with so gret multytude of peple. And his eldest sone gothe be another weye in another Chariot, in the same manere. So that there is betwene hem so gret multitude of folk, that it is marveyle to telle it. And no man scholde trowe the nombre, but he had seen it. And sum tyme it happethe, that whan he wil not go fer; and that it lyke him to have the Emperesse and his Children with him; than thei gon alle to gydere; and here folk ben alle medled in fere,[d] and devyded in 4 parties only.

And zee schulle undirstonde, that the Empire of this gret Chane is devyded in 12 Provynces; and every Provynce hathe mo than 2000 Cytees; and of Townes with outen nombre. This Contree is fulle gret. For it hathe 12 pryncypalle Kynges, in 12 Provynces. And every of tho Kynges han many Kynges undre hem; and alle thei ben obeyssant to the gret Chane. And his Lond and his Lordschipe durethe so ferre, that a man may not gon from on Hed to another, nouther be See ne Lond, the space of 7 Zeer. And thorghe the Desertes of his Lordschipe, there as men may

[d] *Medled in fere*, permixti.

fynde no Townes, there ben Innes ordeyned be every iorneye, to resceyve bothe Man and Hors; in the whiche thei schalle fynde plentee of Vytaylle, and of alle thing, that hem nedethe, for to go be the Contree.

And there is a marveylouse custom in that Contree, (but is profitable) that zif ony contrarious thing, that scholde ben preiudice or grevance to the Emperour, in ony kynde, anon the Emperour hathe tydynges there of and fulle knowleche in a day, thoughe it be 3 or 4 iorneys fro him or more. For his Ambassedours taken here Dromedaries or hire Hors, and thei priken in alle that evere thei may toward on of the Innes: and whan thei comen there, anon thei blowen an Horne; and anon thei of the In knowen wel y now, that there ben tydynges to warnen the Emperour of sum rebellyoun azenst him. And thanne anon thei maken other men redy, in alle haste that thei may, to beren Lettres, and pryken in alle that evere thei may, tille thei come to the other Innes with here Lettres: and thanne thei maken fressche men redy, to pryke forthe with the Lettres, toward the Emperour; whille that the laste bryngere reste him, and bayte his Dromedarie or his Hors. And so fro In to In, tille it come to the Emperour. And thus anon hathe he hasty tydynges of ony thing, that berethe charge, be his Corrours, that rennen so hastyly, thorghe out alle the Contree. And also whan the Emperour sendethe his Corrours hastyly, thorghe out his Lond, everyche of hem hathe a large thong fulle of smale Belles; and whan thei neyghen nere to the Innes of other Corroures, that ben also ordeyned be the iorneyes, thei ryngen here Belles, and anon the other Corrours maken hem redy, and rennen here weye unto another In: and thus rennethe on to other, fulle spedyly and swyftly, till the Emperours entent be served, in alle haste. And theise Currours ben clept Chydydo,[e] aftre here Langage, that is to seye, a Messagere.

Also whan the Emperour gothe from o Contree to another, as I have told zou here before, and he passe thorghe Cytees and Townes, every man makethe a Fuyr before his Dore, and puttethe there inne Pouder of gode Gommes, that ben swete smellynge, for to make gode savour to the Emperour. And alle the peple knelethe doun azenst him, and don him gret reverence. And there where religyouse Cristene men dwellen, as thei don in many Cytees in thei Lond, thei gon before him with processioun with Cros and Holy Watre; and thei seyngen, *Veni Creator, Spiritus*, with an highe Voys, and gon towardes him. And whan he herethe hem, he cōmaundethe to his Lordes to ryde besyde him, that the religiouse men may come to him. And whan thei ben nyghe him, with the Cros, thanne he dothe a down his Galaothe,[f] that syt upon his Hede, in manere of a Chapelet, that is made of Gold and preciouse Stone and grete Perles. And it is so ryche, that men preysen it to the value of a Roialme, in that Contre. And than he knelethe to the Cros. And than the Prelate of the religiouse men seythe before him certeyn Orisouns, and zevethe him a Blessynge with the Cros: and he enclynethe to the Blessynge fulle devoutly. And thanne the

[e] Chipide, L.   [f] Galiotam, L.

Prelate zevethe him sum maner Frute, to the nombre of 9, in a Platere of Sylver, with Peres or Apples or other manere Frute. And he takethe on ; and than men zeven to the othere Lordes, that ben aboute him. For the custom is suche, that no Straungere schalle come before him, but zif he zeve hym sum manere thing, aftre the olde Lawe, that seythe, *Nemo accedat in conspectu meo vacuus.* And thanne the Emperour seythe to the religious men, that thei withdrawe hem azen, that thei ne be hurt ne harmed of the gret multytude of Hors, that comen behynde him. And also in the same maner don the religious men, that dwellen there, to the Emperesses, that passen by hem, and to his eldest Sone; and to every of hem, thei presenten Frute.

And zee schulle undirstonde, that the poeple, that he hathe so many hostes offe, abouten hym and aboute his Wyfes and his Sone, thei dwelle not contynuelle with him : but alle weys, whan him lykethe, thei ben sent fore; and aftre whan thei han don, thei retournen to hire owne Housholdes; saf only thei that ben dwellynge with hym in Houshold, for to serven him and his Wyfes and his Sones, for to governen his Houshold. And alle be it, that the othere ben departed fro him, aftre that thei han perfourmed hire Servyse, zit there abydethe contynuelly with him in Court, 50000 Men at Horse, and 200000 Men a Fote; with outen Mynstrelles, and tho that kepen wylde Bestes and dyverse Briddes, of the whiche I have tolde zou the nombre before.

Undre the Firmament, is not so gret a Lord, ne so myghty, ne so riche, as the grete Chane:

Nought Prestre Johan, that is Emperour of the highe Ynde, ne the Sowdan of Babylone, ne the Emperour of Persye. Alle theise ne ben not in comparisoun to the grete Chane; nouther of Myght, ne of Noblesse, ne of Ryaltee, ne of Richesse: For in alle theise, he passethe alle erthely Princes. Wherfore it is gret harm, that he belevethe not feithefully in God. And natheles he wil gladly here speke of God; and he suffrethe wel, that Cristene men duelle in his Lordschipe, and that men of his Feythe ben made Cristene men, zif thei wile, thorghe out alle his Contree. For he defendethe no man to holde no Lawe, other than him lykethe.

In that Contree, sum man hathe an 100 Wyfes, sūme 60, sūme mo, sūme lesse. And thei taken the nexte of hire Kyn, to hire Wyfes, saf only, that thei out taken hire Modres, hire Doughtres, and hire Sustres of the Modre syde: but hire Sustres on the Fadir syde, of another Wōman, thei may wel take; and hire Bretheres Wyfes also aftre here Dethe; and here Step modres also in the same wyse.

Cap. XXIII.

Of the Lawe and the Customs of the Tartarienes, duellynge in Chatay; and how that men don, whan the Emperour schal dye, and how he schal be chosen.

THE folk of that Contree usen alle longe Clothes, with outen Furroures.[a] And thei ben clothed with precious Clothes of Tartarye, and of Clothes of Gold. And here Clothes ben slytt at the syde; and thei ben festned with Laces of Silk. And thei clothen hem also with Pylches, and the Hyde with outen.[b] And thei usen nouther Cappe ne Hood. And in the same maner as the men gon, the wōmen gon; so that no man may unethe knowe the men fro the Wōmen, saf only tho wōmen, that ben maryed, that beren the tokne upon hire Hedes of a mannes Foot, in signe that thei ben undre mannes fote and undre subieccioun of man. And here Wyfes ne dwelle not to gydere, but every of hem be hire self. And the Husbonde may ligge with whom of hem, that him lykethe. Everyche hathe his Hous, bothe man and wōman. And here Houses ben made rounde of Staves; and it hathe a rounde Wyndowe aboven, that zevethe hem light, and also that servethe for delyverance of Smoke. And the Helynge of here Houses, and the Wowes and the Dores ben alle of Wode.

[a] Pellura, L.
[b] Habent et Pelliceas, quibus utuntur ex transversis, L.; Et vestent des Pellices, le Peil dehors, F.

And whan thei gon to Werre, thei leiden hire Houses with hem upon Chariottes; as men don Tentes or Pavyllouns. And thei maken hire Fuyr, in the myddes of hire Houses. And thei han gret multytude of alle maner of Bestes, saf only of Swyn: for thei bryngen non forthe.[c] And thei beleeven wel, o God, that made and formede alle thinges. And natheles zit han thei Ydoles of Gold and Sylver, and of Tree, and of Clothe. And to tho Ydoles, thei offren alle weys hyre first Mylk of hire Bestes, and also of hire Metes, and of hire Drynkes, before thei eten. And thei offren often tymes Hors and Bestes. And thei clepen the God of Kynde,[d] Yroga. And hire Emperour also, what name that evere he have, thei putten evermore therto Chane. And whan I was there, hire Emperour had to name Thiaut; so that he was clept Thiaut Chane. And his eldeste Sone was clept Tossue. And whañe he schalle ben Emperour, he schalle ben clept Tossue Chane. And at that tyme, the Emperour hadde 12 Sones, with outen him; that were named, Cuncy, Ordii, Chahaday, Buryn, Negu, Nocab, Cadu, Siban, Cuten, Balacy, Babylan and Garegan. And of his 3 Wyfes, the firste and the pryncypalle, that was Prestre Johnes Doughtre, hadde to name Serioche Chan; and the tother Borak Chan; and the tother Karanke Chan.

The folk of that Contree begynnen alle hire thinges in the newe Mone: and thei worschipen moche the Mone and the Sonne, and often tyme knelen azenst hem. And alle the folk of the Contree ryden comounly with outen Spores: but

[c] Quia non nutriunt eos, L.   [d] Nature.

thei beren alle weys a lytille Whippe in hire Hondes, for to chacen with hire Hors. And thei han gret Conscience, and holden it for a gret Synne, to casten a Knyf in the Fuyr, and for to drawe Flessche out of a Pot with a Knyf, and for to smyte an Hors with the handille of a Whippe, or to smyte an Hors with a Brydille, or to breke o Bon with another, or for to caste Mylk or ony Lykour, that men may drynke, upon the Erthe, or for to take and sle lytil Children. And the moste Synne, that ony man may do, is to pissen in hire Houses, that thei dwellen in. And who so that may be founden with that Synne, sykerly thei slen hym. And of everyche of theise Synnes, it behovethe hem to ben schryven of hire Prestes, and to paye gret Sōme of Silver for hire Penance. And it behovethe also, that the place, that men han pissed in, be halewed azen; and elles dar no man entren there inne. And whan thei han payed hire Penance, men maken hem passen thorghe a Fuyr or thorghe 2, for to clensen hem of hire Synnes. And also whan ony Messangere comethe and bryngethe Lettres or ony present to the Emperour, it behovethe him, that he with the thing that he bryngethe, passe thorghe 2 brennynge Fuyres, for to purgen hem, that he brynge no Poysoun ne Venym, ne no wykked thing, that myght be grevance to the Lord. And also, zif ony man or wōman be taken in Avowtery or Fornycacyoun, anon thei sleen him. Men of that Contree ben alle gode Archeres, and schooten righte welle, bothe men and women, als wel on Hors bak, prykynge, as on Fote, rennynge. And the Wōmen maken alle thinges and alle maner Mysteres and

Craftes; as of Clothes, Botes and other thinges; and thei dryven Cartes, Plowes and Waynes and Chariottes: and thei maken Houses and alle maner Mysteres, out taken Bowes and Arwes and Armures, that men maken. And alle the Wōmen weren Breech, as wel as men. Alle the folk of that Contree ben fulle obeyssant to hire Sovereynes; ne thei fighten not ne chiden not, on with another. And there ben nouther Thefes ne Robboures in that Contree; and every man worschipethe other: but no man there dothe no reverence to no Straungeres, but zif thei ben grete Princes. And thei eten Houndes, Lyounes, Lyberdes, Mares and Foles, Asses, Rattes and Mees, and alle maner of Bestes, grete and smale; saf only Swyn, and Bestes that weren defended by the olde Lawe. And thei eten alle the Bestes, with outen and with inne, with outen castynge awey of ony thing, saf only the filthe. And thei eten but litille Bred, but zif it be in Courtes of grete Lordes. And thei have not, in many places, nouther Pesen ne Benes, ne non other Potages, but the Brothe of the Flessche. For littille ete thei ony thing, but Flessche and the Brothe. And whan thei han eten, thei wypen hire Hondes upon hire Skirtes: for thei use non Naperye, ne Towaylles, but zif it be before grete Lordes: but the comoun peple hathe none. And whan thei han eten, thei putten hire Dissches unwasschen in to the Pot or Cawdroun, with remenant of the Flessche and of the Brothe, til thei wole eten azen. And the ryche men drynken Mylk of Mares or of Camaylles or of Asses or of other Bestes. And thei wil ben lightly dronken of Mylk, or of another Drynk, that is made of Hony and of Watre soden to gidre. For in that Contree is nouther Wyn ne Ale. Thei lyven fulle wrecched liche; and thei eten but ones in the day, and that but lytille, nouther in Courtes ne in other places. And in soothe, o man allone in this Contree wil ete more in a day, than on of hem wil ete in 3 dayes. And zif ony straunge Messagre come there to a Lord, men maken him to ete but ones a day, and that fulle litille.

And whan thei werren, thei werren fulle wisely, and alle weys don here besynes, to destroyen hire enemyes. Every man there berethe 2 Bowes or 3, and of Arwes gret plentee, and a gret Ax. And the Gentyles han schorte Speres and large, and fulle trenchant on that o syde: and thei han Plates and Helmes, made of Quyrboylle;[e] and hire Hors covertoures of the same. And who so fleethe fro the Batuyle, thei sle him. And whan thei holden ony Sege abouten Castelle or Toun, that is walled and defensable, thei behoten to hem that ben with inne, to don alle the profite and gode, that it is marveylle to here: and thei graunten also to hem that ben with inne, alle that thei wille asken hem. And aftre that thei ben zolden, anon thei sleen hem alle, and kutten of hire Eres, and sowcen hem in Vynegre, and there of thei maken gret servyse for Lordes. Alle here lust and alle here Ymaginacioun, is for to putten alle Londes undre hire subieccioun. And thei seyn, that thei knowen wel be hire prophecyes, that thei schulle ben overcomen by Archieres, and be strengthe of hem: but they knowe not of what nacioun, ne of what Lawe

[e] Corio bullito, L.

thei schulle ben offe, that schulle overcomen hem. And therfore thei suffren, that folk of alle Lawes may peysibely duellen amonges hem.

Also whan thei wille make hire Ydoles, or an Ymage of ony of hire Frendes, for to have remembrance of hym, thei maken alle weys the Ymage alle naked, with outen ony maner of Clothinge. For thei seyn, that in gode love scholde be no coverynge, that man scholde not love for the faire Clothinge, ne for the riche aray, but only for the body, suche as God hathe made it, and for the gode vertues that the body is endowed with of nature; not only for fair Clothinge, that is not of kyndely nature.

And zee schulle undirstonde, that it is gret drede for to pursue the Tartarines, zif thei fleen in Bataylle. For in fleynge, thei schooten behynden hem, and sleen bothe men and Hors. And whan thei wil fighte, thei wille schokken hem to gidre in a plomp;[e] that zif there be 20000 men, men schalle not wenen, that there be scant 10000. And thei cone wel wynnen lond of Straungeres, but thei cone not kepen it. For thei han grettre lust to lye in Tentes with outen, than for to lye in Castelle or in Townes. And thei preysen no thing the wytt of other naciouns. And amonges hem, Oyle of Olyve is fulle dere: for thei holden it for fulle noble medicyne. And alle the Tartarienes han smale Eyen and litille of Berd, and not thikke hered, but schiere.[f] And thei ben false and traytoures: and thei lasten noghte that thei behoten.[g]

[e] Incedunt pariter, L.   [f] Clare, L.
[g] Et nihil servant quod promittunt, L.

Thei ben fulle harde folk, and moche peyne and wo mow suffren and disese, more than ony other folk: for thei ben taughte therto in hire owne Contree, of Zouthe: and therfore thei spenden, as who seythe, right nought.

And whan ony man schalle dye, men setten a spere besyde him: and whan he drawethe towardes the dethe, every man fleethe out of the Hous, tille he be ded; and aftre that, thei buryen him in the Feldes. And whan the Emperour dyethe, men setten him in a Chayere in myddes the place of his Tent: and men setten a Table before him clene, covered with a clothe, and there upon Flesche and dyverse vyaundes, and a Cuppe fulle of Mares mylk. And men putten a Mare besyde him, with hire Fole, and an Hors sadeled and brydeled; and thei leyn upon the Hors Gold and Silver gret quantytee: and thei putten abouten him gret plentee of Stree: and than men maken a gret pytt and a large; and with the Tent and alle theise other thinges, thei putten him in Erthe. And thei seyn, that whan he schalle come in to another World, he schalle not ben with outen an Hows, ne with owten Hors, ne with outen Gold and Sylver: and the Mare schalle zeven him mylk, and bryngen him forthe mo Hors, tille he be wel stored in the tother World. For thei trowen, that aftre hire Dethe, thei schulle be etynge and drynkynge in that other World, and solacynge hem with hire Wifes, as thei diden here. And aftre tyme, that the Emperour is thus entered, no man schalle be so hardy to speke of him before his Frendes. And zit natheles som-

tyme fallethe of manye, that thei maken hem to
ben entered prevylly be nyghte, in wylde places,
and putten azen the Grasse over the Pytt, for to
growe: or elle men coveren the Pytt with Gravelle and Sond, that no man schalle perceyve
where, ne knowe where the Pytt is, to that entent,
that never aftre, none of his Frendes schulle han
mynde ne remembrance of him. And thanne thei
seyn, that he is ravissht in to another world,
where he is a grettre Lord, than he was here.
And thanne aftre the dethe of the Emperour, the
7 Lynages assemblen hem to gidere, and chesen
his eldest Sone, or the nexte aftre him, of his
Blood: and thus thei seye to him; Wee wolen
and wee preyen and ordeynen, that zee ben oure
Lord and oure Emperour. And thanne he an-
swerethe, Zif zee wile, that I regne over zou, as
Lord, do everyche of zou, that I schalle cōmanden
him, outher to abyde or to go; and whom soever
that I cōmaunde to ben slayn, that anon he be
slayn. And thei answeren alle with o voys, What
so evere zee cōmanden, it schalle be don. Thanne
seythe the Emperour, Now undirstondethe wel,
that my woord from hens forthe, is scharp and
bytynge as a Swerd. After men setten him upon
a blak Stede, and so men bryngen him to a
Cheyere fulle richely arrayed, and there thei
crownen hym. And thanne alle the Cytees and
gode Townes senden hym ryche presentes; so
that at that iourneye, he schalle have more than
60 Chariottes charged with Gold and Sylver, with
outen Jewelles of Gold and precyouse Stones, that
Lordes zeven hym, that ben withouten estyma-

cioun: and with outen Hors and Clothes of Gold and of Camakaas and Tartarynes, that ben with outen nombre.

Cap. XXIV.

Of the Roialme of Thurse and the Londes and Kyngdomes towardes the Septentrionale parties, in comynge down from the Lond of Cathay.

THIS Lond of Cathay is in Asye the depe. And aftre, on this half, is Asye the more. The Kyngdom of Cathay marchethe toward the West, unto the Kyngdom of Tharse; the whiche was on of the Kinges, that cam to presente our Lord in Betheleem. And thei that ben of the Lynage of that Kyng, arn sōme Cristene. In Tharse, thei eten no Flessche, ne thei drynken no Wyn. And on this half, towardes the West, is the Kyngdom of Turquesten, that strecchethe him toward the West, to the Kyngdom of Persie; and toward the Septrentionalle, to the Kyngdom of Chorasme. In the contre of Turquesten, ben but fewe gode Cytees: but the beste Cytee of that Lond highte Octorar. There ben grete Pastures; but fewe Coornes; and therfore, for the most partie, thei ben alle Herdemen: and thei lyzn in Tentes, and thei drynken a maner Ale, made of Hony.

And aftre, on this half, is the Kyngdom of Chorasme, that is a gode lond and a plentevous, with outen Wyn. And it hathe a Desert toward the Est, that lastethe more than an 100 iourneyes.

And the beste Cytee of that Contree is clept Chorasme. And of that Cytee, berethe the Contree his name. The folk of that Contree ben hardy Werryoures. And on this half is the Kyngdom of Comanye, where of the Comayns that dwelleden in Grece, somtyme weren chaced out. This is on of the grettest Kyngdomes of the World: but it is not alle enhabyted. For at on of the parties, there is so gret cold, that no man may dwelle there: and in another partie, there is so gret hete, that no man may endure it. And also there ben so many Flyes, that no man may knowe on what syde he may turne him. In that Contree is but lytille Arberye, ne Trees that beren Frute, ne othere. Thei lyzn in Tentes. And thei brennen the dong of Bestes, for defaute of Wode.

This Kyngdom descendeth on this half toward us, and toward Pruysse, and toward Rossye. And thorghe that Contree rennethe the Ryvere of Ethille, that is on of the grettest Ryveres of the World. And it fresethe so strongly alle Zeres, that many tymes men han foughten upon the Ise with grete hostes, bothe parties on fote, and hire Hors voyded for the tyme: and what on Hors and on Fote, mo than 200000 persones on every syde. And betweene that Ryvere and the grete See Occean, that thei clepen the See Maure, lyzn alle theise Roialmes. And toward the hede benethe in that Roialme, is the mount Chotaz, that is the hiest mount of the world: and it is betwene the See Maure and the See Caspy. There is fulle streyt and dangerous passage, for to go toward Ynde. And therfore Kyng Alysandre leet make there a strong Cytee, that men clepen Alizandre, for to kepe the Contree, that no man scholde passe with outen his leve. And now men clepen that Cytee, the Zate of Helle. And the princypalle Cytee of Comenye is clept Sarak, that is on of the 3 Weyes for to go in to Ynde : but be the Weye, ne may not passe no gret multytude of peple, but zif it be in Wyntre. And that passage men clepen the Derbent. The tother weye is for to go fro the Cytee of Turquesten, be Persie : and be that Weye, ben manye iourneyes be Desert. And the thridde Weye is that comethe fro Comanye, and than to go be the grete See and be the Kyngdom of Abchaz.

And zee schulle undirstonde, that alle theise Kyngdomes and alle theise Londes aboveseyd, unto Pruysse and to Rossye, ben alle obeyssant to the grete Chane of Cathay ; and many othere Contrees, that marchen to other Costes. Wherfore his powere and his Lordschipe is fulle gret, and fulle myghty.

Cap. XXV.

Of the Emperour of Persye, and of the lond of derknesse and of other Kyngdomes, that belongen to the grete Chane of Cathay, and other Londes of his, unto the See of Greece.

Now sithe I have devysed zou the londes and the Kyngdoms toward the parties septentrionales, in comynge down from the lond of Cathay, unto the londes of the Cristene, towardes Pruysse and

Rossye; now schalle I devyse zou of other londes and Kyngdomes, comynge doun be other Costes, toward the right syde, unto the See of Grece, toward the lond of Cristene men: and therfore that, aftre Ynde and aftre Cathay, the Emperour of Persie is the gretteste Lord. Therfore I schalle telle zou of the Kyngdom of Persie. First, where he hathe 2 Kyngdomes; the firste Kyngdom begynnethe toward the Est, toward the Kyngdom of Turquesten, and it strecchethe toward the West, unto the Ryvere of Phison, that is on of the 4 Ryveres, that comen out of Paradys. And on another syde, it strecchethe toward the Septemtrion, unto the See of Caspye: and also toward the Southe, unto the Desert of Ynde. And this Contree is gode and pleyn and fulle of peple. And there ben manye gode Cytees. But the 2 princypalle Cytees ben theise, Boyturra, and Seornergant, that sū men clepen Sormagant. The tother Kyngdom of Persie strecchethe toward the Ryvere of Phison, and the Parties of the West, unto the Kyngdom of Mede: And fro the grete Armenye, and toward the Septemtrion, to the See of Caspie; and toward the Southe, to the lond of Ynde. That is also a gode lond and a plentefous; and it hathe 3 grete principalle Cytees, Messabor, Caphon and Sarmassane.

And thanne aftre is Armenye, in the whiche weren wont to ben 4 Kyngdomes: that is a noble Cuntree, and fulle of Godes. And it begynnethe at Persie, and strecchethe toward the West in lengthe, unto Turkye. And in largenesse, it durethe to the Cytee of Alizandre, that now is clept the Zate of Helle, that I spak offe beforn, undre the Kyngdom of Mede. In this Armenye ben fulle manye gode Cytees: but Tanrizo is most of name.

Aftre this, is the Kyngdom of Mede, that is fulle long: but it is not fulle large, that begynnethe toward the Est, to the lond of Persie, and to Ynde the lesse. And it strecchethe toward the West, toward the Kyngdom of Caldee, and toward the Septemtrion, descendynge toward the litille Armenye. In that Kyngdom of Medee, there ben many grete Hilles, and litille of pleyn Erthe. There duellen Sarazines, and another maner of folk, that men clepen Cordynes. The beste 2 Cytees of that Kyngdom, ben Sarras and Karemen.

Aftre that, is the Kyngdom of George, that begynnethe toward the Est, to the gret Mountayne, that is clept Abzor; where that duellen many dyverse folk of dyverse Naciouns. And men clepen the Contree Alamo. This Kyngdom strecchethe him towardes Turkye, and toward the grete See: and toward the South, it marchethe to the grete Armenye. And there ben 2 Kyngdomes in that Contree; that on is the Kyngdom of Georgie, and that other is the Kyngdom of Abcaz. And alle weys in that Contree ben 2 Kynges, and thei ben bothe Cristene: but the Kyng of Georgie is in subieccioun to the grete Chane. And the King of Abcaz hathe the more strong Contree: and he alle weyes vigerously defendethe his Contree, azenst alle tho that assaylen him; so that no man may make him in subieccioun to no man. In that Kyngdom of Abcaz is a gret Marvaylle. For a Provynce of the Contree, that hathe wel in circuyt

3 iorneyes, that men clepen Hanyson, is alle covered with Derknesse, with outen ony brightnesse or light; so that no man may see ne here, ne no man dar entren in to hem. And natheles, thei of the Contree seyn, that som tyme men heren voys of folk, and Hors nyzenge, and Cokkes crowynge. And men witen wel, that men dwellen there: but thei knowe not what men. And thei seyn, that the Derknesse befelle be Myracle of God. For a cursed Emperour of Persie, that highte Saures, pursuede alle Cristene men, to destroye hem, and to compelle hem to make Sacrifise to his Ydoles; and rood with grete Host, in alle that ever he myghte, for to confounde the Cristene men. And thanne in that Contree, dwelleden manye gode cristene men, the whiche that laften hire Godes, and wolde han fled in to Grece: and whan they weren in a playn, that highte Megon, anon this cursed Emperour mett with hem, with his Hoost, for to have slayn hem, and hewen hem to peces. And anon the Cristene men kneleden to the grounde, and made hire preyeres to God, to sokoure hem. And anon a gret thikke Clowde cam, and covered the Emperour and alle his Hoost: and so thei enduren in that manere, that thei ne mowe not gon out, on no syde; and so schulle thei ever more abyden in Derknesse, tille the day of Dome, be the Myracle of God. And thanne the Cristene men wenten, where hem lykede best, at hire own plesance, with outen lettynge of ony Creature; and hire enemyes enclosed and confounded in Derknesse, with outen ony strok. Wherfore we may wel seye, with David, *A Domino factū est istud; & est mirabile in*

oculis nostris. And that was a gret Myracle, that God made for hem. Wherfore methinkethe, that Cristene men scholden ben more devoute, to serven oure Lord God, than ony other men of ony other Secte. For with outen ony drede, ne were cursednesse and Synne of Cristene men, thei scholden be Lordes of alle the World. For the Banere of Jesu Crist is alle weys displayed, and redy on alle sydes, to the help of his trewe lovynge Servauntes: in so moche, that o gode Cristene man, in gode Beleeve, scholde overcomen and out chacen a 1000 cursed mysbeleevynge men: as David seythe in the Psautere, *Quoniā persequebatur unus mille, & duo fugarent decem milia.* Et, *Cadent a latere tuo mille, & decem milia a dextris tuis.* And how that it myghte ben, that on scholde chacen a 1000, David himself seythe, folewynge, *Quia manus Domini fecit hæc omnia.* And oure Lord himself seythe, be the Prophetes mouthe, *Si in viis meis ambulaveritis, super tribulantes vos misissem manū meā.* So that wee may seen apertely, that zif wee wil be gode men, non enemye ne may not enduren azenst us. Also zee schulle undirstonde, that out of that lond of Derknesse, gothe out a gret Ryvere, that schewethe wel, that there ben folk dwellynge, be many redy tokenes: but no man dar not entre in to it.

And wytethe well, that in the Kyngdoms of Georgie, of Abchaz and of the litille Armenye, ben gode Cristene men and devoute. For thei schryven hem and howsele hem evermore ones or twyes in the Woke. And there ben manye of hem, that howsele hem every day: and so do wee not on this half; alle be it that seynt Poul cōmandethe it, seyenge, *Omnibus diebus dominicis ad cōmunicandū hortor.* Thei kepen that Cōmandement : but wee ne kepen it not.

Also aftre, on this half, is Turkye, that marchethe to the grete Armenye. And there ben many Provynces, as Capadoche, Saure, Brique, Quesiton, Pytan and Gemethe. And in everyche of theise ben many gode Cytees. This Turkye strecchethe unto the Cytee of Sachala, that sittethe upon the See of Grece; and so it marchethe to Syrie. Syrie is a gret Contree and a gode, as I have told zou before. And also it hathe, aboven toward Ynde, the Kyngdom of Caldee, that strecchethe fro the Mountaynes of Calde, toward the Est, unto the Cytee of Nynyvee, that sittethe upon the Ryvere of Tygre : and in largenesse, it begynnethe toward the Northe, to the Cytee of Maraga; and it strecchethe toward the Southe, unto the See Occean. In Caldee is a pleyn Contree, and fewe Hilles and few Ryveres.

Aftre is the Kyngdom of Mesopotayme, that begynnethe toward the Est, to the Flom of Tygre, unto a Cytee that is clept Moselle : and it strecchethe toward the West, to the Flom of Eufrate, unto a Cytee that is clept Roianz : and in lengthe it gothe to the mount of Armenye, unto the Desert of Ynde the lesse. This is a gode Contree and a pleyn : but it hathe fewe Ryveres. It hathe but 2 Mountaynes in that Contree: of the whiche, on highte Symar, and that other Lyson And this Lond marchethe to the Kyngdom of Caldee.

Zit there is, toward the parties meridionales, many Contrees and many Regyouns ; as the lond of Ethiope, that marchethe, toward the Est, to the

grete Desertes; toward the West, to the Kyngdom
of Nubye; toward the Southe, to the Kyngdom of
Moretane; and toward the North, to the rede See.
Aftre is Moretane, that durethe fro the Mountaynes of Ethiope, unto Lybie the hize. And that
Contree lyȝth a long fro the See Occean, toward
the Southe; and toward the Northe, it marchethe
to Nubye, and to the highe Lybye. (Theise men
of Nubye ben Cristene.) And it marchethe fro
the londes aboveseyd to the Desertes of Egypt.
And that is the Egypt, that I have spoken of
before. And aftre is Libye the hye, and Lybye
the lowe, that descendethe down lowe, toward the
grete See of Spayne. In the whiche Contree ben
many Kyngdomes and many dyverse folk. Now
I have devysed ȝou many Contrees, on this half
the Kyngdom of Cathay: of the whiche, many
ben obeyssant to the grete Chane.

Cap. XXVI.

*Of the Contrees and Yles, that ben bezonde the Lond
of Cathay; and of the Frutes there; and of 22
Kynges enclosed within the Mountaynes.*

Now schalle I seye ȝou sewyngly of Contrees and
Yles, that ben bezonde the Contrees that I have
spoken of. Wherfore I seye ȝou, in passynge be
the Lond of Cathaye, toward the highe Ynde, and
toward Bacharye, men passen be a Kyngdom, that
men clepen Caldilhe; that is a fulle fair Contree.

And there growethe a maner of Fruyt, as thoughe it weren Gowrdes: and whan thei ben rype, men kutten hem a to, and men fynden with inne a lytylle Best, in Flessche, in Bon and Blode, as

though it were a lytylle Lomb, with outen Wolle. And men eten bothe the Frut and the Best: and that is a gret Marveylle. Of that Frute I have eten; alle thoughe it were wondirfulle: but that I knowe wel, that God is marveyllous in his Werkes. And natheles I tolde hem, of als gret a Marveylle to hem, that is amonges us: and that was of the Bernakes. For I tolde hem, that in oure Contree weren Trees, that beren a Fruyt, that becomen Briddes fleeynge: and tho that fellen in the Water, lyven; and thei that fallen on the Erthe, dyen anon: and thei ben right gode to Mannes mete. And here of had thei als gret marvaylle, that sūme

of hem trowed, it were an impossible thing to be.
In that Contree ben longe Apples, of gode savour;
where of ben mo than an 100 in a Clustre, and als
manye in another; and thei han grete longe Leves
and large, of 2 Fote long or more. And in that
Contree, and in other Contrees there abouten,
growen many Trees, that beren Clowe Gylofres
and Notemuges, and grete Notes of Ynde and of
Canelle and of many other Spices. And there ben
Vynes, that beren so grete Grapes, that a strong
man scholde have y now to done, for to bere o
clustre with alle the Grapes. In that same regioun
ben the Mountaynes of Caspye, that men clepen
Uber in the Contree. Betwene tho Mountaynes,
the Jewes of 10 Lynages ben enclosed, that men
clepen Gothe and Magothe: and thei mowe not
gon out on no syde. There weren enclosed 22
Kynges with hire peple, that duelleden betwene
the Mountaynes of Sythye. There Kyng Alisandre
chacede hem betwene tho Mountaynes; and there
he thoughte for to enclose hem thorghe werk of
his men. But whan he saughe, that he myghte
not don it, ne bryng it to an ende, he preyed to
God of Nature, that he wolde parforme that that
he had begonne. And alle were it so, that he was
a Payneme and not worthi to ben herd, zit God of
his grace closed the Mountaynes to gydre: so that
thei dwellen there, alle faste y lokked and enclosed
with highe Mountaynes alle aboute, saf only on o
syde; and on that syde, is the See of Caspye.
Now may sum men asken, Sithe that the See is on
that o syde, wherfore go thei not out on the See
syde, for to go where that hem lykethe? But
to this questioun, I schal answere, That See of

Caspye gothe out be Londe, undre the Mountaynes, and rennethe be the Desert at o syde of the Contree; and aftre it strecchethe unto the endes of Persie. And alle thoughe it be clept a See, it is no See, ne it touchethe to non other See: but it is a Lake, the grettest of the World. And thoughe thei wolden putten hem in to that See, thei ne wysten never, where that thei scholde arryven. And also thei conen no Langage, but only hire owne, that no man knowethe but thei: and therfore mowe thei not gon out. And also zee schulle undirstonde, that the Jewes han no propre Lond of hire owne for to dwellen inne, in alle the World, but only that Lond betwene the Mountaynes. And zit thei zelden Tribute for that Lond to the Queen of Amazoine, the whiche makethe hem to ben kept in cloos fulle diligently, that thei schalle not gon out on no syde, but be the Cost of hire Lond. For hire Lond marchethe to tho Mountaynes. And often it hathe befallen, that sūme of the Jewes han gon up the Mountaynes, and avaled down to the Valeyes: but gret nombre of folk ne may not do so. For the Mountaynes ben so hye and so streghte up, that thei moste abyde there, maugre hire Myghte. For thei mowe not gon out, but be a littille issue, that was made be strengthe of men; and it lastethe wel a 4 grete Myle. And aftre, is there zit a Lond allo Desert, where men may fynde no Watre, ne for dyggynge, ne for non other thing. Wherfore men may not dwellen in that place: so is it fulle of Dragounes, of Serpentes and of other venymous Bestes, that no man dar not passe, but zif it be be strong Wyntre. And that streyt passage, men clepen in that Contree, Clyron. And that is the passage, that the Queen of Amazoine makethe to ben kept. And thoghe it happene, sum of hem, be Fortune, to gon out; thei conen no maner of Langage but Ebrow: so that thei can not speke to the peple. And zit natheles, men seyn, thei schalle gon out in the tyme of Antecrist, and that thei schulle maken gret slaughtre of Cristene men. And therfore alle the Jewes, that dwellen in alle Londes, lernen alle weys to speken Ebrew, in hope that whan the other Jewes schulle gon out, that thei may undirstonden hire Speche, and to leden hem in to Cristendom, for to destroye the Cristene peple. For the Jewes seyn, that they knowen wel, be hire Prophecyes, that thei of Caspye schulle gon out and spreden thorghe out alle the World; and that the Cristene men schulle ben undre hire Subieccioun, als longe as thei han ben in subieccioun of hem. And zif that zee wil wyte, how that thei schulle fynden hire Weye, aftre that I have herd seye, I schalle telle zou. In the time of Antecrist, a Fox schalle make there his trayne, and mynen an hole, where Kyng Alisandre leet make the Zates: and so longe he schalle mynen and perce the Erthe, till that he schalle passe thorghe, towardes that folk. And whan thei seen the Fox, thei schulle have gret marveylle of him, be cause that thei saughe never suche a Best. For of alle othere Bestes, thei han enclosed amonges hem, saf only the Fox. And thanne thei schullen chacen him and pursuen him so streyte, tille that he come to the same place, that he cam fro. And thanne thei schullen dyggen and mynen so strongly, tille that thei fynden the Zates, that Kyng Alisandre leet make of grete Stones and passynge huge, wel symented and made stronge for the maystrie. And tho Zates thei schulle breken, and so gon out, be fyndynge of that issue.

Fro that Lond, gon men toward the Lond of Bacharie, where ben fulle yvele folk and fulle cruelle. In that Lond ben Trees, that beren Wolle, as thoghe it were of Scheep; where of men maken Clothes, and alle thing that may ben made of Wolle. In that Contree ben many Ipotaynes, that dwellen somtyme in the Watre, and somtyme on the Lond: and thei ben half Man and half Hors, as I have seyd before: and thei

eten men, whan thei may take hem. And there ben Ryveres of Watres, that ben fulle byttere, three sythes more than is the Watir of the See. In that Contree ben many Griffounes, more plentee than in ony other Contree. Sum men seyn, that thei han the Body upward, as an Egle, and benethe as a Lyoun: and treuly thei seyn sothe, that thei ben of that schapp. But o Griffoun hathe the body more gret and is more strong thanne 8 Lyouns, of suche Lyouns as ben o this half; and more gret and strongere, than an 100 Egles, suche as we han amonges us. For o Griffoun there wil bere, fleynge to his Nest, a gret Hors, or 2 Oxen zoked to gidere, as thei gon at the Plowghe. For he hathe his Talouns[a] so longe and so large and grete, upon his Feet, as thoughe thei weren Hornes of grete Oxen or of Bugles or of Kyzn; so that men maken Cuppes of hem, to drynken of: and of hire Ribbes and of the Pennes of hire Wenges, men maken Bowes fulle stronge, to schote with Arwes and Quarelle. From thens gon men, be many iourneyes, thorghe the Lond of Prestre John, the grete Emperour of Ynde. And men clepen his Roialme, the Yle of Pentexoire.

[a] One 4 Foot long, in the Cotton Library, has a Silver Hoop about the end, whereon is engraven, *Griphi Unguis, Divo Cuthberto Dunelmensi sacer*. Another about an Ell long, is mentioned by Dr. Grew, in his History of the Rarities of the Royal Society, pag. 26; tho' the Doctor there supposes it rather the Horn of a Rock-Buck or of the *Ibex mas*.

Cap. XXVII.

Of the Ryalle estate of Prestre John; and of a riche man, that made a marveyllous Castelle, and cleped it Paradys; and of his Sotyltee.

THIS Emperour Prestre John holt fulle gret Lond, and hathe many fulle noble Cytees and gode Townes in his Royalme, and many grete dyverse Yles ond large. For alle the Contree of Ynde is devysed in Yles, for the grete Flodes, that comen from Paradys, that departen alle the Lond in many parties. And also in the See, he hathe fulle manye Yles. And the beste Cytee in the Yle of Pentexoire is Nyse, that is a fulle Ryalle Cytee and a noble, and fulle riche. This Prestre John hathe undre him many Kynges and many Yles and many dyverse folk of dyverse condiciouns. And this Lond is fulle gode and ryche; but not so riche as is the Lond of the grete Chane. For the Marchauntes come not thidre so comounly, for to bye Marchandises, as thei don in the Lond of the gret Chane: for it is to fer to travaylle to. And on that other partie, in the Yle of Cathay, men fynden alle maner thing, that is nede to man; Clothes of Gold, of Silk, and Spycerie. And therfore, alle be it that men han grettre chep in the Yle of Prestre John, natheles men dreden the longe wey and the grete periles in the See, in tho parties. For in many places of the See ben grete Roches of Stones of the Adamant, that of his propre nature drawethe Iren to him. And therfore there passen no Schippes, that han outher Bondes or Nayles of Iren with in hem : and zif there do, anon the Roches of the Adamantes drawen hem to hem, that never thei may go thens. I my self have seen o Ferrom in that See, as thoughe it hadde ben a gret Yle fulle of Trees and Buscaylle, fulle of Thornes and Breres, gret plentee. And the Schipmen tolde us, that alle that was of Schippes, that weren drawen thidre be the Adamauntes, for the Iren that was in hem. And of the rotenesse and other thing that was with in the Schippes, grewen suche Buscaylle and Thornes and Breres and grene Grasse and suche maner of thing; and of the Mastes and the Seylle Zerdes : it semed a grete Wode or a Grove. And suche Roches ben in many places there abouten. And therfore dur not the Marchauntes passen there, but zif thei knowen wel the passages, or elle that thei han gode Lodes men. And also thei dreden the longe weye : and therfore thei gon to Cathay; for it is more nyghe: and zit is not so nyghe, but that men moste ben travayllynge be See and Lond, 11 Monethes or 12, from Gene or from Venyse, or he come to Cathay. And zit is the Lond of Prestre John more ferr, be many dredfulle iourneyes. And the Marchauntes passen be the Kyngdom of Persie, and gon to a Cytee that is clept Hermes : for Hermes the Philosophre founded it. And aftre that, thei passen an Arm of the See, and thanne thei gon to another Cytee that is clept Golbache :[a] and there thei fynden Marchandises, and of Popengayes, as gret plentee

[a] Gohathe, L.

as men fynden here of Gees. And zif thei will passen ferthere, thei may gon sykerly i now. In that Contree is but lytylle Whete or Berley: and therfore thei eten Ryzs and Hony and Mylk and Chese and Frute.

This Emperour Prestre John takethe alle weys to his Wif, the Doughtre of the grete Chane: and the gret Chane also in the same wise, the Doughtre of Prestre John. For theise 2 ben the grettest Lordes undir the Firmament.

In the Lond of Prestre John, ben many dyverse thinges and many precious Stones, so grete and so large, that men maken of hem Vesselle; as Plateres, Dissches and Cuppes. And many other marveylles ben there; that it were to combrous and to long to putten it in scripture of Bokes.

But of the princypalle Yles and of his Estate and of his Lawe, I schalle telle zou som partye. This Emperour Prestre John is Cristene; and a gret partie of his Contree also: but zit thei have not alle the Articles of oure Feythe, as wee have. Thei beleven wel in the Fadre, in the Sone and in the Holy Gost: and thei ben fulle devoute, and righte trewe on to another. And thei sette not be no Barettes, ne by Cawteles, ne of no Disceytes. And he hathe undre him 72 Provynces; and in every Provynce is a Kyng. And theise Kynges han Kynges undre hem; and alle ben tributaries to Prestre John. And he hathe in his Lordschipes many grete marveyles. For in his Contree, is the See that men clepen the Gravely See, that is alle Gravelle and Sond, with outen ony drope of Watre: and it ebbethe and flowethe in grete Wawes, as other Sees don: and it is never stille ne in pes, in no maner cesoun. And no man may passe that See be Navye, ne be no maner of craft: and therfore may no man knowe, what Lond is bezond that See. And alle be it that it have no Watre, zit men fynden there in and on the Bankes, fulle gode Fissche of other maner of kynde and schappe, thanne men fynden in ony other See; and thei ben of right goode tast, and delycious to mannes mete.

And a 3 iourneys long fro that See, ben gret Mountaynes; out of the whiche gothe out a gret Flood, that comethe out of Paradys: and it is fulle of precious Stones, with outen ony drope of Water: and it rennethe thorghe the Desert, on that o syde; so that it makethe the See gravely: and it berethe in to that See, and there it endethe. And that Flōme rennethe also, 3 dayes in the Woke, and bryngethe with him grete Stones, and the Roches also therewith, and that gret plentee. And anon as thei ben entred in to the gravely See, thei ben seyn no more; but lost for evere more. And in tho 3 dayes, that that Ryvere rennethe, no man dar entren in to it: but in the other dayes, men dar entren wel y now. Also bezonde that Flōme, more upward to the Desertes, is a gret Pleyn alle gravelly betwene the Mountaynes: and in that Playn, every day at the Sonne risynge, begynnen to growe smale Trees; and thei growen til mydday, berynge Frute: but no man dar taken of that Frute; for it is a thing of Fayrye. And aftre mydday, thei discrecen and entren azen in to the Erthe; so that at the goynge doun of the Sonne, thei apperen no more: and so thei don every day; and that is a gret marvaylle.

T

In that Desert ben many wylde men, that ben hidouse to loken on: for thei ben horned;[b] and thei speken nought, but thei gronten, as Pygges. And there is also gret plentee of wylde Houndes. And there ben manye Popegayes, that thei clepen Psitakes in hire Langage: and thei speken of hire propre nature, and salven men that gon thorghe the Desertes, and speken to hem als appertely, as thoughe it were a man. And thei that speken wel, han a large Tonge, and han 5 Toos upon a Fote. And there ben also of other manere, that han but 3 Toos upon a Fote; and thei speken not, or but litille: for thei cone not but cryen.

This Emperour Prestre John, whan he gothe in to Battayle, azenst ony other Lord, he hathe no Baneres born before him: but he hathe 3 Crosses of Gold, fyn, grete and hye, fulle of precious Stones: and every of the Crosses ben sett in a Chariot, fulle richely arrayed. And for to kepen every Cros, ben ordeyned 10000 men of Armes, and mo than 100000 men on Fote, in maner as men wolde kepe a Stondard in oure Contrees, whan that wee ben in Lond of Werre. And this nombre of folk is with outen the pryncipalle Hoost, and with outen Wenges ordeynd for the Bataylle. And whan he hathe no Werre, but ridethe with a pryvy Meynee, thanne he hathe bore before him but o Cross of Tree, with outen peynture, and with outen Gold or Silver or precious Stones; in remembrance, that Jesu Crist suffred Dethe upon a Cros of Tree. And he hathe born before him also a Plater of Gold fulle of Erthe, in tokene that his Noblesse and his Myghte and his Flessche

---

[b] The Latin Version does not make them *horned*.

schalle turnen to Erthe. And he hathe born before him also a Vesselle of Silver, fulle of noble Jewelles of Gold fulle riche, and of precious Stones, in tokene of his Lordschipe and of his Noblesse and of his Myght. He duellethe comounly in the Cytee of Suse; and there is his principalle Palays, that is so riche and so noble, that no man wil trowe it by estymacioun, but he had seen it. And aboven the chief Tour of the Palays, ben 2 rounde Pomeles of Gold; and in everyche of hem ben 2 Carboncles grete and large, that schynen fulle brighte upon the nyght. And the principalle Zates of his Palays ben of precious Ston, that men clepen Sardoyne: and the Bordure and the Barres ben of Ivorye: and the Wyndowes of the Halles and Chambres ben of Cristalle: and the Tables, where on men eten, sōme ben of Emeraudes, sūme of Amatyst and sōme of Gold, fulle of precious Stones; and the Pileres, that beren up the Tables, ben of the same precious Stones. And the Degrees to gon up to his Throne, where he sittethe at the Mete, on is of Oniche, another is of Cristalle, and another of Jaspre grene, another of Amatyst, another of Sardyne, another of Corneline, and the sevene that he settethe on his Feet, is of Crisolyte. And alle theise Degrees ben bordured with fyn Gold, with the tother precious Stones, sett with grete Perles oryent. And the sydes of the Sege of his Throne ben of Emeraudes, and bordured with Gold fulle nobely, and dubbed with other precious Stones and grete Perles. And alle the Pileres in his Chambre, ben of fyne Gold with precious Stones, and with many Carboncles, that zeven gret lyght upon the nyght to alle peple.

And alle be it that the Charboncle zeve lyght right y now, natheles at alle tymes brennethe a Vesselle of Cristalle fulle of Bawme, for to zeven gode smelle and odour to the Emperour, and to voyden awey alle wykkede Eyres and corrupciouns. And the forme of his Bedd is of fyne Saphires bended with Gold, for to make him slepen wel, and to refreynen him from Lecherye. For he wille not lyze with his Wyfes, but 4 sithes in the Zeer, aftre the 4 Cesouns: and that is only for to engendre Children. He hathe also a fulle fayr Palays and a noble, at the Cytee of Nyse, where that he dwellethe, whan him best lykethe: but the Ayr is not so attempree, as it is at the Cytee of Suse. And zee schulle undirstonde, that in alle his Contree, ne in the Contrees there alle aboute, men eten noghte but ones in the day, as men don in the Court of the grete Chane. And so thei eten every day in his Court, mo than 30000 persones, with outen goeres and comeres. But the 30000 persones of his Contree, ne of the Contree of the grete Chane, ne spenden noghte so moche Gode, as don 12000 of oure Contree. This Emperour Prestre John hathe evere more 7 Kynges with him, to serve him: and thei departen hire Service be certeyn Monethes. And with theise Kynges serven alle weys 72 Dukes and 360 Erles. And alle the dayes of the Zeer, there eten in his Houshold and in his Court, 12 Erchebysshoppes and 20 Bisshoppes. And the Patriark of seynt Thomas is there, as is the Pope here. And the Erchebisshoppes and the Bisshoppes and the Abbottes in that Contree, ben alle Kynges. And everyche of theise grete Lordes knowen wel y now the attendance of hire Servyce. The on is Mayster of his Houshold, another is his Chamberleyn, another servethe him of a Dyssche, another of the Cuppe, another is Styward, another is Mareschalle, another is Prynce of his Armes : and thus is he fulle nobely and ryally served. And his Lond durethe in verry brede 4 Monethes iorneyes, and in lengthe out of mesure : that is to seyn, alle the Yles undir Erthe, that wee supposen to ben undir us.

Besyde the Yle of Pentexoire, that is the Lond of Prestre John, is a gret Yle long and brode, that men clepen Milsterak; and it is in the Lordschipe of Prestre John. In that Yle is gret plentee of Godes. There was dwellynge somtyme a ryche man, and it is not longe sithen, and men clept him Gatholonabes; and he was fulle of Cauteles and of sotylle Disceytes : and he hadde a fulle fair Castelle, and a strong, in a Mountayne, so strong and so noble, that no man cowde devise a fairere ne a strengere. And he had let muren alle the Mountayne aboute with a strong Walle and a fair. And with inne tho Walles he had the fairest Gardyn, that ony man myghte beholde; and therein were Trees berynge alle maner of Frutes, that ony man cowde devyse: and there in were also alle maner vertuous Herbes of gode smelle, and alle other Herbes also, that beren faire Floures. And he had also in that Gardyn, many faire Welles ; and beside tho Welles, he had lete make faire Halles and faire Chambres, depeynted alle with Gold and Azure. And there weren in that place many a dyverse thinges and many dyverse stories: and of Bestes and of Bryddes, that songen fulle delectabely, and meveden be craft, that it semede that thei weren quyke. And he had also in his Gardyn alle maner of Foules and of Bestes, that ony man myghte thenke on, for to have pley or desport to beholde hem. And he had also in that place, the faireste Damyseles, that myghte ben founde undir the Age of 15 Zere, and the faireste zonge striplynges, that men myghte gete of that same age: and alle thei weren clothed in Clothes of Gold fully richely: and he seyde, that tho weren Aungeles. And he had also let make 3 Welles, faire and noble, and alle envyround with ston of Jaspre, of Cristalle, dyapred with Gold, and sett with precious Stones and grete orient Perles. And he had made a Conduyt undir Erthe, so that the 3 Welles, at his list, on scholde renne Milk, another Wyn, and another Hony. And that place he clept Paradys. And whan that ony gode Knyght, that was hardy and noble, cam to see this Rialtee, he wolde lede him into his Paradys, and schewen him theise wondirfulle thinges, to his desport, and the marveyllous and delicious Song of dyverse Briddes, and the faire Damyseles, and the faire Welles of Mylk, Wyn and hony, plentevous rennynge. And he wolde let make dyverse Instrumentes of Musick to sownen in an highe Tour, so merily that it was joye for to here; and no man scholde see the craft thereof: And tho, he seyde, weren Aungeles of God, and that place was Paradys, that God had behighte to his Frendes, seyenge, *Dabo vobis Terram fluentem lacte & Melle.* And thanne wolde he maken hem to drynken of certeyn drynk, where of anon thei scholden be dronken. And thanne wolde hem thinken gretter delyt, than thei hadden before. And than wolde he seye to hem, that zif thei wolde dyen for him and for his love, that aftir hire Dethe, thei scholde come to his Paradys; and thei scholde ben of the age of the Damyseles, and thei scholde pleyen with hem, and zit ben Maydenes. And aftir that, zit scholde he putten hem in a fayrere Paradys, where that thei schold see God of Nature visibely, in his Magestee and in his Blisse. And than wolde he schewe hem his entent, and seye hem, that zif thei wolde go sle suche a Lord or suche a man, that was his Enemye, or contrarious to his list, that thei scholde not drede to don it, and for to be slayn therefore hemself: for aftir hire Dethe, he wolde putten hem into another Paradys, that was an 100 fold fairere than ony of the tothere: and there schode thei dwellen with the most fairest Damyselles that myghte be, and pley with hem ever more. And thus wenten many dyverse lusty Bacheleres for to sle grete Lords, in dyverse Countrees, that weren his enemyes, and maden hem self to ben slayn, in hope to have that Paradys. And thus often tyme, he was revenged of his enemyes, be his sotylle disceytes and false Cauteles. And whan the worthi men of the Contree hadden perceyved this sotylle falshod of this Gatholonabes, thei assembled hem with force, and assayleden his Castelle, and slowen him, and destroyden alle the fair places, and alle the nobletees of that Paradys. The place of the Welles and of the Walles and of many other thinges, ben zit apertly sene: but the richesse is voyded clene. And it is not longe gon, sithe that place was destroyed.

Cap. XXVIII.

Of the Develes Hede in the Valeye perilous; and of the Customs of folk in dyverse Yles, that ben abouten, in the Lordschipe of Prestre John.

BESYDE that Yle of Mistorak, upon the left syde, nyghe to the Ryvere of Phison, is a marveylous thing. There is a Vale betwene the Mountaynes, that durethe nyghe a 4 Myle: and summen clepen it the Vale enchaunted; some clepen it the Vale of Develes, and some clepen it the Vale perilous. In that Vale, heren men often tyme grete Tempestes and Thondres and grete Murmures and Noyses, alle dayes and nyghtes: and gret noyse, as it were sown of Tabours and of Nakeres and Trompes, as thoughe it were of a gret feste. This Vale is alle fulle of Develes, and hathe ben alle weys. And men seyn there, that it is on of the entrees of Helle. In that Vale is gret plentee of Gold and Sylver: wherefore many mys belevynge men, and manye Cristene men also, gon in often tyme, for to have of the Thresoure, that there is: but fewe comen azen; and namely of the mys belevynge men, ne of the Cristene men nouther: for thei ben anon strangled of Develes. And in mydde place of that Vale, undir a Roche, is an Hed and the Visage of a Devyl bodyliche, fulle

horrible and dreadfulle to see, and it schewethe not but the Hed, to the Schuldres. But there is no man in the World so hardy, Cristene man ne other, but that he wolde ben a drad for to beholde it; and that it wolde semen him to dye for drede; so is it hidouse for to beholde. For he beholdethe every man so scharply, with dreadfulle Eyen, that ben evere more mevynge and sparklynge, as Fuyr, and chaungethe and sterethe so often in dyverse manere, with so horrible Countenance, that no man dar not neighen towardes him. And fro him comethe out Smoke and Stynk and Fuyr, and so moche Abhomynacioun, that unethe no man may there endure. But the gode Cristene men, that ben stable in the Feythe, entren welle withouten perile. For thei wil first schryven hem, and marken hem with the tokene of the Holy Cros;

so that the Fendes ne han no Power over hem. But alle be it that thei ben with outen perile, zit natheles ne ben thei not with outen drede, whan that thei seen the Develes visibely and bodyly alle aboute hem, that maken fulle many dyverse Assautes and Manaces in Eyr and in Erthe, and agasten hem with strokes of Thondre blastes and of Tempestes. And the most drede is, that God wole taken Vengeance thanne, of that men han mys don azen his Wille. And zee schulle undirstonde, that whan my Fellows and I weren in that Vale, wee weren in gret thought, whether that wee dursten putten oure Bodyes in aventure, to gon in or non, in the proteccioun of God. And some of oure Fellowes accordeden to enter, and somme noght, So there weren with us 2 worthi men, Frere Menoures, that weren of Lombardye, that seyden, that zif ony man wolde entren, thei wolde gon in with us. And when thei hadden seyd so, upon the gracyous trust of God and of hem, wee leet synge Masse, and made every man to ben schryven and houseld : and thanne wee entreden 14 personnes; but at oure goynge out, wee weren but 9. And so wee wisten nevere, whether that oure Fellowes weren lost, or elle turned azen for drede: but wee ne saughe hem never after: and tho weren 2 men of Grece and 3 of Spayne. And oure other Fellows, that wolden not gon in with us, thei wenten by another Coste, to ben before us, and so thei were. And thus wee passeden that perilouse Vale, and founden thereinne Gold and Sylver and precious Stones and riche Jewelles gret plentee, both here and there, as us semed : but whether that it was, as us semede, I wot nere: for I touched none, because that the Develes ben so subtyle to make a thing to seme otherwise than it is, for to disceyve mankynde: and therfore I towched none; and also because that I wolde not ben put out of my Devocioun: for I was more devout thanne, than evere I was before or after, and alle for the drede of Fendes, that I saughe in dyverse Figures; and also for the gret multytude of dede Bodyes, that I saughe there liggynge be the Weye, be alle the Vale, as thoughe there had ben a Bataylle betwene 2 Kynges and the myghtyest of the Contree, and that the gretter partye had ben discomfyted and slayn. And I trowe, that unethe scholde ony Contree have so moche peple with in him, as lay slayn in that Vale, as us thoughte; the whiche was an hidouse sight to seen. And I merveylled moche, that there weren so manye, and the Bodyes all hole, with outen rotynge. But I trowe, that Fendes made hem semen to ben so hole, with outen rotynge. But that myghte not ben to myn avys, that so manye scholde have entred so newely, ne so manye newely slayn, with outen stynkynge and rotynge. And manye of hem weren in habite of Cristene men: but I trowe wel, that it weren of suche, that wenten in for covetyse of the Thresoure, that was there, and hadden over moche feblenesse in Feithe; so that hire Hertes ne myghte not enduren in the Beleve for drede. And therfore weren wee the more devout a gret del: and zit wee weren cast doun and beten down many tymes to the hard Erthe, be Wyndes and Thondres and Tempestes: but evere more God of his grace halp us: and so wee passed that perilous Vale, with outen perile and with outen encombrance. Thanked be alle myghty Godd.

Aftre this, bezonde the Vale, is a gret Yle, where the folk ben grete Geauntes of 28 Fote longe or of 30 Fote longe; and thei han no Clothinge, but of Skynnes of Bestes, that thei hangen upon hem: and thei eten no Breed, but alle raw Flesche: and thei drynken Mylk of Bestes; for thei han plentee of alle Bestaylle. And thei have none Houses, to lyen inne. And thei eten more gladly mannes Flessche, thanne ony other Flesche. In to that Yle dar no man gladly entren: and zif thei seen a Schipp and Men there inne, anon thei entren in to the See, for to take hem.

And men seyden us, that in an Yle bezonde that, weren Geantes of grettere Stature: sūme of 45 Fote, or 50 Fote long, and as some men seyn, sūme of 50 Cubytes long: but I saghe none of tho; for I hadde no lust to go to tho parties, because that no man comethe nouther in to that Yle ne in to the other, but zif he be devoured anon. And among tho Geauntes ben Scheep, als grete as Oxen here; and thei beren gret Wolle and roughe. Of the Scheep I have seyn many tymes. And men han seyn many tymes tho Geauntes taken men in the See out of hire Schippes, and broughte hem to lond, 2 in on hond and 2 in another, etynge hem goynge, alle rawe and alle quyk.

Another Yle is there toward the Northe, in the See Occean, where that ben fulle cruele and ful evele Wommen of Nature; and thei han precious Stones in hire Eyen: and thei ben of that kynde, that zif thei beholden ony man with wratthe, thei slen him anon with the beholdynge, as dothe the Basilisk.[a]

Another Yle is there, fulle fair and gode and gret, and fulle of peple, where the custom is suche, that the firste nyght that thei ben maryed, thei maken another man to lye be hire Wifes, for to have hire Maydenhode: and therfore thei taken gret Huyre and gret Thank. And ther ben certeyn men in every Town, that serven of non other thing; and thei clepen hem Cadeberiz, that is to seyne, the Foles of Wanhope. For thei of the Contree holden it so gret a thing and so perilous, for to haven the Maydenhode of a Woman, that hem semethe that thei that haven first the Maydenhode, puttethe him in aventure of his Lif. And zif the Husbonde fynde his Wif Mayden, that other next nyghte, aftre that sche scholde have ben leyn by of the man, that is assigned therefore, perauntes for Dronkenesse or for some other cause, the Husbonde schalle pleyne upon him, that he hathe not don his Deveer, in suche cruelle wise, as thoughe he wolde have him slayn therfore. But after the firste nyght, that thei ben leyn by, thei kepen hem so streytely, that thei ben not so hardy to speke with no man. And I asked hem the cause, whi that thei helden suche custom: and thei seyden me, that of old tyme, men hadden ben dede for deflourynge of Maydenes, that hadden Serpentes in hire Bodyes, that stongen men upon

---

[a] Plin. lib. vii. c. 2: In eadem Affrica familias quasdam effascinantium, Isigonus et Nymphodorus tradunt, quarum laudatione, intereant Probata, arescant Arbores, emoriantur Infantes. Esse ejusdem generis in Triballis et Illyriis adjicit Isigonus, qui visu quoque effascinent interimantque, quos diutius intueantur, iratis præcipue oculis.

hire Zerdes, that thei dyeden anon: and therfore thei helden that custom, to make other men, ordeyn'd therfore, to lye be hire Wyfes, for drede of Dethe, and to assaye the passage be another, rather than for to putte hem in that aventure.

Aftre that, is another Yle, where that Wōmen maken gret Sorwe, whan hire Children ben y born: and whan thei dyen, thei maken gret Feste and gret Joye and Revelle, and thanne thei casten hem in to a gret Fuyr brennynge. And tho that loven wel hire Husbondes, zif hire Husbondes ben dede, thei casten hem also in the Fuyr, with hire Children, and brennen hem. And thei seyn, that the Fuyr schalle clensen hem of alle filthes and of alle Vices, and thei schulle gon pured and clene in to another World, to hire Husbondes, and thei schulle leden hire Children with hem. And the cause whi that they wepen, when hire Children ben born, is this, For whan thei comen in to this World, thei comen to labour, sorwe and hevynesse: And whi thei maken ioye and gladnesse at hire dyenge, is be cause that, as thei seyn, thanne thei gon to Paradys, where the Ryveres rennen Mylk and Hony, where that men seen hem in ioye and in habundance of Godes, with outen sorwe and labour. In that Yle men maken hire Kyng evere more be eleccioun: and they ne chese him nought for no Noblesse ne for no Ricchesse, but suche an on as is of gode maneres and of gode Condiciouns, and therewith alle rightfulle; and also that he be of gret Age, and that he have no Children. In that Yle men ben fulle rightefulle, and thei don rightfulle Iuggementes in every cause, bothe of riche and pore, smale and grete, aftre the quantytee of the trespas that is mys don. And the Kyng may nought deme no man to Dethe, with outen assent of his Barouns and other wyse men of Conseille, and that alle the Court accorde therto. And zif the Kyng him self do ony Homycydie or ony Cryme, as to sle a man, or ony suche cas, he schalle dye therefore; but he schalle not be slayn, as another man, but men schulle defende in peyne of Dethe, that no man be so hardy to make him Companye, ne to speke with hym, ne that no man zeve him ne selle him ne serve him nouther of Mete ne Drynk: and so schalle he dye in myschef. Thei spare no man that hath trespaced, nouther for love ne for favour ne for ricchesse ne for Noblesse, but that he schalle have aftre that he hathe don.

Bezonde that Yle, is another Yle, where is gret multytude of folk; and thei wole not for nothing eten Flesche of Hares, ne of Hennes, ne of Gees: and zit thei bryngen forthe y now, for to seen hem and to beholden hem only. But thei eten Flesche of alle other Bestes, and drynken Mylk. In that Contre, thei taken hire Doughtres and hire Sustres to here Wyfes, and hire other Kynneswōmen. And zif there ben 10 or 12 men or mo dwellynge in an Hows, the Wif of everyche of hem schalle ben comoun to hem alle, that duellen in that Hows; so that every man may liggen with whom he wole of hem, on o nyght, and with another another nyght. And zif sche have ony Child, sche may zeve it to what man sche list, that hathe companyed with hire; so that no man knoweth there, whether the Child be his or anotheres. And zif ony man seye to hem, that thei norisschen other mennes Children, thei answeren, that so don other men hires. In that Contre and be all Ynde, ben gret plentee of Cokodrilles, that is a maner of a long Serpent, as I have seyd before. And in the nyght, thei dwellen in the Watir, and on the day, upon the Lond, in Roches and Caves. And thei ete no mete in alle the Wynter: but thei lyzn as in a Drem, as don the Serpentes. Theise Serpentes slen men, and thei eten hem wepynge: and whan thei eten, thei meven the over Jowe, and noughte the nether Jowe; and thei have no Tonge. In that Contree, and in many other bezonde that, and also in manye on this half, men putten in werke the Sede of Cotoun: and thei sowen it every Zeer, and than growethe it in smale Trees, that beren Cotoun. And so don men every Zeer; so that there is plentee of Cotoun, at alle tymes. Item, in this Yle and in many other, there is a manner of Wode, hard and strong: who so coverethe the Coles of that Wode undir the Assches there offe, the Coles wil duellen and abyden alle quyk, a Zere or more. And that Tre hathe many Leves, as the Gynypre hathe. And there ben also many Trees, that of nature thei wole never brenne ne rote in no manere. And there ben Note Trees, that beren Notes, als grete as a Mannes Hed. There also ben many Bestes, that ben clept Orafles. In Arabye, thei ben clept Gerfauntz; that is a Best pomelee or spotted; that is but a litylle more highe, than is a Stede: but he hathe the Necke a 20 Cubytes long: and his Croup and his Tayl is as of an Hert: and he may loken over a gret highe

Hous. And there ben also in that Contree manye Camles, that is a lytille Best as a Goot, that is wylde, and he lyvethe be the Eyr, and etethe nought ne drynkethe nought at no tyme. And he chaungethe his colour often tyme: for men seen him often scithes, now in o colour and now in another colour: and he may chaunge him in to alle maner of coloures that him list, saf only in to red and white. There ben also in that Contree passynge grete Serpentes, sūme of 120 Fote long, and thei ben of dyverse coloures, as rayed, rede, grene and zalowe, blewe and blake, and alle spekelede. And there ben othere, that han Crestes upon hire Hedes: and thei gon upon hire Feet upright: and thei ben wel a 4 Fadme gret or more: and thei duellen alle weye in Roches or in Mountaynes: and thei han alle wey the Throte open, of whens thei droppen Venym alle weys. And there ben also wylde Swyn, of many coloures, als grete as ben Oxen in oure Contree, and thei ben alle spotted, as ben zonge Fownes. And there ben also Urchounes, als grete as wylde Swyn here. Wee clepen hem Poriz de Spyne. And there ben Lyouns alle whyte gret and myghty. And there ben also of other Bestes, als grete and more

gretter than is a Destrere:[b] and men clepen hem Loerancz: and sum men clepen hem Odenthos: and thei han a blak Hed and 3 longe Hornes trenchant in the Front, scharpe as a Sword; and the Body is sclender. And he is a fulle felonous Best: and he chacethe and sleethe the Olifaunt. There ben also manye other Bestes, fulle wykked and cruelle, that ben not mocheles more than a Bere; and thei han the Hed lyche a Bore; and thei han 6 Feet: and on every Foote 2 large Clawes trenchant: And the Body is lyche a Bere,

[b] Equus dextrarius.

and the Tayl as a Lyoun. And there ben also Myse, als grete as Houndes; and zalowe Myse, als grete as Ravenes. And there ben Gees alle rede, thre sithes more gret than oure here: and thei han the Hed, the Necke and the Brest alle blak. And many other dyverse Bestes ben in tho Contrees, and elle where there abouten: and manye dyverse Briddes also; of the whiche, it were to longe for to telle zou: and therefore I passe over at this tyme.

Cap. XXIX.

Of the Godenesse of the folk of the Yle of Bragman. Of Kyng Alisandre: and wherfore the Emperour of Ynde is clept Prestre John.

AND bezonde that Yle, is another Yle, gret and gode, and plentyfous, where that ben gode folk and trewe, and of gode lyvynge, aftre hire Beleve, and of gode Feythe. And alle be it that thei ben not cristned, ne have no perfyt Lawe, zit natheles of kyndely Lawe, thei ben fulle of alle Vertue, and thei eschewen alle Vices and alle Malices and alle Synnes. For thei ben not proude ne coveytous ne envyous ne wrathefulle ne glotouns ne leccherous; ne thei don to no man other wise than thei wolde that other men diden to hem: and in this poynt, thei fullefillen the 10 Commandementes of God: and thei zive no charge of Aveer ne of Ricchesse: and thei lye not, ne thei swere not, for non occasioun; but thei seyn symply, ze and nay. For thei seyn, He that swerethe, wil disceyve his Neyghbore: and therfore alle that thei don, thei don it with outen Othe. And men clepen that Yle, the Yle of Bragman: and sōme men clepen it the Lond of Feythe. And thorgh that Lond, rennethe a gret Ryvere, that is clept Thebe. And in generalle, alle the men of tho Yles and of alle the Marches there abouten, ben more trewe than in ony othere Contrees there abouten, and more righte fulle than othere, in alle thinges. In that Yle is no Thief, ne Mordrere, ne comoun Woman, ne pore beggere, ne nevere was man slayn in that Contree. And thei ben so chast, and leden so gode lif, as tho thei weren religious men: and thei fasten alle dayes. And because thei ben so trewe and so rightfulle and so fulle of alle gode condiciouns, thei weren nevere greved with Tempestes ne with Thondre ne with Leyt ne with Hayl ne with Pestylence ne with Werre ne with Hungre ne with non other tribulaccioun, as wee ben many tymes amonges us, for our Synnes. Wherfore it semethe wel, that God lovethe hem and is plesed with hire Creance, for hire gode Dedes. Thei beleven wel in God, that made alle thinges; and him thei worschipen. And thei preysen non erthely Ricchesse; and so thei ben alle right fulle. And thei lyven fulle ordynatly, and so sobrely in Met and Drynk, that thei lyven right longe. And the most part of hem dyen with outen Syknesse, whan nature faylethe hem for elde. And it befelle in Kyng Alisandres tyme, that he purposed him to conquere that Yle, and to maken hem to holden of him. And whan thei of the Contree herden it, thei senten Messangeres to him with Lettres, that seyden thus: What may ben y now to that man, to whom alle the

World is insuffisant: thou schalt fynde no thing in us, that may cause the to warren azenst us: for wee have no Ricchesse, ne none wee coveyten.: and alle the Godes of our Contree ben in comoun. Oure Mete, that we susteyne with alle oure Bodyes, is our Ricchesse: and in stede of tresoure of Gold and Sylver, wee maken oure Tresoure of Accord and Pees, and for to love every man other. And for to apparaylle with oure Bodyes, wee usen a sely litylle Clout, for to wrappen in oure Careynes. Oure Wyfes ne ben not arrayed for to make no man plesance, but only connable Array, for to eschewe Folye. Whan men peynen hem to arraye the Body, for to make it semen fayrere than God made it, thei don gret Synne. For man scholde not devise ne aske grettre Beautee, than God hath ordeyned man to ben at his Birthe. The Erthe mynystrethe to us 2 thinges; our Liflode, that comethe of the Erthe that wee lyve by, and oure Sepulture aftre oure Dethe. Wee have ben in perpetuelle Pees tille now, that thou come to disherite us; and also wee have a Kyng, nought for to do Justice to every man, for he schalle fynde no forfete amonge us; but for to kepe noblesse, and for to schewe that wee ben obeyssant, wee have a Kyng. For Justice ne hathe not among us no place: for wee don no man other wise than wee desiren that men don to us; so that rightwisnesse ne Vengeance han nought to don amonges us; so that no thing thou may take fro us, but oure gode Pes, that alle weys hath dured amonge us. And whan Kyng Alisandre had rad theise Lettres, he thoughte that he scholde do gret Synne, for to trouble hem: and thanne he sente hem Surteez, that thei scholde not ben aferd of him, and that thei scholde kepen hire gode maneres and hire gode Pees, as thei hadden used before of custom; and so he let hem allone.

Another Yle there is, that men clepen Oxidrate; and another Yle, that men clepen Gynosophe, where there is also gode folk, and fulle of gode Feythe: and thei holden for the most partye the gode condiciouns and customs and gode maneres, as men of the Contree above seyd: but thei gon alle naked. In to that Yle entred Kyng Alisandre, to see the manere. And when he saughe hire gret Feythe and hire Trouthe, that was amonges hem, he seyde that he wolde not greven hem: and bad hem aske of him, what that they wolde have of hym, Ricchesse or ony thing elles; and thei scholde have it with gode wille. And thei answerden, that he was riche y now, that hadde Mete and Drynke to susteyne the Body with. For the Ricchesse of this World, that is transitorie, is not worthe: but zif it were in his power to make hem inmortalle, there of wolde thei preyen him, and thanken him. And Alisandre answerde hem, that it was not in his powere to don it; because he was mortelle, as thei were. And thanne thei asked him, whi he was so proud and so fierce and so besy, for to putten alle the World undre his subjeccioun, righte as thou were a God; and hast no terme of this lif, neither day ne hour; and wylnest to have alle the World at thi commandement, that schalle leve the with outen fayle, or thou leve it. And righte as it hathe ben to other men before the, righte so it schalle ben to othere aftre the : and from hens schal tow bere no thyng; but as thou were born naked, righte so alle naked schalle thi Body ben turned in to Erthe, that thou were made of. Wherfore thou scholdest thenke and impresse it in thi mynde, that nothing is inmortalle, but only God, that made alle thing. Be the whiche answere, Alisandre was gretly astoneyed and abayst; and alle confuse departe frō hem. And alle be it that theyse folk han not the Articles of oure Fythe, as wee han, natheles for hire gode Feythe naturelle, and for hire gode entent, I trowe fulle, that God lovethe hem, and that God take hire Servyse to gree, right as he did of Job, that was a Paynem, and held him for his trewe Servaunt. And therfore alle be it that there ben many dyverse Lawes in the World, zit I trowe, that God lovethe alweys hem that loven him, and serven him mekely in trouthe : and namely, hem that dispysen the veyn Glorie of this World; as this folk don, and as Job did also : and therfore seyde oure Lorde, be the mouthe of Ozee the Prophete, *Ponam eis multiplices Leges meas.* And also in another place, *Qui totum Orbem subdit suis Legibus.* And also our Lord seythe in the Gospelle, *Alias Oves habeo, que non sunt ex hoc Ovili;* that is to seyne, that he hadde othere Servauntes, than tho that ben undre Cristene Lawe. And to that acordethe the Avisioun, that seynt Petir saughe at Jaffe, how the Aungel cam from Hevene, and broughte before him diverse Bestes, as Serpentes and other crepynge Bestes of the Erthe, and of other also gret plentee, and bad him take and ete. And Seynt Petir answerde; I ete never, quoth he, of unclene Bestes. And thanne seyde the Aungelle, *Non dicas inmunda, que Deus mundavit.* And that was in tokene, that no man scholde have in despite non erthely man, for here diverse Lawes: for wee knowe not whom God lovethe, ne whom God hatethe. And for that ensample, whan men seyn, *De profundis*, thei seyn it in comoun and in generalle, with the Cristene, *pro animabus omnium defunctorum, pro quibus sit orandum.* And therfore seye I of this folk, that ben so trewe and so feythefulle, that God lovethe hem. For he hathe amonges hem many of the Prophetes, and alle weye hathe had. And in tho Yles, thei prophecyed the Incarnacioun of oure Lord Jesu Crist, how he scholde ben born of a Mayden; 3000 Zeer or more or oure Lord was born of the Virgyne Marie. And thei beleeven wel in the Incarnacioun, and that fulle perfitely: but thei knowe not the manere, how he suffred his Passioun and Dethe for us.

And bezonde theise Yles, there is another Yle, that is clept Pytan. The folk of that Contree ne tyle not, ne laboure not the Erthe: for thei eten no manere thing: and thei ben of gode colour, and of faire schap, aftre hire gretnesse: but the smale ben as Dwerghes: but not so litylle, as ben the Pigmeyes. Theise men lyven be the smelle of wylde Apples; and whan thei gon ony fer weye, thei beren the Apples with hem. For zif thei hadde lost the savour of the Apples, thei scholde dyen anon.[a] Thei ne ben not fulle resonable: but thei ben symple and bestyalle.

[a] Plin. lib. vii. c. 2: Ad extremos fines Indiæ, ab Oriente, circa fontem Gangis, Astomorum gentem sine ore, corpore toto

Aftre that, is another Yle, where the folk ben alle skynned roughe Heer, as a rough Best, saf only the Face and the Pawme of the Hond.

Theise Folk gon als wel undir the Watir of the See, as thei don above the Lond, alle drye. And thei eten bothe Flessche and Fissche alle raughe. In this Yle is a great Ryvere, that is wel a 2 Myle and an half of brede, that is clept Beumare.[b] And fro that Rivere a 15 journeys in lengthe, goynge be the Desertes of the tother syde of the Ryvere, (whoso myght gon it, for I was not there: but it

---

hyrtam vestiri frondium lanugine, halitu tantum viventem et odore quem naribus trahant. Nullum illis Cibum nullumque Potum: tantum Radicum florumque varios odores et Sylvestrium Malorum, quæ secum portant longiore itinere ne, desit Olfactus: graviore paulo odore haud difficulter exanimari.

Weman, L.

was told us of hem of the Contree, that with inne tho Desertes) weren the Trees of the Sonne, and of the Mone, that spaken to Kyng Alisandre, and warned him of his Dethe. And men seyn, that the folk that kepen tho Trees, and eten of the Frute and of the Bawme that growethe there, lyven wel 400 Zeere or 500 Zeere, be vertue of the Frut and of the Bawme. For men seyn, that Bawme growethe there in gret plentee, and no where elles, saf only at Babyloyne, as I have told zou before. Wee wolde han gon toward the Trees fulle gladly, zif wee had myght: but I trowe, that 100000 men of Armes myghte not passen the Desertes safly, for the gret multytude of wylde Bestes, and of grete Dragouns, and of grete Serpentes, that there ben, that slen and devouren alle that comen aneyntes hem. In that Contre ben manye white Olifantes with outen nombre, and of Unycornes, and of Lyouns of many maneres, and many of suche Bestes, that I have told before, and of many other hydouse Bestes with outen nombre.

Many othere Yles there ben in the Lond of Prestre John, and many grete Merveyles, that weren to long to tellen alle, both of his Ricchesse and of his Noblesse, and of the gret plentee also of precious Stones, that he hathe. I trowe that zee knowe wel y now, and have herd seye, wherefore this Emperour is clept Prestre John. But nathales for hem that knowen not, I schalle seye zou the cause. It was somtyme an Emperour there, that was a worthi and a fulle noble Prynce, that hadde Cristene Knyghtes in his companye, as he hathe that is now. So it befelle, that he hadde gret list for to see the Service in the Chirche, among

Cristenmen. And than dured Cristendom bezonde the See, alle Turkye, Surrye, Tartarie, Jerusalem, Palestyne, Arabye, Halappee, and alle the Lond of Egypte. So it befelle, that this Emperour cam, with a Cristene Knyght with him, into a Chirche in Egypt: and it was the Saterday in Wyttson woke. And the Bishop made ordres. And he beheld and listend the servyse fulle tentyfly: And he askede the Cristene Knight, what men of Degree thei scholden ben, that the Prelate had before him. And the Knyght answerde and seyde, that thei scholde ben Prestes. And than the Emperour seyde, that he wolde no longer ben clept Kyng ne Emperour, but Preest; and that he wolde have the name of the first Preest, that went out of the Chirche: and his name was John. And so evere more sithens, he is clept Prestre John.

In his Lond ben manye Cristene men of gode Feythe and of gode Lawe; and namely of hem of the same Contree; and han comounly hire Prestes, that syngen the Messe, and maken the Sacrement of the Awtier of Bred, right as the Grekes don: but thei seyn not so many thinges at the Messe, as men don here. For thei seye not but only that, that the Apostles seyden, as oure Lord taughte hem: righte as seynt Peter and seynt Thomas and the other Apostles songen the Messe, seyenge the Pater-noster, and the wordes of the Sacrement. But wee have many mo addiciouns, that dyverse Popes han made, that thei ne knowe not offe.

Cap. XXX.

Of the Hilles of Gold, that Pissemyres kepen: and of the 4 Flodes, that comen from Paradys terrestre.

TOWARD the Est partye of Prestre Johnes Lond, is an Yle gode and gret, that men clepen Taprobane, that is fulle noble and fulle fructuous: and the Kyng thereof is fulle ryche, and is undre the obeyssance of Prestre John. And alle weys there thei make hire King be Eleccyoun. In that Ile ben 2 Someres and 2 Wyntres; and men hervesten the Corn twyes a Zeer. And in alle the Cesouns of the Zeer ben the Gardynes florisht. There dwellen gode folke and resonable, and manye Cristene men amonges hem, that ben so riche, that thei wyte not what to done with hire Godes. Of olde tyme, whan men passed from the Lond of Prestre John unto that Yle, men maden ordynance for to passe by Schippe, 23 dayes or more: but now men passen by Schippe in 7 dayes. And men may see the botme of the See in many places: for it is not fulle depe.

Besyde that Yle, toward the Est, ben 2 other Yles: and men clepen that on Orille, and that other Argyte; of the whiche alle the Lond is Myne of Gold and Sylver. And tho Yles ben right where that the rede See departethe fro the See Occean. And in tho Yles men seen ther no Sterres so clerly as in other places: for there apperen no Sterres, but only o clere Sterre, that men clepen Canapos. And there is not the Mone seyn in alle the Lunacioun, saf only the seconde quarteroun. In the Yle also of this Taprobane, ben grete Hilles of Gold, that Pissemyres kepen fulle diligently. And thei fynen the pured Gold, and casten away the unpured. And theise Pissemyres ben grete as Houndes :^c so that no man dar come to tho Hilles : for the Pissemyres wolde assaylen hem and devouren hem anon; so that no man may gete of that Gold, but be gret sleighte. And therfore whan it is gret hete, the Pissemyres resten hem in the Erthe, from pryme of the Day in to Noon : and than the folk of the Contree taken Camayles, Dromedaries and Hors and other Bestes, and gon thidre, and chargen hem in alle haste that thei may. And aftre that thei fleen awey, in alle haste that the Bestes may go, or the Pissemyres comen out of the Erthe. And in other tymes, whan it is not so hote, and that the Pissemyres ne resten hem not in the Erthe, than thei geten Gold be this Sotyltee; Thei taken Mares, that han zonge Coltes or Foles, and leyn upon the Mares voyde Vesselles made therfore; and thei ben alle open aboven, and hangynge lowe to the Erthe: and thanne thei sende forth tho Mares, for to pasturen aboute tho Hilles, and with holden the Foles with hem at home. And whan the Pissemyres sen tho Vesselles, thei lepen in anon, and thei han this kynde, that thei lete no thing ben empty among hem, but anon thei fillen it, be it what maner of thing that it be : and so thei fillen tho Vesselles with Gold. And whan that the folk supposen, that the Vesselle

[c] Plin. lib. xi. c. 31 : Indicæ Formicæ—Aurum ex cavernis egerunt terræ—Ipsis autem color Felium, magnitudo Ægypti Luporum.

ben fulle, thei putten forthe anon the zonge Foles, and maken hem to nyzen aftre hire Dames; and

than anon the Mares retornen towardes hire Foles, with hire charges of Gold; and than men dischargen hem, and geten Gold y now be this sotyltee. For the Pissemyres wole suffren Bestes to gon and pasturen amonges hem; but no man in no wyse.

And bezonde the Lond and the Yles and the Desertes of Prestre Johnes Lordschipe, in goynge streyght toward the Est, men fynde nothing but Mountaynes and Roches fulle grete: and there is the derke Regyoun, where no man may see, nouther be day ne be nyght, as thei of the Contree seyn. And that Desert, and that place of Derknesse, duren fro this Cost unto Paradys terrestre; where that Adam oure foremest Fader, and Eve weren putt, that dwelleden there but lytylle while; and that is towards the Est, at the begynnynge of the Erthe. But that is not that Est, that wee clep oure Est, on this half, where the Sonne risethe to us: for whenne the Sonne is Est in tho partyes, toward Paradys terrestre, it is thanne mydnyght in oure parties o this half, for the rowndenesse of the Erthe, of the whiche I have towched to zou before. For oure Lord God made the Erthe alle round, in the mydde place of the Firmament. And there as Mountaynes and Hilles ben, and Valeyes, that is not but only of Noes Flode, that wasted the softe ground and the tendre, and felle doun into Valeyes: and the harde Erthe, and the Roche abyden Mountaynes, whan the soft Erthe and tendre wax nessche, throghe the Water, and felle and becamen Valeyes.

Of Paradys ne can not I speken propurly: for I was not there. It is fer bezonde; and that forthinkethe me: and also I was not worthi. But as I have herd seye of wyse men bezonde, I schalle telle zou with gode Wille. Paradys terrestre, as wise men seyn, is the highest place of Erthe, that is in alle the World: and it is so highe, that it touchethe nyghe to the cercle of the Mone, there as the Mone makethe hire torn. For sche is so highe, that the Flode of Noe ne myght not come to hire, that wolde have covered alle the Erthe of the World alle aboute, and aboven and benethen, saf Paradys only allone. And this Paradys is enclosed alle aboute with a Walle; and men wyte not wherof it is. For the Walles ben covered alle over with Mosse; as it semethe. And it semethe not that the Walle is Ston of Nature. And that Walle strecchethe fro the Southe to the Northe; and it hathe not but on entree, that is closed with Fyre brennynge; so that no man, that is mortalle, ne dar not entren. And in the moste highe place of Pardys, evene in the myddel place, is a Welle, that castethe out the 4 Flodes, that rennen be dyverse Londes: of the whiche, the first is clept Phison or Ganges, that is alle on; and it rennethe thorghe out Ynde or Emlak: in the whiche Ryvere ben manye preciouse Stones, and mochel of Lignū Aloes, and moche gravelle of Gold. And that other Ryvere is clept Nilus or Gyson, that gothe be Ethiope, and aftre be Egypt. And that other is clept Tigris, that rennethe be Assirye and be Armenye the grete. And that other is clept Eufrate, that rennethe also be Medee and be Armonye and be Persye. And men there bezonde seyn, that all the swete Watres of the World aboven and benethen, taken hire begynnynge of the Welle of Paradys: and out of that Welle, alle Watres comen and gon. The firste Ryvere is clept Phison, that is to seyne in hire langage, Assemblee: For many othere Ryveres meten hem there, and gon in to that Ryvere. And sum men clepen it Ganges; for a Kyng that was in Ynde, that highte Gangeres, and that it ran thorge out his Lond. And that Water is in sum place clere, and in sum place trouble: in sum place hoot, and in sum place cole. The seconde Ryvere is clept Nilus or Gyson: for it is alle weye trouble: and Gyson, in the langage of Ethiope, is to seye trouble: and in the langage of Egipt also. The thridde Ryvere, that is clept Tigris, is as moche for to seye as faste rennynge: for he rennethe more faste than ony of the tother. And also there is a Best, that is cleped Tigris, that is faste rennynge. The fourthe Ryvere is clept Eufrates, that is to seyne, wel berynge: for there growen manye Godes upon that Ryvere, as Cornes, Frutes, and othere Godes y nowe plentee.

And zee schulle undirstonde, that no man that is mortelle, ne may not approchen to that Paradys. For be Londe no man may go for wylde bestes, that ben in the Desertes, and for the highe Mountaynes and gret huge Roches, that no man may passe by, for the derke places that ben there, and that manye: And be the Ryveres may no man go; for the water rennethe so rudely and so scharply, because that it comethe doun so outrageously from the highe places aboven, that it rennethe in so grete Wawes, that no Schipp may not rowe ne seyle azenes it: and the Watre rorethe so, and makethe so huge noyse, and so gret tempest, that no man may here other in the Schipp, thoughe he cryede with alle the craft that he cowde, in the hyeste voys that he myghte. Many grete Lordes han assayed with gret wille many tymes for to passen be tho Ryveres toward Paradys, with fulle grete Companyes: but thei myghte not speden in hire Viage; and manye dyeden for werynesse of rowynge azenst tho stronge Wawes; and many of hem becamen blynde, and many deve, for the noyse of the Water: and sūme weren perisscht and loste, with inne the Wawes: So that no mortelle man may approche to that place, with outen specyalle grace of God: so that of that place I can seye zou no more. And therfore I schalle holde me stille, and retornen to that that I have seen.

x

Cap. XXXI.

Of the Customs of Kynges, and othere that dwellen in the Yles costynge to Prestre Johnes Lond. And of the Worschipe, that the Sone dothe to the Fader, whan he is dede.

FROM tho Yles, that I have spoken of before, in the Lond of Prestre John, that ben undre Erthe as to us, that ben o this half, and of other Yles, that ben more furthere bezonde; who so wil, pursuen hem, for to comen azen right to the parties that he cam fro; and so environne alle Erthe: but what for the Yles, what for the See, and what for strong rowynge, fewe folk assayen for to passen that passage; alle be it that men myghte don it wel, that myght ben of power to dresse him thereto; as I have seyd zou before. And therfore men returnen from tho Yles aboveseyd, be other Yles costynge fro the Lond of Prestre John. And thanne comen men in returnynge to an Yle, that is clept Casson: and that Yle hathe wel 60 jorneyes in lengthe, and more than 50 in brede. This is the beste Yle, and the beste Kyngdom, that is in alle tho partyes, out taken Cathay. And zif the Merchauntes useden als moche that Contre as thei don Cathay, it wolde ben better than Cathay, in a schort while. This Contree is fulle well enhabyted, and so fulle of Cytees, and of gode Townes, and enhabyted with peple, that whan a man gothe out of o Cytee, men seen another

Cytee, evene before hem : and that is what partye that a man go, in alle that Contree. In that Yle is gret plentee of alle Godes for to lyve with, and of alle manere of Spices. And there ben grete Forestes of Chesteynes. The Kyng of that Yle is fulle ryche and fulle myghty : and natheles he holt his Lond of the grete Chane, and is obeyssant to hym. For it is on of the 12 Provynces, that the gret Chane hathe under him, with outen his propre Lond, and with outen other lesse Yles, that he hathe: for he hathe fulle manye.

From that Kyngdom comen men, in returnynge, to another Yle, that is clept Rybothe: and it is also under the grete Chane. That is a fulle gode Contree, and fulle plentefous of alle Godes and of Wynes and Frut, and alle other Ricchesse. And the folk of that Contree han none Houses : but thei dwellen and lyggen all under Tentes, made of black Ferne, by alle the Contree. And the princypalle Cytee, and the most royalle, is alle walled with black ston and white. And alle the Stretes also ben pathed of the same Stones. In that Cytee is no man so hardy, to schede Blode of no man, ne of no Best, for the reverence of an Ydole, that is worschipt there. And in that Yle dwellethe the Pope of hire Lawe, that they clepen Lobassy. This Lobassy zevethe alle the Benefices, and alle other Dignytees, and alle other thinges, that belongen to the Ydole. And alle tho that holden ony thing of hire Chirches, Religious and othere, obeyen to him ; as men don here to the Pope of Rome.

In that Yle thei han a Custom, be alle the Contree, that whan the Fader is ded of ony man, and the Sone list to do gret Worschipe to his Fader, he sendethe to alle his Frendes, and to alle his Kyn, and for religious men and Preestes, and for Mynstralle also, gret plentee. And thanne men beren the dede Body unto a gret Hille, with gret joye and solempnyte. And when thei han brought it thider, the chief Prelate smythe of the Hede, and leythe it upon a gret platere of Gold and of Sylver, zif so be he be a riche man; and than he

takethe the Hede to the Sone: and thanne the Sone and his other Kyn syngen and seyn manye Orisouns: and thanne the Prestes, and the religious men, smyten alle the Body of the dede man in peces: and thanne thei seyn certeyn Orisouns. And the Fowles of raveyne of alle the Contree abouten knowen the custom of long tyme before, and comen fleenge aboven in the Eyr, as Egles, Gledes, Ravenes and othere Foules of raveyne, that eten Flesche. And than the Preestes casten the gobettes of the Flesche; and than the Foules eche of hem takethe that he may, and gothe a litille thens and etethe it: and so thei don whils ony pece lastethe of the dede Body. And aftre that, as Preestes amonges us syngen for the dede, *Subvenite sancti Dei*, &c. right so the Preestes syngen with highe voys in hire Langage, Beholdethe how so worthi a man, and how gode a man this was, that the Aungeles of God comen for to sechen him, and for to bryngen him in to Paradys. And thanne semethe it to the Sone, that he is highliche worschipt, whan that many Briddes and Foules and Raveyne comen and eten his Fader. And he that hathe most nombre of Foules, is most worschiped. Thanne the Sone bryngethe hoom with him alle his Kyn, and his Frendes, and alle the othere to his Hows, and makethe hem a gret Feste. And thanne alle his Frendes maken hire avaunt and hire Dalyance, how the Fowles comen thider, here 5, here 6, here 10, and there 20, and so forthe: and thei rejoyssen hem hugely for to speke there of. And whan thei ben at Mete, the Sone let brynge forthe the Hede of his Fader, and there of he zevethe of the Flesche to his most specyalle Frendes, in stede of Entre Messe,[a] or a Sukkarke. And of the Brayn panne, he letethe make a Cuppe, and there of drynkethe he and his other Frendes also, with great Devocioun, in remembrance of the holy man, that the Aungeles of God han eten. And that Cuppe the Sone schalle kepe to drynken of, alle his lif tyme, in remembrance of his Fadir.

From that Lond, in returnynge be 10 jorneys

[a] Deynte, F. 1, 2, 3, 4.

thorge out the Lond of the grete Chane, is another
gode Yle, and a gret Kyngdom, where the Kyng
is fulle riche and myghty. And amonges the riche
men of his Contree, is a passynge riche man, that
is no Prince, ne Duke ne Erl; but he hathe mo
that holden of him Londes and other Lordschipes:
for he is more riche. For he hathe every zeer of
annuelle Rente 300000 Hors charged with Corn
of dyverse Greynes and of Ryzs: and so he ledethe
a fulle noble Lif, and a delycate, aftre the custom
of the Contree. For he hathe every day, 50 fair
Damyseles, alle Maydenes, that serven him everemore at his Mete, and for to lye be hem o nyght,
and for to do with hem that is to his plesance.
And whan he is at the Table, they bryngen him
hys Mete at every tyme, 5 and 5 to gedre. And
in bryngynge hire Servyse, thei syngen a Song.
And aftre that, thei kutten his Mete, and putten it

in his Mouthe; for he touchethe no thing ne handlethe nought, but holdethe evere more his Hondes before him, upon the Table. For he hathe so longe Nayles, that he may take no thing, ne handle no thing. For the Noblesse of that Contree is to have longe Nayles, and to make hem growen alle weys to ben as longe as men may. And there ben manye in that Contree, that han hire Nayles so longe, that thei envyronne alle the Hond: and that is a gret Noblesse. And the Noblesse of the Wōmen, is for to haven smale Feet and litille: and therfore anon as thei ben born, they leet bynde hire Feet so streyte, that thei may not growen half as nature wolde: And alle weys theise Damyseles, that I spak of beforn, syngen alle the tyme that this riche man etethe: and whan that he etethe no more of his firste Cours, thanne other 5 and 5 of faire Damyseles bryngen him his seconde Cours, alle weys syngynge, as thei dide beforn. And so thei don contynuelly every day, to the ende of his Mete. And in this manere he ledethe his Lif. And so dide thei before him, that weren his Auncestres; and so schulle thei that comen aftre him, with outen doynge of ony Dedes of Armes: but lyven evere more thus in ese, as a Swyn, that is fedde in Sty, for to ben made fatte. He hathe a fulle fair Palays and fulle riche, where that he dwellethe inne: of the whiche, the Walles ben in cyrcuyt 2 Myle: and he hathe with inne many faire Gardynes, and many faire Halles and Chambres, and the pawment of his Halles and Chambres ben of Gold and Sylver. And in the myd place of on of hys Gardynes, is a lytylle Mountayne, where there is a litylle Medewe: and in that Medewe, is a litylle Toothille[b] with Toures and Pynacles, alle of Gold: and in that litylle Toothille wole he sytten often tyme, for to taken the Ayr and to desporten hym: for that place is made for no thing elles, but only for his Desport.

Fro that Contree men comen be the lond of the grete Chane also, that I have spoken of before.

And zee schulle undirstonde, that of alle theise Contrees, and of alle theise Yles, and of alle the dyverse folk, that I have spoken of before, and of dyverse Lawes, and of dyverse Beleeves that thei han; zit is there non of hem alle, but that thei han sum Resoun with in hem and undirstondynge, but zif it be the fewere: and that han certeyn Articles of oure Feithe and sūme gode poyntes of oure Beleeve: and that thei beleeven in God, that formede alle thinges and made the World; and clepen him God of Nature, aftre that the Prophete seythe, *Et metuent eum omnes fines Terre:* and also in another place, *Omnes gentes servient ei;* that is to seyn, *Alle folk schalle serven him.* But zit thei cone not speken perfytly; (for there is no man to techen hem) but only that thei cone devyse be hire naturelle Wytt. For thei han no knouleche of the Sone, ne of the Holy Gost: But thei cone alle speken of the Bible: and namely of Genesis, of the Prophetes Lawes, and of the Bokes of Moyses. And thei seyn wel, that the Creatures, that thei worschipen, ne ben no Goddes: but thei worschipen hem, for the Vertue that is in hem, that may not be, but only be the grace of God. And of Simulacres and of Ydoles, thei seyn,

[b] Place, E. 1, 2, 3, 4; Monasterium, L. 1, 2; Mouster, F. 1, 2.

that there ben no folk, but that thei han Simulacres: and that thei seyn, for we Cristène men han Ymages, as of oure Lady, and of othere Seyntes, that wee worschipen; nohte the Ymages of Tree or of Ston, but the Seyntes, in whoos name thei ben made aftre. For righte as the Bokes of the Scripture of hem techen the Clerkes, how and in what manere thei schulle beleeven, righte so the Ymages and the Peyntynges techen the lewed folk to worschipen the Seyntes, and to have hem in hire mynde, in whoos name that the Ymages ben made aftre. Thei seyn also, that the Aungeles of God speken to hem in tho Ydoles, and that thei don manye grete Myracles. And thei seyn Sothe, that there is an Aungele with in hem: for there ben 2 maner of Aungeles, a gode and an evelle; as the Grekes seyn, Cacho and Calo; this Cacho is the wykked Aungelle, and Calo is the gode Aungelle: but the tother is not the gode Aungelle, but the wykked Aungelle, that is with inne the Ydoles, for to disceyven hem, and for to meyntenen hem in hire errour.

There ben manye other dyverse Contrees and manye other Marveyles bezonde, that I have not seen: wherfore of hem I can not speke propurly, to telle zou the manere of hem. And also in the Contrees where I have ben, ben manye dyversitees of manye wondir fulle thinges, mo thanne I make mencioun of. For it were to longe thing to devyse zou the manere. And therfore that that I have devised zou of certeyn Contrees, that I have spoken of before, I beseche zoure worthi and excellent Noblesse, that it suffise to zou at this tyme. For zif that I devysed zou alle that is bezonde the See, another man peraunter, that wolde peynen him and travaylle his Body for to go in to tho Marches, for to encerche tho Contrees, myghten ben blamed be my Wordes, in rehercynge manye straunge thinges. For he myghten not seye no thing of newe, in the whiche the hereres myghten haven outher solace or desport or lust or lykynge in the herynge. For men seyn alle weys, that newe thynges and newe tydynges ben plesant to here. Wherfore I wole holde me stille, with outen ony more rehercyng of dyversiteez or of marvaylles, that ben bezonde, to that entent and ende, that who so wil gon in to the Contrees, he schalle fynde y nowe to speke of, that I have not touched of in no wyse.

And zee schulle undirstonde, zif it lyke zou, that at myn Hom comynge, I cam to Rome, and schewed my Lif to oure holy Fadir the Pope, and was assoylled of alle that lay in my Conscience, of many a dyverse grevous poynt: as men mosten nedes, that ben in company, dwellyng amonges so many a dyverse folk of dyverse Secte and of Beleeve, as I have ben. And amonges alle, I schewed hym this Tretys, that I had made aftre informacioun of men, that knewen of thinges, that I had not seen my self; and also of Marveyles and Customes, that I hadde seen my self; as fer as God wolde zeve me Grace: and besoughte his holy Fadirhode, that my Boke myghten be examyned and corrected be avys of his wyse and discreet Conseille. And oure holy Fadir, of his special grace, remytted my Boke to ben examyned and preved be the Avys of his seyd Conseille. Be the whiche, my Boke was preeved for trewe; in so

moche that thei schewed me a Boke, that my
Boke was examynde by, that comprehended fulle
moche more, be an hundred part; be the whiche,
the *Mappa Mundi* was made after. And so my
Boke (alle be it that many men ne list not to zeve
credence to no thing, but to that that thei seen
with hire Eye, ne be the Auctour ne the persone
never so trewe) is affermed and preved be oure
holy Fadir, in maner and forme as I have seyd.

And I John Maundevylle Knyghte aboveseyd,
(alle thoughe I bē unworthi) that departed from
oure Contrees and passed the See, the Zeer of
Grace 1322, that have passed many Londes and
manye Yles and Contrees, and cerched manye
fulle straunge places, and have ben in many a fulle
gode honourable Companye, and at many a faire
Dede of Armes, (alle be it that I dide none my
self, for myn unable insuffisance) now I am comen
Hom (mawgree my self) to reste: for Gowtes,
Artetykes, that me distreynen, tho diffynen the
ende of my labour, azenst my wille (God knowethe). And thus takynge Solace in my wrecched
reste, recordynge the tyme passed, I have fulfilled
theise thinges and putte hem wryten in this Boke,
as it wolde come in to my mynde, the Zeer of
Grace 1356 in the 34 Zeer that I departede from
oure Contrees. Wherfore I preye to alle the
Rederes and Hereres of this Boke, zif it plese
hem, that thei wolde preyen to God for me: and
I schalle preye for hem. And alle tho that seyn
for me a *Pater noster*, with an *Ave Maria*, that
God forzeve me my Synnes, I make hem parte-
neres and graunte hem part of alle the gode Pilgrymages and of alle the gode Dedes, that I have

don, zif ony be to his plesance : and noghte only of tho, but of alle that evere I schalle do unto my lyfes ende. And I beseche Almighty God, fro whom alle Godenesse and Grace comethe fro, that he vouchesaf, of his excellent Mercy and habundant Grace, to fulle fylle hire Soules with inspiracioun of the Holy Gost, in makynge defence of alle hire gostly Enemyes here in Erthe, to hire Salvacioun, bothe of Body and Soule; to worschipe and thankynge of him, that is three and on, with outen begynnynge and withouten endynge; that is, with outen qualitee, good, and with outen quantytee, gret; that in alle places is present, and alle thinges conteynynge; the whiche that no goodnesse may amende, ne non evelle empeyre; that in perfeyte Trynytee lyvethe and regnethe God, be alle Worldes and be alle tymes. Amen, Amen, Amen.

FINIS.

Additional Notes.

Page 1, line 3. *Beheste or promise.* *Bethtony* in Bib. Reg. 17 C. xxxviii., but in no other MS. in the Museum.

P. 1, l. 9. *Envyrone.* The above-mentioned MS. has *honoure,* which must evidently be the proper reading.

P. 4, l. 21. The MSS. vary considerably in the enumeration of countries, but not so as to affect the narrative.

P. 5, l. 5-18. The whole of this passage is omitted in every other MS. that I have seen.

P. 6, l. 17. *Slesie.* Alfeigh; MS. Reg. 17 C. xxxviii.

P. 6. l. 22. "And a greet part3 of the kyngdome of Rome." Same MS.

P. 8, l. 2. *Bezanson.* In some MSS. *Bessamoran.*

P. 8, l. 7. *Covered with gold,* i.e. *gilded.*

P. 9, l. 5. *Est.* In some MSS. *West.*

P. 9. l. 10. The cross, coat, and nails, are sometimes omitted, and several variations in different MSS.

P. 10, l. 23. The title in Bib. Reg. 17 C. xxxviii. is *Jehu nazarenus rex Judeorum.*

P. 12, l. 3. *Four grains and four trees* in some MSS.

P. 13, l. 11, and in other places, for *o* read *oon.*

P. 20, l. 14-22. Omitted in the majority of MSS., probably from the transcribers' ignorance of the Greek language.

P. 21. The chapters are very differently divided in various MSS. Some have no divisions at all. Some MSS. make the first three chapters in this only one, and commence their second with our fourth.

P. 23. The story of the Knight and Dragon is very similar to one told in the Arabian Nights' Entertainments. The same may also be remarked of some other tales in this book.

P. 47. The note at the bottom of this page is probably erroneous; for the only MS. of the tract mentioned that I am aware of being in that collection, is of a much more recent period.

P. 53. In many MSS. the characters of the Egyptian letters are given, though generally somewhat rudely.

P. 109. The names of the Hebrew letters and their forms vary considerably in different MSS. See MS. Harl. 3954, where the difference is very striking.

P. 142. At the end of Chapter the 12th, in MS. Harl. 3954, are given the Arabic letters and names—" and sythyn I have told ʒow apertly of here lawe and customys, I schal tellyn ʒow now of here lettrys."

P. 161, l. 3. The Ademaund is here mentioned as the "Schipmannes ston;" and this early allusion, connected with what follows, is curious; but for a proper consideration of it, viewed with other notices of a similar kind, I refer to the very able paper in the first volume of the British Annual, by my learned friend Professor Davies, of the Royal Military Academy, Woolwich.

P. 163, l. 15. This tradition of a mountain of magnetic ore is very general among the Chinese and throughout Asia. The Chinese assign its position to a specific place, which they call Tchanghaï, in the Southern Sea, between Tonquin and Cochin China, which is precisely the same geographical region that the author of the Voyages of Sinbad the Sailor indicates. See Professor Davies's History, p. 256. See also p. 271 of this volume, where Maundevile again mentions this mountain.

P. 180, l. 21. This passage and the remainder is most exceedingly curious: it proves, beyond a doubt, that Maundevile had a distinct notion of the New World, and if he had had means, he would probably have anticipated by a century the brilliant discovery of Columbus.

P. 180, l. 26. *The Astrolabe.* An astronomical instrument for taking altitudes, &c. Chaucer translated a treatise expressly on it, of which the original has been found in Sanscrit. See his Works, and Gentleman's Magazine for April 1839.

P. 228, l. 9. Veneration for peculiar numbers was a very general superstition, and the number *nine* in particular was in universal repute; when we consider its very singular properties, it is not wonderful that a people of extravagancies should have this extreme reverence for it. See, however, the Rev. Professor Peacock's valuable and learned history of Arithmetic, where more may be found on this subject.

P. 228, l. 22. This story of the King and the Twelve Arrows is told in very nearly the same manner in the Arabian Nights' Entertainments; and the substance of a well-known fable will be easily recognised in it.

P. 270. The best information that we have relative to Unkhan,

Prester or Presbyter John, is to be found in the work of Matthew Paris, a monk of St. Alban's, who wrote before the middle of the thirteenth century. Marco Polo, in his travels, mentions the former subjection of the Tartars to him. See Marsden's edition, book i. ch. xliii. Roger Bacon did not believe the extraordinary tales which were current relative to Prester John,—*de quo tanta fama solebat esse, et multa falsa dicta sunt et scripta.* Opus Majus, edit. Jebb, p. 232. See, for a most profound and learned dissertation on the personage and history of Prester John, M. D'Avezac's Introduction to his Edition of the History of the Tartars, by John de Plan-de-Carpin, 4to. 1838, p. 165-168.

P. 315. It is a matter of doubt whether the *Mappa Mundi* mentioned here was an adjunct originally to Maundevile's work, or whether he refers to another treatise. According to Herbert, the English edition of 1503, printed by Wynken de Worde, possesses a map of the world, and it is not improbable that it belonged to the original work, although the only approach to it among the MSS. that I have seen is in one in Corpus Christi College, Cambridge.

Glossary.

In this Glossary, z in the text will be found often interchanged with the middle-age character ȝ. See Introd. p. viii.

abasscht, 226, 28; *abashed, ashamed.* See Chaucer's Dreme, 1289.
aboon, *above.*
ac, *but.*
ademand, *the loadstone.*
adown, *down.*
affligit, *afflicted.*
agaste, *aghast, frightened.*
agayneward, *on the contrary.*
aȝen, *again.*
aȝenst, *against.*
airn, *iron.*
alandes, *greyhounds.*
Alisaundre, *Alexander.*
all, *quite.*
allane, *alone.*
allinge, *altogether.*
all onely, *alone.*
Almaine, *German.*
als, *as.*
amyralles, *admirals.*
amys, *amiss.*
anenst, *over against.*
apertly, *openly, plainly.* Apert is also sometimes use adverbially.
appulle, *apple.*
apropred, *appropriated.*

arbery, *trees, arbour.*
arly, *early.*
arrere, *to rear, to raise.* A.S. arǽran.
aschen, *ashes.*
assay, *try.*
assche, *ash.*
assoylled, 314, 28; *loosed, acquitted, absolved.*
astounded, *astonished.*
attempree, 276, 29; *temperate.*
augurynes, *fortune-tellers.*
autour, *an author.*
avaunten, 176, 30; *boast,* pl.
aved, *had.*
aventure, *chance.*
avowtrie, 54, 31; *adultery.*
avys, *advice.*
awen, *own.*
awtere, autier, *altar.*
axe, *to ask.*
ayenward, *on the contrary.*
ayren, *eggs.*

baar, 30, 3; *bear.*
babby, *a babe.*
babewyne, *baboon.*
bald, *bold.*
barette, *fraud, strife.*

be, *by*.
bebledd, 3, 10 ; *coloured, covered with blood*.
beelippe, 52, 4; *curdle*.
beheste, 1, 3 ; *promise*.
behighten, 3, 12 ; *promised*
behotynge, *promising*.
bended, 276, 23; *bound*.
berde, *beard*.
beren, *bearing*.
beste, *beast*.
bestyalle, *cattle*.
betaughten, *gave to, delivered*.
betoke, *gave*.
bewtee, *beauty*.
boys, *voice*.
boyst, *box*.
brace, *arm*.
brede, *breadth*.
brenning, *a burning*.
bridde, *a bird;* briddis, *birds*.
brigge, *a bridge*.
broylly, *broiled*.
buscaylle, 271, 13 ; *bushes*.
byggere, *buyer*.

calveren, *calves*.
careynes, 293, 11 ; *carcases*.
cauteles, 277, 17 ; *crafts*. For this and several other words, see Mr. Wright's Glossary to the third publication of the Camden Society.
cawdroun, *caldron*.
cesoun, *season*.
chayere, cheyere, *chair*.
chees, ches, *chose*.
chesteynes, *chestnuts*.
cheve, *rise*.
cheventeyn, *chieftain*.

cheynes, *chains*.
claretee, *brightness*.
clepen, clepe, *to call;* cleped, *called*.
cokodrilles, *crocodiles*.
comynliche, *commonly*.
conchen, *lie*, pl.
connable, *convenient*.
connen, 213, 14 ; *know*, pl.
contre, *country*.
cost, *coast, region*.
costage, 125, 25 ; *expense*.
costynge, 127, 17 ; *coasting, bordering*.
cowde, *could*.
culver, colver, 11, 12 ; *dove, pigeon;* see p. 118. A.S. culfra.
cumanc, *ten thousand*.
cylours, *ceiling*.

dauis, *days*.
dede, *did*.
defaute, *want, deficiency*.
delyverly, *deliberately*.
deme, *to judge*.
demer, *a judge*.
departeth, *divideth*.
dere, *dare*.
dereworthe, *valuable, precious*.
derkelitch, *darkly*.
desparpleth, 4, 1 ; *disperses*.
desport, *pastime*.
destrere, *a horse*.
deve, 306, 3 ; *deaf*.
deveer, *duty*. Fr. devoir.
disherite, *disinherit*.
dispytous, 112, 24; *quarrelsome, spiteful*.
doel, 202, 5 ; *sorrow*.

doughty, *mighty*.
drede, *dread*.
duelle, *dwell*.
dure, *endure*.
dwerghes, *dwarfs*.
dyghte, 12, 32 ; *set*.
dysceytes, *deceits*.
dyversitee, *diversity*.

Ebreu, *Hebrew*.
eft, *again*.
eftsones, 51, 20 ; *soon after, again*. A.S. eft-sona.
elde, *old age*.
ellis, *else*.
emerunde, *emerald*.
enleved, *inlaid*.
enter, *inter*.
ere, *to plough*.
erchebysschoppes, *archbishops*.
eremyte, *hermit*.
eris, *ears*.
eschewe, *avoid*.
everyche, *every*.
eyen, *eyes*.
eyr, *air*.
eyren. *See* ayren.
eyselle, *vinegar*.
eysements, 214, 17 ; *conveniences, accommodations*. Easement is a law-term now in use ; see *Encyc. Cowel*.
ewtes, 61, 18 ; *newts, lizards*. A.S. efeta.

fader, *father*.
fadme, *fathom*.
fele, *many*.
fer, *far*.
fere, *companions*.

ferrest, *farthest*.
fertre, 225, 19 ; *bier*.
fetten, *fetch*, pl.
flessche, *flesh*.
fleyghe, *flew*.
flom, *river*.
florysscht, *flourished*.
fole, *fool*.
forcelette, *fort*.
fordon, 56, 7 ; *to undo, destroy*. A.S. for-dón.
forȝettynge, *forgetting*.
formyour, *former*.
forthinke, *repent*.
fosse, *ditch*.
freeltee, *frailty*.
frist, *first*.
frotethe, 60, 7 ; *rubbeth*. A.S. freoðan.
furneys, *furnaces*.
fuyr, *fire*.
fynt, *finds*.

ȝaf, *gave*.
ȝalowe, 48, 24 ; *yellow*.
ȝate, *gate* ; ȝatis, *gates*.
geauntz, *giants*.
ȝe, *ye*.
ȝeer, *year* ; ȝeris, *years*.
ȝeve, *to give*.
ȝevynge, *giving*.
gerneres, *granaries*.
ȝif, *if*.
ȝifte, *gift*.
gildene, *gilded*.
ȝit, *yet*.
gobettes, 309, 2 ; *pieces*.
gode, *good*.
ȝonge, *young*.
ȝou, *you*.

Glossary. 323

ʒoure, *your;* ʒouris, *yours.*
grave, 12, 2; *bury.*
gravely, *gravelly.*
grece, *step.*
grette, *great.*
Grew, Greu, *Greek.*
greynes, *grains.*
grucched, 57, 7; *grumbled.* Mr. Wright, in his before-mentioned Glossary, has *grudge,* where the word occurs twice.
gyngevere, *ginger.*
gyses, guyses, *fashions.*

halfendel, *half.*
han, *have,* pl.
hede, heed, *head.*
heer, *hair.*
hele, *health.*
helynge, *covering.*
hem, *them.*
herberyhgage, *entertainment.*
here, *their.*
heved, *head.* A.S. heafod.
hidre, *hither.*
hidreward, *hitherward.*
hight, *called.*
howsele, 261, 31, 33; *communicate.*

ichonne, *each one.*
insuffisance, 315, 18; *insufficiency.*

jogulours, 237, 22; *ministrels, jugglers.*
joukes, 13, 5; *rushes.*
joutes, 58, 31; *gourds.*

kembed, 24, 16; *combed.*
kepe, *heed.*
knouleche, *knowledge.*

knoulechen, 134, 30; *know.*
kutte, *cut.*
kynde, *nature.*
kyndely, *naturally.*
kynrede, *kindred.*

ladde, *led.*
lasten, *keep.*
Latyneres, *Latiners, men who speak Latin.*
leder, *leader.*
leef, *leaf.*
leet, *let.*
leeven, *believe.*
leme, *limb.*
lemman, *lover.*
lentone, 19, 20; *Lent-time.*
leve, *live.*
lever, *rather.*
lewed, 137, 15; lewe, *lay, laity.*
leytes, 129, 24; *lightnings.* A.S. leohtan.
licke, *like.*
list, *will.*
lite, *little.*
lodes-man, *pilot.*
loggen, 193, 23; *lodge,* pl. A.S. logian.
lusty, *pleasant:* it must not be confounded with the modern term.
lyche, *like.*
lycour, *liquor.*
lyggynge, 11, 18; *lying.*
lyʒn, *lie,* pl.
lyʒs, *lice.*

mareyes, 130, 19; *meres, boundaries.*
mawgre, 24, 9; *in spite of.*

mawndee, *last supper*. Glossary to the former edition.
meche, *much*.
meddle, *mingle*.
mede, *meed, reward*.
medewe, *meadow*.
meridionale, *southern*.
mervaylle, *marvel, wonder*.
meselle, *leprous*.
meveden, 278, 1 ; *move* (pl.).
meynee, 14, 10 ; *retinue, household*.
mo, *more*.
mochel, *much*.
moutance, *amount*.
morwe, *morrow*.
moten, *must* (pl.).
mowe, *may*.
moysted, 3, 10 ; *moistened*.
muren, 277, 21 ; *wall*.
myȝth, *might;* myȝthen (pl.), *they might*.
mynen, 267, 34 ; *excavate*.
myrs, 49, 6 ; *marshes, bogs*. A.S. mersc.
mysdoeres, 9, 6 ; *misdoers*.
mysteres, *mysteries*.

nadde, *contracted from* ne hadde ; *had not*.
natheless, *nevertheless*.
nempne, *to name;* nempned, *named*.
nessche, *nice, delicate*.
neyghen, 243, 33 ; *approach* (pl.).
nobelyche, *nobly*.
noryscht, *nourished*.
note, *nut*.
nought, *not*.
nys, ne is, *is not*.

obeyssant, *obedient, subject*.
oftere, *oftener*.
oon, *one*.
or, *before*.
outtake, *except*.

paas, *paces*.
pathe, *pave*.
pawme, *palm*.
pawment, 311, 32 ; *pavement*.
pens, *pence*.
peraunter, 314, 1 ; *perhaps*.
perte, *party*.
pes, pees, *peace*.
pese, 158, 12 ; *peas*.
pete, *pity*.
peyne, 3, 16 ; *to try*.
peynen, *pain* (pl.).
peynte, *painted*.
peysibely, 252, 3 ; *peaceably*.
pighte, 183, 6 ; *fixed*.
plenerly, *fully*.
plesance, *liking*.
pleyn, *full*.
pleyne, *complain*.
prevytees, 124, 9 ; *privacies, secrets*.
profren, 193, 18 ; *offer*.
propurlyche, 220, 1 ; *properly*
psawtere, *psalter*.
pupplische, 2, 17 ; *publish*.
pupplischt, 2, 25 ; *published*.
purpre, *purple*.

quyk, 22, 21 ; *alive*.

ravysscht, *ravished*.
recchen, 64, 13 ; *care* (pl.).
rede, *read*.
reme, *see* rewme.

Glossary. 325

remeven, *remove.*
renegate, *renegate.*
resceyve, *receive.*
rewme, reme, *realm.*
rightefulle, *righteous.*
rightewisnesse, *righteousness.*
roche, *rock.*
rosere, *rose-tree.*
ryden, *ridden.*
ry3s, 272, 4; *rice.*

saff, *safe.*
saughe, *saw.*
schadew, *shadow.*
schappes, *shapes.*
scherethorsday, 19, 1; *Shrove-Thursday.*
scholde, *should.*
schore, *shore.*
schryven, 249, 15; 261, 31; *confessed* (pl.).
sclaundre, *slander.*
scleyes, 130, 31; *sledges.*
scomfyte, *discomfit.*
scripture, 272, 16; *writing.*
seche, *seek.*
seke, *sick.*
sekurly, *surely.*
semblee, *assembly.*
septemtrionale, *northern.*
sewyng, 191, 3; *following.*
seyden, *said.*
seyn, 308, 11; *sing.*
si3th, *sight.*
sikerly, *see* sykerly.
simulacres, 161, 15; *see* p. 164 for a distinction between these and idols.
sithe, *since.*
skylle, 64, 3; *reason.*

sleighte, 301, 9; *cunning.*
sleu, *slay.*
sloughe, *slew.*
smyth, 45, 3; *sink* (?).
somdelle, *somewhat, some part.*
sothe, *truth, sooth.*
sothefastness, *truth.*
sotyle, *subtle.*
soudan, *sultan.*
sowd, *war* (?).
sowkedest, *suckest.*
sown, *sound.*
specyalte, *rarity.*
spores, *spurs.*
stankes, 209, 5; *pools.*
stedes, *places.*
stedes, *horses.*
stered, *stirred.*
stye, 134, 15; *to ascend.* A.S. stigan.
subgettes, *subjects.*
suget, *subject.*
sukkarke, 309, 26; *dainty.*
sweloghe, 33, 2; *whirlpool.*
swythe, 27, 12; *quickly.*
syde, *brim.*
syker, 193, 19; *secure, sure.*
sykerly, *securely, surely.*
symented, *cemented.*

ther, *there, where.*
therf, 19, 1; *unleavened.* A.S. peorf. Therf-breed, *panis sine fermento,* Reliquiæ Antiquæ, p. 6. Pickering, 1839.
thilke, *that.*
tho, *those, they.*
thorewe, *through.*
thralled, 2, 34; *enslaved.*
thristelle, *thistle.*

toke, *gave*.
transmontayne ster, *the Pole-star*.
travers, 48, 29; *streaks*.
trepassable, *that may be passed over*.
tresour, *treasure*.
trow, *think*.
truffule, *truth*.

undernemen, *reprove* (?).
unethe, 281, 13; 283, 14; *with difficulty, scarcely*. A.S. uneaðe.

vacrie, 18, 17; *vicar*.
verres, *glass*.
vif, *live*.
vissage, *face*.
vowte, *vault*.

wane, *to empty* (?).
wanhope, *despair*.
wawe, *wave*.
wedde, 13, 2; *pledge*.

wedre, *weather*.
wene, *think, imagine*.
werche, *to work*.
werre, *war*; werren, *to make war*.
wexe, 44, 21; *increase*.
whassched, *washed*. Also wesshe.
wlcane, *volcano*.
wo, *woe*.
woke, *week*.
wolden, *would*.
woneth, *dwelleth*.
wossche, *wash*.
wot, *know*.
wowe, *wall* (?).
wratthed, 37, 29; *provoked*.
wyle, *while*.
wyndwe, 107, 9; *winnow, blow away*. A.S. windwian.
wyte, *know*; wytethe, *know ye*; wyttyn, *to know*.

ylke, *same*.
ynow, *enough*.

THE END.

www.ingramcontent.com/pod-product-compliance
Lightning Source LLC
Chambersburg PA
CBHW020244240426
43672CB00006B/637